Steve James is the cricket columnist for the *Sunday Telegraph* and a sports writer for the *Daily Telegraph*.

He read Classics at Swansea University before becoming a postgraduate at Cambridge, where he won a Blue in the side captained by Mike Atherton. He played county cricket with Glamorgan for eighteen years, scoring nearly 16,000 runs at an average of over 40, and captaining them for three seasons, winning a National League trophy in 2002, before retiring due to injury.

In 1997, James helped Glamorgan to win the County Championship for the first time in nearly thirty years and was named the Professional Cricketers' Association Player of the Year. He also won a National League trophy in 2002 and still holds the record for highest score by a Glamorgan batsman (309 not out against Sussex at Colwyn Bay in 2000) and also won two caps for England.

www.transworldbooks.co.uk

Also by Steve James

Third Man to Fatty's Leg: An Autobiography
Ashes Regained (*with Duncan Fletcher*)
Behind the Shades (*with Duncan Fletcher*)

THE PLAN

How Fletcher and Flower
Transformed English Cricket

STEVE JAMES

BANTAM BOOKS

LONDON • TORONTO • SYDNEY • AUCKLAND • JOHANNESBURG

TRANSWORLD PUBLISHERS
61–63 Uxbridge Road, London W5 5SA
A Random House Group Company
www.transworldbooks.co.uk

THE PLAN
A BANTAM BOOK: 9780857500861

First published in Great Britain
in 2012 by Bantam Press
an imprint of Transworld Publishers
Bantam edition published 2013

Addresses for Random House Group Ltd companies outside the UK
can be found at: www.randomhouse.co.uk
The Random House Group Ltd Reg. No. 954009

The Random House Group Limited supports The Forest Stewardship Council®
(FSC®), the leading international forest-certification organisation. Our books
carrying the FSC label are printed on FSC®-certified paper. FSC is the
only forest-certification scheme supported by the leading environmental
organisations, including Greenpeace. Our paper-procurement policy
can be found at www.randomhouse.co.uk/environment

Typeset in Times New Roman by Falcon Oast Graphic Art Ltd.
Printed and bound by CPI Group (UK) Ltd, Croydon, CR0 4YY.

2 4 6 8 10 9 7 5 3 1

To my mum. I wish you could have
read this in its finished form.
And to my dad, always an inspiration.

Contents

Acknowledgements

Firstly thank you to Scyld Berry, my colleague at the *Sunday Telegraph*, whose idea this book was, and to whom I first wrote in 1996 when wanting to work in the national press. He has been a help and inspiration ever since. But the man who gave me my first break was Peter Mitchell, of the *Sunday Telegraph*. He is now sports editor there, and I cannot thank him enough for his backing, advice and friendship. Thank you also to Ben Clissitt, Adam Sills and Jim Bruce-Ball and everyone else at the *Telegraph* for their kindness and patience in allowing me to pursue this project.

Thanks too to David Luxton, of DLA, for his determination that this book should see the light of day. But I still cannot forgive him for being part of the Christ College, Brecon side that once inflicted upon me the most humiliating defeat of my cricketing career. 'That was not a defeat; it was a surrender,' my Monmouth School cricket master said.

Thanks also to Giles Elliott at Transworld for embracing the idea. His enthusiasm from the off was extraordinary, his editing always thorough and sensible, and his knowledge outstanding. We'll go on that bike ride one day, I promise. Thanks also to Daniel Balado-Lopez for his wonderful editing.

I am indebted to many people whom I interviewed or informally spoke to for the purposes of this book: David Morgan, Hugh Morris, Ashley Giles, Geraint Jones, Marcus Trescothick, Matthew Maynard, Dean Conway, Bill and Jean Flower, Grant Flower,

Alistair Campbell, Lord MacLaurin of Knebworth, Tim Lamb, Ken Schofield, Brian Bolus, Peter Moores, Nasser Hussain, Michael Vaughan, Mark Garaway, James Boiling, Mark Wallace, Matthew Streeton, Andrew Walpole and Paul Grayson. There are also a number who wish to remain anonymous. They know who they are. Many thanks.

And thank you to a number of other journalists and commentators who have helped and advised: Richard Gibson, Simon Wilde (who passed on James Lawton's excellent advice: 'Get up at six a.m. every morning and do two hours' work before the day starts!'), Ian Ward, Paul Newman, Mike Atherton and David Lloyd. Thanks also to my parents who perused the text with their usual diligence and sharp eyes. Indeed they did, except that there is a tragic twist to this tale. My mum read the last few chapters while in hospital. She returned home, delighted that I had taken her advice and made all the suggested changes to the submitted manuscript. But a couple of weeks later, on 22 November 2011, she passed away. I hope this book would have made her proud.

A word for Duncan Fletcher and Andy Flower too, the two central characters in this story. I have known both of them for many years and regard them as close friends. Neither was interviewed directly for this book but both gladly endorsed the writing of it. Flower has told me that he does not want to write an autobiography (or authorize a full biography) after an earlier attempt was halted because of his uneasiness with the project, and his co-author, Keith Meadows, has now sadly passed away. The current England team like to be discreet (thus Flower's mild rebuke of Graeme Swann in the autumn of 2011 when, in his autobiography, he made some criticism of team-mate Kevin Pietersen) and Flower was wary of talking about his team and their methods, but we do, of course, talk. Fletcher is always willing to talk. To me at least!

Finally, thanks and apologies to my wife, Jane, and children Bethan and Rhys for their love, support and tolerance. I'll get up later from now on . . .

Introduction

I'd like 'to begin at the beginning', as Dylan Thomas did in *Under Milk Wood*. And given that much of the thinking for and indeed some of the writing of this book took place in a favourite holiday retreat in the west Wales village of Laugharne, where Thomas lived, it would be apt. But the truth is that we are not beginning at the beginning. Rather we are beginning at the bottom. At a bottom so low that it was certainly made of rock.

We begin on a day so dark that it was indeed the 'bible-black' imagined by Thomas at the start of his celebrated play. In Test cricket, the format that really matters, England have rarely suffered a darker day. On Sunday, 22 August 1999 they lost a Test match to New Zealand at the Oval, and with it the series. Embarrassing at the best of times, yes, but that was not the half of it. In doing so they also slipped to the bottom of what was then called the Wisden World Championship, below even Zimbabwe in the rankings of the nine Test-playing nations. It was probably just as well that Bangladesh still had another year to wait before playing their inaugural Test.

As captain Nasser Hussain went to the pavilion balcony for the after-match presentations, he was roundly booed. It was the appropriate sound to end a quite dreadful summer, which had begun with an unedifying row between England's players and the England and Wales Cricket Board over pay for the home World Cup. Then those very same players acquitted themselves so poorly in that tournament that, after a performance of remarkable ineptitude in defeat to India at Edgbaston, they were eliminated the day before the tournament song was released. 'Let's get things fully in proportion,' wrote John Etheridge in the *Sun*. 'This was only the most catastrophic day ever for English cricket.' He was wrong. That would actually come later in the summer, at the Oval.

And the administrators didn't exactly cover themselves in glory, producing a World Cup opening ceremony at Lord's that can only go down in the history column marked 'Cock-Ups'. It really did consist of little more than a couple of banger fireworks and a dodgy public address system that failed when Prime Minister Tony Blair tried to speak.

After the Oval defeat the ECB's chief executive Tim Lamb said that there was nothing wrong with English (and Welsh of course!) cricket 'except the shop window' (the analogy always used of the England team by ECB chairman Lord MacLaurin of Knebworth, unsurprisingly so given that he had been chairman of Tesco). It was brave defiance, but essentially misguided. Subsequent off-field improvements, like central contracts, the establishment of a National Academy and a two-divisional set-up for the county championship, which were to come soon afterwards, have proved that there was much wrong with the rest of the shop too.

The truth is that the game as a whole in England and Wales was still coming to terms with the fact that the shop window had to be of paramount importance. The state of English and Welsh cricket (from now on I will just say 'English' if that is OK, hoping my friends in the Principality will understand) is judged by the performance of its national team. And back then that window was a horrible sight. There was glass everywhere. It had been smashed to smithereens. As Lamb now admits, 'It was a disastrous summer', and MacLaurin recalls walking away from the ground to his London apartment afterwards, wanting to hide his head in embarrassment. 'It was horrific,' he says.

Alec Stewart paid for England's incompetence on the field in the World Cup with his job as skipper, and coach David Lloyd also departed with his contract time incomplete. It appears he would not have been offered a renewal anyway, judging by the haste with which the ECB accepted his resignation ('he simply had to go' says Lamb now) and agreed to pay out the remaining few months of his contract, even if that meant a coaching void for the New Zealand series, with no replacement settled upon at the time. Not since 1986 had England entered a series without a coach.

Lloyd had many good ideas as a coach, but lacked the finance and necessary support. And, if truth be told, he was a little too emotional and temperamental. He immediately moved into Sky's commentary box, and, with his natural wit, even if it sometimes borders on a lovable madness, found his true vocation.

There was some succour at hand, however. But it was not all immediate or obvious. Hussain and Duncan Fletcher were announced as captain and coach, but unfortunately only Hussain could start straight away: out of loyalty Fletcher would not leave Glamorgan until the end of the season. So England made do with selector Graham Gooch overseeing practices and chairman of selectors David Graveney acting as manager.

England won the first Test at Edgbaston, but then Hussain broke a finger in the second Test at Lord's (which New Zealand won by nine wickets), and asked Graham Thorpe to take over. The bungling selectors (Mike Gatting formed an unholy triumvirate) didn't like that, though, and instead asked Mark Butcher to captain the third Test at Old Trafford.

During that Test Gooch and Gatting were sacked as selectors. So was Butcher as captain, and indeed as a player too, as he was dropped for Hussain to return for the grim denouement at the Oval. There followed a stultifying piece of selection so that England, with three genuine number elevens in Alan Mullally, Phil Tufnell and Ed Giddins, possessed a tail longer than that of your average alligator. Debuts were handed to Giddins and Darren Maddy, as horribly miscast as a Test opener as the team's number seven Ronnie Irani was as a Test all-rounder.

Shambolic? You bet. On the Monday morning following the Oval defeat, the *Sun* devoted the whole of its front page to a mock obituary of English cricket, with a huge picture of burning bails in a parody of the famous 1882 *Sporting Times* piece that spawned the Ashes and all its subsequently rich history. 'In affectionate remembrance of English cricket which died at the Oval, 22nd August 1999,' the *Sun* said. 'Deeply lamented by a large circle of sorrowing friends and acquaintances, RIP. NB The body will be cremated and the Ashes taken to New Zealand.' Yes, English cricket was in a rare old state.

I didn't write much about it then. I was only a part-time journalist, mainly filing rushed rugby reports on chilly winter Saturday afternoons. I had begun writing for the *Sunday Telegraph* earlier that summer when providing some offerings for their World Cup pages, and I was also writing a weekly column for the *South Wales Argus* that lasted a delightful sixteen years, but that mostly concerned more parochial matters at my county, Glamorgan.

Primarily I was still a professional cricketer. Indeed I was a professional cricketer desperate to get back into that awful England team. I'd been awarded two caps the previous year, and fancied more. Heck, my county coach was about to take over.

'If you pick that Vaughan it will be an absolute disgrace,' I said to Fletcher soon after the Oval debacle and just as deliberations on the winter tour party to South Africa and Zimbabwe were being finalized. Yes, not the smartest piece of selectorial observation about a player who would go on to enjoy a highly distinguished Test career, but cricketers are mostly, by their very nature, selfish. I was thinking only of myself. And Michael Vaughan had just made the sum total of two runs in two innings for Yorkshire as we thumped them at Headingley. He hadn't looked too good in that game.

Unfortunately for me, after nearly two years at Glamorgan, Fletcher knew how good I was: an above-average county cricketer who had probably made more of his meagre talents than he should have. But, at that stage, he didn't know quite as much about many others around the county circuit, so there were a few – like Maddy, Chris Adams, Gavin Hamilton and even Graeme Swann at that stage of his career – who were extremely fortunate to board the plane that winter.

Thankfully there was, however, enough proof that England were about to enter a bright new period in terms of selection. Fletcher would never again allow England to possess a tail like that at the Oval in the summer of 1999. Lower-order runs became essential. And just watching Vaughan at net practice had been enough for him. Fletcher had seen something he liked, a talent that he could develop in readiness for Test match cricket, just as he had a week earlier when Glamorgan played Somerset at Taunton and a chunky left-hander named Marcus Trescothick had bludgeoned our bowlers, most especially Jacques Kallis in his only season for the Welsh county, to all parts. By the following summer Trescothick would be exhibiting his talents on the international stage.

Sadly Glamorgan were about to lose their coach, though. I was about to lose a travelling companion and fellow rugby addict. Fletcher might have been off to join England, but we didn't lose touch. Sometimes he might call about a bowler they were considering for selection; on other occasions we might meet in the Sophia Gardens gym as he still rented a property in

Cardiff during his England tenure, although, contrary to common perception, he never did buy one there. He wanted to, but was advised against doing so by his great friend and ally, the physiotherapist Dean Conway. Within a year or two the property which he had eyed almost doubled in value!

In 2004 Fletcher unexpectedly called asking me to ghost his autobiography. I don't think I was first choice. Mike Atherton was, but at least my old Cambridge University mate had the decency to recommend me, speaking favourably of my own autobiography, published earlier that year following my retirement from the game due to knee trouble.

There was no hesitation. Ghosting books can often be an unsatisfactory experience, but, as a journalist making his way, this was a no-brainer. When Fletcher's agent called, I simply accepted his first offer. He could easily have snared my services for much less. There began a fascinating period until the book, *Behind the Shades*, was published amid great controversy in 2007. Insight into the workings of the England cricket team does not come much sharper than straight from the coach's mouth.

I had not even heard of Fletcher when I first went to his country of birth, Zimbabwe, in 1990 to play club cricket and do some coaching in local schools. He had left the country in 1984 to work in Cape Town, but he had clearly left his mark. The admiration for him, especially among the older guard who had played under his captaincy in the national team, was evident. His name just kept cropping up in bar-room conversations. The small cricketing fraternity there yearned for his return as a coach. But, to their chagrin, his only cricket-related appearance in the country during my five winters there was as coach of Western Province on an early-season tour.

Instead I befriended the group of young Zimbabwean coaches that the Zimbabwe Cricket Union had just employed to try to spread the game's popularity to the country's more densely populated areas. Among them were two brothers, Andy and Grant Flower. They seemed decent cricketers. They seemed even better blokes.

I gleefully joined their daily rituals. Mornings were spent training maniacally at the Harare city centre gym of Zimbabwe cricketer Malcolm Jarvis. Lunchtimes were occupied with nets at Harare Sports Club, where those national cricketers with 'proper' jobs, like the trio of lawyers John Traicos, Andy Pycroft and Kevin Arnott, would fit in their extra cricket practice. Afternoons were for coaching in the various schools to which we were allocated, and then late afternoon was time for more net practice with one's club side. Evenings? Well, let us just say they were convivial. And let us say that I was quickly introduced to a favourite local drink, the soapie, a ridiculously intoxicating concoction of cane, lemon barley and soda water.

Thursday nights were different, however. They were quiet. And mostly, thanks to the wonderful kindness of Mr and Mrs Flower, Bill and Jean, they were spent at the Flower family home in the Mount Pleasant suburb of Harare, having dinner and then watching the weekly transmission of the magazine programme *Transworld Sport*. Satellite television was rare in Zimbabwe then. And on the local channels this was the only guaranteed taste of televised sport all week. In that sport-mad Flower household only the monthly arrival of the *Cricketer* magazine, as it was then called, from the UK created as much excitement.

The image of the white Zimbabwean then, before Robert Mugabe began his wicked land reclamation policies, was of a person of wealth. And many, especially those in the farming community, fitted that bill neatly. But not the Fletchers or the Flowers. There are many differences between Duncan Fletcher and Andy Flower, but here is the first of a number of similarities between the two African families that would rear two outstanding cricket coaches for England.

Both Fletcher and Flower have been prepared to challenge common political allegiances. Fletcher's family stayed loyal to the United Federal Party rather than Ian Smith's Rhodesia Front movement which oversaw white rule, and they eventually had to move into Salisbury because they became ostracized in the area.

Flower, along with Zimbabwe team-mate Henry Olonga, famously railed against Mugabe's regime and the perceived 'death of democracy' in his country when wearing black armbands in a World Cup match in Harare in 2003. But long before that both Flower and his father Bill had helped the predominantly black, high-density-area-based side Winstonians at a time when accusations of racism were rife in Zimbabwean cricket. It ended in a good deal of acrimony, as most things did in Zimbabwean cricket at the time, but the Flowers had walked avenues others would not even contemplate walking.

Both Fletcher and Flower are from big families: Fletcher was one of six children, Flower one of five. Fletcher grew up on a farm (Carswell Farm near Nyabira, north of Salisbury), but only one of 'modest return' as he puts it. The Flowers' was also an ordinary existence. Bill, an accountant and enthusiastic schoolboy coach, worked hard to provide for his family, but no silver spoons were included in that provision.

Cricket equipment is expensive at the best of times. So just imagine the cost of importing it to a third-world country like Zimbabwe, even back then when the ludicrous days of an exchange rate for Zimbabwe dollar to pound of 700,000,000,000:1 were far away and a reasonable rate of about 10:1 existed. So the Flower brothers were not the only cricketers in the country to be envious of the English professionals like me arriving with their bagfuls of kit courtesy of generous sponsorship deals.

Therefore when Zimbabwe were preparing to go to Australia and New Zealand for the 1991/92 World Cup, I did not feel it in the slightest way patronizing to offer Andy Flower a pair of my Reebok boots. He accepted readily, and wearing them duly scored 115 not out against Sri Lanka at New Plymouth. It was the closest I came to a World Cup hundred! Indeed I was watching it back in Zimbabwe with Grant, agonizingly forced to pull out at the last minute after having his arm broken by Northern Transvaal B quick bowler Chris van Noordwyk while playing for the Zimbabwe Under 24 team. He considered soapies the requisite balm to his pain. I thought I'd join him.

His brother's international playing career was ignited, even though Andy, like Grant and another batsman of huge potential, Alistair Campbell, was still paid first and foremost to coach rather than to play. And how English cricket was to benefit eventually from that rather unusual beginning to an international cricket career.

But first, what a playing career it turned out to be. Flower simply delights in surprising, and in defying perceptions and expectations. I will happily admit that the first time I saw him bat, in 1990 in a match between his Old Georgians and my team 'Bionics', he did not stand out at all. He stood out when inside-edging my Glamorgan and Bionics colleague Adrian Dale, but that was his most memorable contribution. He just looked a half-decent left-hander, with hands conspicuously low on the handle. Nostradamus himself might have been hard pushed to predict that a future number one ranked batsman in the world was in action that day. But he was. Flower ended a sixty-three-match Test career with a batting average of 51.54, higher in the lists than Sunil Gavaskar, Steve Waugh, Allan Border and Sir Vivian Richards, just to name but a few greats of the game.

The ancient French apothecary and seer might also have struggled to foresee Flower's exploits as England coach when in late 2008 and early 2009 he was Peter Moores' assistant as an almighty row erupted between the coach and captain Kevin Pietersen. Flower was being tarred with Moores' brush and, with both Moores and Pietersen sacked (although the official line was that Pietersen resigned), he could easily have lost his job altogether. Instead he uneasily took temporary charge of a tour to the West Indies where almost immediately England were bowled out for just 51 in his first Test in charge.

Ah, from the most barren soil can the most productive Flower grow. Soon he was in permanent charge, and even sooner after that he was overseeing consecutive winning Ashes series, at home in 2009 and away in 2010/11, as well as capturing a first global trophy at the International Cricket Council World Twenty20 in the West Indies in 2010. In 2011 England became the number one ranked Test team in the world. It was a remarkable *bouleversement*.

Since the debacle of 1999 England have had three coaches. It is a quirk that two of them are Zimbabwean, although Flower was actually born in Cape Town, South Africa. And just as curious that they should unexpectedly find themselves in opposition during the summer of 2011, when Fletcher arrived as coach of India to face England, after being suddenly tempted out of semi-retirement by the departure from the Indian job of one of his protégés Gary Kirsten immediately after India's World Cup triumph at home.

Even now Fletcher and Flower barely know each other. Indeed one of the few occasions when they talked at any length before becoming direct adversaries in that 2011 India series was before a T20 international against Pakistan in Cardiff in 2010 when I happened to be meeting Fletcher at the England team hotel. They chatted warmly enough, and Fletcher congratulated Flower on his achievements with England. Another occasion was in Perth in 2006 when Flower was with the National Academy squad shadowing the senior Ashes side. Fletcher was outlining his favoured batting technique of the 'forward press'; Flower wasn't entirely convinced apparently.

Flower had asked for Fletcher's telephone number before the 2009 Ashes, but did not eventually speak to him because his skipper Andrew Strauss did so first, picking Fletcher's brains on the best methods to defeat the Australians. When Strauss went with Flower to speak to Fletcher and his India captain Mahendra Singh Dhoni at Trent Bridge in the second Test in 2011, things were a little more frosty. Ian Bell had been given run out after wandering out of his crease towards the pavilion, thinking an Eoin Morgan shot had gone for four and that it was tea-time, so Strauss and Flower went asking for the decision to be overturned. I have spoken to both Fletcher and Flower privately about this incident, and neither wants his thoughts recorded, which is fair enough. But I also think it is fair enough to say that Christmas cards are unlikely to be exchanged in the future.

The other coach since that dark day at the Oval was, of course, Peter Moores, whose tenure was brief but eventful, ending in that double departure. Moores, though, appointed Flower as his assistant, and in fact undertook his first foreign coaching assignment in Zimbabwe in the mid-eighties, at Lomagundi College, while also playing for Old Hararians with Graeme Hick, then a Worcestershire colleague and close friend (Cheshire-born Moores played at Worcestershire for three seasons before enjoying a fourteen-year playing career at Sussex). He didn't meet Flower then, but when they did so later in their careers there was a huge mutual respect. To this day Flower considers Moores his coaching mentor. Moores also appointed the excellent fielding coach Richard Halsall, born in Zimbabwe but brought up in England, and made some player selections that were to be of considerable benefit then and later. There was good in his tenure.

It is by pure chance that I know Fletcher and Flower so well. As a journalist covering the England team I have been very lucky in that respect. But not as lucky as English cricket in general. Between them the two Zimbabweans oversaw three Ashes series victories in four, when the previous eight had all been lost. Their influence has been huge. They have helped transform English cricket since that day in 1999 when their own humble country of Zimbabwe was deemed, however fleetingly, better at Test cricket, with the New Zealanders sandwiched between them at the foot of the table.

There is a much-used Zimbabwean phrase called 'Making a Plan', one especially used in times of trouble. Between them Fletcher and Flower made 'The Plan' for English cricket. Between them they made England the number one ranked side in the world, a position Strauss's side reached in August 2011 when they thrashed India at Edgbaston by an innings and 242 runs to overtake the Indians at the summit. That Fletcher was present in the opposition was ironic, but there was little he could do. He had not been with that team long enough. And he did exact some sort of revenge with a thumping 5–0 defeat for England in the one-day series that followed soon afterwards in India. His presence in the heavily beaten opposition at England's moment of crowning should not in any way diminish his contribution to England cricket. He played his part all right. That he did.

1

Who's Fletcher?

England were very fortunate to acquire the services of Duncan Fletcher as coach. For it was hardly his lifetime's ambition. Indeed when his name was first mentioned as a possible candidate, he was startled. He thought it was some kind of ruse. The kid from a Zimbabwean farm as coach of the England cricket team? Pah!

The first inkling came on 17 March 1999. I remember it well because, although it was not exactly the sort of occasion to inspire Max Boyce into song, 'I was there'. It was at the Stellenbosch Farmers' Winery ground outside Cape Town where Glamorgan were playing a three-day match on a pre-season tour. Fletcher was about to begin his second season with us (having helped us win the county championship in 1997, he had taken a year off), but, because he was still coach of Western Province in the southern hemisphere summer, he was taking a short rest and only popping in for the odd day during that tour.

Back in England, the national coach David Lloyd had recently met with ECB chairman Lord MacLaurin and it had been mutually agreed that he would leave after the World Cup. So the frantic search had begun for a new coach, and, if one thinks about it, it was little surprise that Fletcher's name should have been raised as a possibility. For in place at the ECB at the time was a small Welsh enclave.

David Morgan was deputy chairman, poised to take over as chairman from MacLaurin in 2002, and already in position as technical director for two years was Hugh Morris, my old opening partner who had played under Fletcher at Glamorgan in 1997 and then made a fairy-tale ending to an excellent seventeen-year career by scoring 165 in his final match to help secure the championship. 'To Lord's with a Title' he went, as evidenced by the title of a semi-autobiographical diary he wrote of that season.

Morris and Morgan did mention Fletcher's name in ECB corridors, but so, according to MacLaurin, did Glamorgan's Robert Croft, the off-spinning all-rounder who was then a member of the England side. That is surprising given that Croft was later the only person who advised Fletcher not to take the England job, and was then hardly a close friend of Fletcher's after they had clashed on a couple of occasions during 1997, most notably in a championship match against Northampton-shire at Abergavenny when Croft, in a prevalent dressing-room prank of the time, snipped the bottoms of Fletcher's socks so that when he attempted to pull them on at the end of the day's play they flew up beyond his knees.

To say Fletcher was not impressed would be an under-statement of which Jack Lemmon would have been proud. During that game I was travelling with him daily from Cardiff to Abergavenny and back, and he did not say one word for the rest of the match. He was fuming. I was sure he was about to return home. It was not just necessarily a sense of humour failure, more a feeling that his authority had been undermined, and that it had been a collective jape. It hadn't. Croft had acted independently. 'There are two things you don't mess with,' Fletcher later announced sternly. 'My woman and my kit.'

And in relating that quote, I hope I am not upsetting his delightful wife Marina, whom Fletcher positively dotes upon. In a world where machismo often dictates a supposedly cool insouciance towards relationships, I have not seen many professional sportsmen as devoted to their wives as Fletcher, or indeed so protective.

Anyway, Croft got the message. Thereafter there was always a mutual, if at times grudging, respect between them. Fletcher will even admit now that Croft altered his opinion on finger-spinners. He came to Wales considering them as relevant in the modern game as green spiked batting gloves, but Croft's skills persuaded him otherwise, even if, as regards Monty Panesar, the media would never believe as much in future years.

Morris backed Fletcher throughout the selection process, not knowing then that he would be on the interview panel. He was called only forty-eight hours beforehand to join MacLaurin, Simon Pack (ECB international teams director), Brian Bolus (chairman of EMAC, the England Management Advisory Committee), David Acfield (chairman of Essex) and Dennis Amiss (chief executive of Warwickshire) because it was felt there was a lack of coaching experience on the panel. Morris's job brief at that time was the rather large task of 'raising the standard of playing and coaching cricket from the playground to the Test arena'.

But Fletcher was not the man the ECB really wanted. MacLaurin wanted Bob Woolmer, then the coach of South Africa, although he was to resign very soon afterwards when they were bundled out of the World Cup after somehow managing to tie a semi-final with Australia that they should have won. 'I'd known Bob from my Kent days,' explains MacLaurin (who had played for Kent second eleven), 'and he was a high-flying coach at the time.' That's a rather circuitous way of admitting he wanted Woolmer. For once his chief executive Tim Lamb takes a more direct route. 'There was no doubt that Ian favoured Bob,' he says.

So MacLaurin sent Pack, the former major-general whom he'd bizarrely recruited despite a lack of cricketing experience or knowledge, to see Woolmer in South Africa about the job. The trouble was that no one else but Lamb was told, not even Bolus, who was supposed to be in charge of the new coach's recruitment.

Bolus was understandably furious when he learnt of the trip, quite by accident, from Amiss, of all people. 'I was chairman and knew nothing about this,' blasts Bolus. 'So I had a blistering row with the General [as Bolus always called Pack]. But it was not his fault. He was only acting under orders. He was a man I always admired and got on with, but he was under the influence of MacLaurin [whom Bolus often called "the Grocer"].'

Contrary to many people's opinions, most of them held to this day, Lamb says that Woolmer was not offered the job there and then. 'Simon had no mandate to offer Bob the job,' contends Lamb, 'but in hindsight it was a mistake to send him. We should have consulted the other members of EMAC. The perceived clandestine nature of the visit caused problems. I could have just had a conversation over the phone with Bob, whom I knew well from my playing days [Lamb was a seam bowler for Oxford University, Middlesex and Northamptonshire]. But I seem to recall that he [Woolmer] said, "Of course I'd be interested, but not immediately."'

What was worse was that, in going to South Africa, Pack missed an important meeting over pay for the World Cup with England's players in Sharjah, where they were competing in the Coca-Cola Cup in preparation for the World Cup.

Woolmer felt he could only begin as coach after England's tour to South Africa that winter, meaning England would have to endure another series without a coach. It should not even have been a starter. As it was, the ECB suffered enough criticism for being without a coach for one series. Just imagine if it had been for two series. But still Woolmer was slated to be interviewed. Goodness, they wanted him all right. The interviews were even arranged to fit into his schedule, 16 June being the day before that tied semi-final. But at the eleventh hour Woolmer pulled out. 'He phoned and said, "No, I can't really accept,"' says MacLaurin. 'He said, "Thanks for thinking of me."'

It is common knowledge that Bolus initially had in mind a 'dream team' as coach and team manager. As coach he wanted Jack Birkenshaw, the Leicestershire coach, and as manager James Whitaker, then still a player at the same county but having undertaken some managerial duties while suffering with the knee injury that eventually ended his career. He had done this most notably when Leicestershire won the county championship in 1998 for the second time in three years under his captaincy.

'Yes, I'd made my mind up that at that time the best management group in English cricket was Whitaker and Birkenshaw,' admits Bolus. 'They were a very good combination at a fairly impoverished county. Leicestershire were getting far more out of their players than they had any right to and it was down to those two. But if I'd have wanted Jack Birkenshaw as coach, I'd have got Jack Birkenshaw as coach.'

That last sentence is typical Bolus. A batsman who played for three counties, Yorkshire, Nottinghamshire and Derbyshire, and made seven appearances for England in the mid-sixties, he is certainly a no-nonsense, if also eccentric, character. 'He's got a screw loose,' wrote Nasser Hussain in his autobiography *Playing with Fire*, and he certainly gives that impression. 'He used to throw ideas into meetings and then sort of giggle in the corner and you never knew whether he was being serious or not,' added Hussain. 'He was a total loose cannon. We were trying to analyse people properly and getting selection back on an even keel, and this bloke was running around telling everyone what was said in meetings. The press played him brilliantly. They knew he could be quite uninhibited about what he said, and they would ring him and nearly always get something out of him.'

I know the feeling. Half the stuff Bolus told me I would not dream of repeating here, and he did say to me beforehand, 'I'll answer everything you ask, but please show some discretion in using it. I don't want any shit.' It was certainly an entertaining half hour that I spent chatting with him, as I suppose you would expect from a once-much-booked after-dinner speaker. He confused, baffled, shocked, tickled and enlightened me all at once.

What he did make clear was the situation regarding Birkenshaw. His preference for him and Whitaker held only while the World Cup was still taking place. 'I spoke to them [Birkenshaw and Whitaker] and said I was interested in them taking the job,' Bolus says. 'But then we had that debacle at Birmingham [when England tumbled out of the World Cup] and I said to Amiss and [David] Graveney, "What about this lot then?" It was obvious that the dressing room needed reform. Bob Woolmer, God bless him, had given everything to South Africa, but I felt we needed a fresh pair of legs, someone with plenty left in the tank, with ambitions to fulfil. So I went to see Jack [Birkenshaw] and said, "Sorry Jack, but I can't go along with that original suggestion. I need a different animal." Jack said, "Can I apply on my own?" I said "Yes, of course" and so we put him on the shortlist.'

Fletcher's name was mentioned to Bolus and it should be of little surprise to learn that he said 'Who's Fletcher?' and then giggled. He did know. Our 1997 championship win may have been a little surprising, but it didn't go completely unreported.

Bolus began doing some research. 'Myself and the General worked extremely hard in gathering background on him,' he says. 'It emerged that Fletcher had the reputation not just for being very successful but for being a strong man too. A lot of people gave him full marks for his attention to detail, planning and his strength of character.'

So Fletcher most definitely was in the frame, but back out in South Africa when Matthew Maynard and Dean Conway, Glamorgan's captain and physiotherapist respectively, indicated to him at Stellenbosch that this might be the case, the Zimbabwean just laughed. It was a situation laced with irony, given that Conway would become Fletcher's physiotherapist with England – indeed his presence was eventually a stipulation in Fletcher's acceptance of the job – and Maynard would one day become his assistant. But it was no joke.

Within a month Simon Pack had called Fletcher to ask if he was interested in the job. By June Fletcher was attending his interview at the ECB, with the clowning Pack famously greeting him 'Hello Dav', mistaking him for another interviewee, Dav Whatmore (Birkenshaw was also interviewed).

Fletcher was confused. Throughout this whole process he had been convinced, with some justification, that others were ahead of him in the pecking order. He had heard about the Woolmer approach and spent some forty-five minutes on the phone one day being persuaded by Morris, who, for some reason, was standing on the Western Terrace at Headingley amid the mayhem after Pakistan had beaten Australia in their World Cup pool match, that he should stay in the running and attend his interview. And when Glamorgan played Leicestershire at Grace Road, Leicester, Fletcher was somewhat perturbed to open the door of the home coach's office to find Bolus talking in serious and hushed tones with Birkenshaw and Whitaker.

But Fletcher went for his interview, and went with a very relaxed attitude. He immediately set out the principles that have always underpinned his coaching modus operandi: that the captain must be the managing director of the business that is the professional cricket team, and that he as coach must be the consultant, but must also be in charge of all off-field management, with all staff reporting to him. Fletcher told the interview panel that he would have to complete the season at Glamorgan, and then said, 'These are my current earning capacities with Glamorgan and Western Province. This is what I want.' It was thought to be an annual salary well into six figures.

Fletcher then made his way back to Canterbury where Glamorgan were playing Kent, worried that his demands had been too high. He need not have worried. Only a few hours later Pack called to offer him the job. A decision had been unanimous immediately upon the interviews being concluded.

The following day I happened to see Pack at the back of the Canterbury pavilion. I wondered why he was there. I simply could not believe that he was offering Fletcher the job so swiftly. But he was. He was offering Fletcher exactly the package he wanted in a three-year contract; not even Fletcher's added request that Conway be his physiotherapist was a problem. The ECB had clearly decided that money was no object, especially when one considers that the previous incumbent had been retained on as little as £60,000 p.a. 'We recognized that we had to pay our England coach well,' admits Lamb.

Fletcher was shocked, and asked for five days to consider. Not that anyone in the Glamorgan dressing room, skipper Maynard apart, knew. We obviously knew where he had been when he missed that day's play at Canterbury, but otherwise Fletcher was in full *omertà* mode.

It was only after Pack called again that he began to open up. He'd asked Pack for another three days: this was getting serious then. We were playing a NatWest Trophy match at Southampton against the Hampshire Board XI, and the night before Fletcher canvassed a group of senior players. He was clearly in a state of rare indecision. He never did anything without a lot of research, and it was obvious that this research had led him to a consensus that the group of England players at that time were mostly bad eggs.

I didn't really know what to say when he quizzed me. I didn't know the majority of the England players well enough to pass considered judgement, and at the back of my mind was the thought of impending trouble at Glamorgan. He had not returned to us in 1998 and we had faltered. And we were already showing such signs in 1999. We needed Fletcher to guide our youngsters.

We were to get him only for the rest of the season, and even that in hindsight was a mistake. Fletcher awoke the next morning and phoned Pack to say that he was taking the job, but he only wanted a two-year deal. 'I thought that after two years I would know whether I could do the job or not,' he later said. 'I did not want to let anyone down.'

It was probably the easiest negotiations the ECB ever had with him. 'He wouldn't take any prisoners in a business negotiation,' says Lamb now. 'He could be gruff but also very impressive. We all know that there's Duncan in a business situation and there's Duncan in a social situation. I'd be a liar if I said I didn't have some difficult moments with him.' But this was no such occasion.

Now England had to find a captain to work alongside Fletcher. He had been asked about his preference among the group and shrewdly had been noncommittal. He was never a man to make speculative judgements. And he certainly did not champion Maynard's cause as skipper. That was the word around the county circuit at the time. It was misguided rumour.

It was MacLaurin's manner to interview prospective captains. He had done so when Alec Stewart was appointed in 1998, and did so again now. There were two interviewees, Hussain and Mark Ramprakash, although in MacLaurin's rather hazy memory there were three. He thinks that Kent's Matthew Fleming was also interviewed, but he wasn't. 'Do you think I would have kept that quiet all these years?' joked Fleming when I asked him. The truth is that MacLaurin, as a Kent man, wished Fleming had been more involved in the England set-up (he won eleven one-day international caps) and at the time Fleming was chairman of the Professional Cricketers' Association, so their dealings were frequent. And it does have to be said that a man like MacLaurin – as well as being chairman of Tesco and the ECB, he has been chairman of Vodafone and the UK Sports Council and has served on the boards of Enterprise Oil, Guinness, National Westminster Bank and Whitbread – must have interviewed an awful lot of people in his time.

'Running into the interview Nasser was not favourite,' says MacLaurin. 'I think we were looking at Ramps to be quite honest with you. Nasser was not the favourite son then. But we asked them about their vision for English cricket and what they felt for the future and Nasser was fantastic, absolutely fantastic.'

This is how Hussain saw it: 'Basically I said the same stuff I told them the first time [when interviewed with Stewart the year before, clearly aware of his selfish and hot-headed reputation he had said, "You have to realize that someone, when you give them the responsibility, has it in them to behave differently"]. I think to an extent the ECB went for me as what they saw as the lesser of two evils. I gather they thought both of us would constitute a gamble but that perhaps I was calmer than Ramps by this stage of our careers and was a bit more established in the team.'

Both did indeed constitute gambles. I'd known Hussain since playing against him for Welsh Schools when he was the curly-haired leg-spinner and middle-to-late-order batsman in an English Schools Under 15 side which also included Michael Atherton. The three of us had later become team-mates in the Combined Universities side which enjoyed considerable success in the 1989 Benson & Hedges Cup. And I'm not sure our characters have changed a lot over the years: Atherton calm, studious, ever loyal and utterly confident; me quiet, always observing from a distance, utterly lacking in confidence. The

basis of Hussain's personality has remained – fiercely determined, often stroppy but with a good sense of humour when the
mood was and is right – but he has matured, and certainly found
self-deprecation a useful ally as a commentator. And along the
way as England captain he found a way to hide some of the less
appropriate parts of his character at the right times. The red
mist could be dispersed quickly if need be.

As Conway explains, Hussain's ability to alter his mood was
quite remarkable. 'Nass would be throwing things round,' he
says, 'but then he'd put his Vodafone cap on and march out of
the dressing room to a press conference and he would be
amazing. I couldn't believe the change in him sometimes. Mind
you, he'd shut the door of the press conference and he'd be
kicking off again!'

The acronym FEC on Atherton's Old Trafford locker may not
have meant what people wanted – the actual middle word was
'educated', surrounded by two unrepeatables – but there
was little doubt that he was a Future England Captain. And
back then there was little doubt in my mind that Hussain was
going to be a special cricketer. That he lost his leg-spin
completely and became a batsman instead reveals all about his
simmering desire to succeed.

If only hell hath the fury of a batsman unfairly dismissed,
then Hussain was indeed cricket's Cerberus. I was astonished
when I made my Test debut in 1998 against South Africa as to
the length and ferocity of Hussain's rage upon his first-innings
dismissal, enacted in the toilet and shower area at the back of
the Lord's dressing rooms. I remarked upon it in my autobiography, and not long after its publication I chanced upon Hussain
at Edgbaston during Twenty20 Finals Day. 'You been having a
go at me in your book Jamo?' he asked matter-of-factly. To be
truthful, I was just grateful he'd read part of my book, or at least
been informed of some of its contents. 'I was just showing that
you cared,' I blurted in response. And I was. I've not known

a cricketer who cared as much. Except maybe Ramprakash.

So it was that on Friday, 25 June 1999 Hussain and Fletcher were formally announced at Lord's as captain and coach of England. Both were very nervous. Before that morning they had never met. Hussain had been captain of Essex and Fletcher coach of Glamorgan during a tempestuous NatWest Trophy semi-final at Chelmsford in 1997, but with so much else going on – Croft and Mark Ilott pushing and shoving each other, after Darren Thomas had accidentally punched Ronnie Irani's helmet in celebration at trapping him lbw – it was little surprise that neither had taken much notice of the other. Mind you, when I spoke to Hussain for the purposes of this book, he could not even remember playing in that game! He thought he'd broken a finger around that time. He did have what he himself calls 'poppadom' fingers, mind. And he was always rather focused on playing for England.

'I was surprised when it was announced that Duncan had got the job,' wrote Hussain later. 'At that stage I wouldn't have recognized him if he'd walked in the Chelmsford dressing room, and I thought to myself, "Oh my God. Not only are you going into a job you know nothing about, but you are going to do it with a bloke you don't know at all."'

Fletcher travelled up on the train from Cardiff 'with doubts and anxieties filling my head', he later said. Before the official unveiling they were introduced by Morris and left to talk for about half an hour in his office. Fletcher outlined his philosophy and emphasized how important the captain's body language is at all times on a cricket field, because everyone, from colleagues to spectators and the media, is watching you.

'When the name Fletcher was announced, I joked that I thought they'd got Keith Fletcher!' says Hussain now, referring to the former England and Essex batsman and coach. 'But it was actually quite nice. There was a clean slate. I was worried at the time that too much of English cricket was too insular. You appointed from within, so that if you played for that county then you coached there. I wasn't a fan of all that. Now two blokes who'd never met before met at Lord's and were told: "Right, you're going to be in charge of English cricket for a while!" And straight away I knew that Fletch was different. He wasn't your average ex-cricketer talking in average ex-cricketer's clichés. He clearly had a different angle on things. He talked to me about being out of the game for a while and looking at it from the outside, and it was clear he had a business brain.'

When they then met the press, Hussain mentioned the importance of body language. Fletcher was impressed. Hussain clearly was too.

It was the start of a remarkable relationship.

2

Shiny Shoes and a Perma-tan

Nasser Hussain and Duncan Fletcher could not have transformed England cricket without central contracts. Fact. No one single decision by the ECB in recent times has been more important for the improvement of the England cricket team. Together and individually Hussain and Fletcher were pretty good anyway, but their timing was impeccable. They arrived just as this radical new initiative was about to be introduced, and they benefited accordingly. But, as always, with the gain goes the pain, and Fletcher in particular had an extraordinarily tough task in overseeing the new contracts' implementation.

Make no mistake; central contracts were a radical initiative. They were radical because since county cricket had begun in the nineteenth century, the counties had always been the players' primary employers. Some of the better players sometimes went off to play for England – for which they received some additional monetary reward – but they always returned swiftly, and went straight back into county action. They went back to their day job.

Now it was being proposed that the ECB take control of those players, maybe even deciding that they miss the odd county game so that they could be in some sort of decent physical condition for the next international. The revolutionary notion was being floated that maybe an England player could win a Test match and celebrate with his colleagues that evening rather than rush off to join his county brethren in readiness for a match the following morning. Maybe he could even report for duty for a Test match a little before noon on the day before the match. Maybe he could even report for duty feeling a little less than knackered. Goodness, maybe he could even feel part of the England team rather than some temporary intruder, as many did, including me when I played twice in 1998.

Please forgive my sarcasm. These notions seem so sensible and routine nowadays, but, believe it or not, there was a time when they were not even considered. 'We weren't really a team,' wrote Graham Thorpe of those times. 'They [Tests for England] were more like representative matches.'

Somebody had needed to see the bigger picture. And England captain Mike Atherton had. In his report after the winter tour of South Africa and then the Asian World Cup of 1995/96, he wrote: 'Although we suffered fewer injuries than on the previous tour, we do suffer more than other teams (we were the only team to send two players home from the World Cup). Clearly this is no mere accident; it is a result of overplaying. Considering especially the need to look after our premier players (in particular the fast bowlers), it seems to me the sooner we can ensure these players are under TCCB [the Test and County Cricket Board, which was incorporated into the ECB in 1997] contracts all year round the better.' But it still went down like the proverbial lead balloon.

Central contracts were considered in the Acfield Review (set up under David Acfield, then Essex's chairman of cricket, to look at the management of the England team) that was published in July 1996, but, even though there were two former England captains in David Gower and Mike Gatting on that committee, there was no recommendation for contracts, only that the chairman of selectors should have the right to withdraw players from county cricket if he felt it best for their long-term welfare. Even that idea was summarily rejected by the counties in August. And to think that Kerry Packer had lit the way for international cricketers some nineteen years previously, when using three-year contracts to entice the world's best players for his World Series Cricket. Talk about slow on the uptake.

Somehow English cricket had to be dragged kicking and screaming into the modern world, and to Lord MacLaurin, who became chairman of the ECB upon its creation in 1997, befell that fiendishly difficult task. 'Never trust a man with shiny shoes and a perma-tan' are the oft-repeated words concerning MacLaurin, as penned by Atherton in his autobiography. But, wonderful wordsmith that he has become, they were not Atherton's own, as indeed he admits if you read closely. They were prefaced by 'Someone once told me . . .', and that someone was Derek Pringle, the current cricket correspondent of the *Daily Telegraph*.

But they were still delightfully apposite. MacLaurin did have, indeed still has, both. He was, and still can be, smooth and political. But for the ECB at the time he was the perfect figure. He modernized English cricket. He made eighteen stubborn and anachronistic counties realize that the England team was much more important than them as a collective.

'I visited all the county chairmen when I took over,' MacLaurin says on a bright, sunny day when we meet near his home at Farleigh Hungerford outside Bath, 'and frankly none of them was interested in a winning England side. They were only interested in their own counties winning the championship.' Why is that not a surprise? It is still a view not exactly unknown today.

I'll tell you a little story to illustrate the point. Remember the 2005 Ashes and all its glory for England? Well, England might not have won that series had one county had its myopic way. Before the decisive fifth Test at the Oval, with England leading the series 2–1 and Australia desperate to win in order to share the series and so keep the urn that they held, Australia wanted to give their second leg-spinner, Stuart MacGill, some match practice. They were considering playing him at the Oval, but he hadn't played in any of the previous Tests.

Somerset stepped forward, eagerly offering MacGill a game (he had played one match for them against Pakistan A in 1997). Even if Auckland did give James Anderson some such match practice on England's tour of New Zealand in 2008, can you imagine an England reserve spinner being given a game or two in the Sheffield Shield while on an Ashes tour? The answer is no. A definitive no. But here were Somerset thinking only of themselves. MacGill was actually on his way to Taunton when the deal fell through, with it becoming clear that he was available for only one week, when the ECB regulations at the time specified a minimum of three weeks for overseas signings. You do wonder what might have happened if MacGill had played in the dramatically drawn Oval Test instead of the wayward seamer Shaun Tait.

At least by 2011 Somerset had changed their outlook considerably, allowing the short-of-match-practice England captain Andrew Strauss to appear as a guest against India before the first Test against the same opponents.

The Somerset chairman in 2005? Giles Clarke. The same Giles Clarke who was to become ECB chairman in 2007, and the same Giles Clarke who phoned both Middlesex and Kent in outrage when they signed the Australians Phillip Hughes and Stuart Clark to play ahead of the 2009 Ashes in this country. Hughes scored a bucketful of runs for Middlesex, but was then exposed in the Tests, and dropped. Clark did not arrive because he was called up to Australia's one-day squad in South Africa.

Back to the ECB's first chairman, and MacLaurin knew that his 'shop window' needed his full attention. Otherwise the 'shambles' of an operation, as he describes the ECB then, with its budget of 'just £30 million', stood no chance.

He chaired the last meeting of the TCCB in December 1996, then thought it best to check on the well-being of the England team, who were touring Zimbabwe at the time. It did not take him long to discover it was a sick patient. He telephoned Lord's in order to organize his accommodation on the tour and was shocked to be asked where he would like to stay. 'With the team, of course,' he answered. He was then told politely that that had never happened before. The management always stayed somewhere else in much more salubrious surroundings, while the team slummed it, always sharing rooms, as well as always flying in economy class.

'The gap between the players and the administrators was quite frightening,' MacLaurin says. 'But my late wife and I booked into the team hotel. I went around all the rooms and couldn't believe it. I went to Tim Lamb immediately and said, "I'm appalled that we treat our boys like this." He said, "It's tradition." I just said, "That tradition stops now, and they will all have single rooms."' They also began to travel business class as well as enjoying a whole host of what Lamb calls 'fringe benefits'. And too right too.

In an instant MacLaurin had smashed down an unfathomable but long-lasting class barrier. At last an administrator was more concerned with the players' welfare than his perks and expenses. 'I didn't know these guys from a bar of soap,' he says, 'so I thought I'd better get to know them. I spent time with each and every one of them. I started with Mike Atherton. "What is the vision for England cricket?" I asked him. "Tell me what, if you like in business terms, is the mission statement?" He looked at me across the breakfast table and said, "Chairman, you're the first person to talk to me about that." And he'd been captain for three years!'

MacLaurin also had to alter England's image on a tour that became infamous for coach David Lloyd's 'We flippin' murdered 'em' comment after England had drawn – yes, drawn – with Zimbabwe in the Bulawayo Test. It was an outburst now termed 'disastrous' by Lamb. Relations between the two sides were probably best summed up by the home skipper, Alistair Campbell, who accused England of possessing a 'superiority complex'. And he was right. But it was a stance without foundation. England truly were a poorly performing side then.

They were also scruffy. 'If you saw the boys on the field,' says MacLaurin, 'they went out with jockey caps on. They had white helmets, pink helmets and green helmets. There was no discipline at all. I went about branding the whole thing. That was not popular with a lot of people, but a lot of things I did weren't popular.'

England may have ceased being called MCC away from home after the 1976/77 tour of Australia, but they were still wearing the club's colours of yellow and red (or egg and bacon) on their sweaters and caps with the St George and Dragon crest in Zimbabwe and later that winter in New Zealand. MacLaurin knew that had to end, with the three lions and crown always being worn, even if it inevitably upset the MCC. 'Not only did we need a winning England team but we also needed a common brand in order to attract the right sorts of sponsors,' he says.

And sponsors were leaving cricket at an alarming rate at the time. Texaco had withdrawn their sponsorship of the one-day internationals, AXA of the Sunday League and Britannic Assurance of the county championship. But, as you would expect, MacLaurin had some rather decent contacts. He was not yet chairman of Vodafone (he became so in the summer of 1998) but he knew its chief executive, Christopher Gent, a keen cricket supporter who was educated at Archbishop Tenison's

Grammar School not a stone's throw away from the Oval, well enough to broker a deal. So Vodafone's first tour as England sponsors was to the West Indies in early 1998. It was a relationship that lasted twelve years.

Even more importantly, in that same year MacLaurin persuaded Chris Smith, the Secretary of State for Culture, Media and Sport, to move cricket from the government's broadcasting A list, which restricted the live coverage of sport to terrestrial channels, to the B list. It was only on the proviso that 'the majority of Test cricket was on terrestrial TV', as MacLaurin says now.

That has obviously caused much debate and rancour since, because that is anything but the case these days with Sky ruling the roost, but this was only a gentlemen's agreement. It was hugely significant, though. Suddenly the field was open, and the sole bid was not coming from the BBC, who had first televised Test cricket in 1938 and provided sixty years of excellent coverage. Much to the chagrin of the BBC, a joint deal was done with BSkyB and Channel 4, whose unexpected bid outdid the BBC's by several million pounds. 'Our budget suddenly went up from approx £30 million to £130 million,' says MacLaurin.

The ECB had money to do things, most notably to introduce central contracts. In 2006, when terrestrial television was abandoned completely and the whole rights package sold to BSkyB in a four-year deal worth £208 million, they had even more. For the period 2009 to 2013 the deal is worth £260 million.

Like it or not, sporting excellence requires dosh. And lots of it. As an example there is none better than Clive Woodward's famous switching of hotels for his England rugby team in South Africa in 1998, paid for on his own Amex card. Only the best will do if the real mountain tops are to be reached, and this was a statement of intent that was still resonating in 2003 when England won the rugby World Cup. So in 2010 Hugh Morris, by then the managing director of England cricket, was spending

£24.8 million on all England teams. In 2005 that figure had been only £10.9 million. It makes a difference. It really does.

In October 1998 the First Class Forum had at last agreed in principle to the introduction of central contracts. Unsurprisingly the ECB did what every good English sporting organization does: they formed a committee. Yes, the Contracts Review Group was set up under the chairmanship of Don Trangmar, chairman of Sussex and a director of Marks and Spencer, and included Surrey's Paul Sheldon and Somerset's Peter Anderson. Quite naturally, the road they travelled was long and bumpy.

David Morgan was then chairman of the First Class Forum, the body that served as the guardian of county cricket until 2005 and had to provide clearance and permission to implement any significantly different changes in the game. Central contracts certainly came under that umbrella. 'Having them approved was not an easy task,' says Morgan with typical understatement. 'There were many county chairmen and chief executives – mainly those that had played at first-class level – who didn't believe it was right that Team England should be separate from the eighteen first-class counties. They believed that England had done great things in the past and would continue to do great things in the future without this.' Ah, the vision of those men.

But by May 1999 the FCF had confirmed their imminent arrival. MacLaurin was to have what he wanted, as mentioned by Morgan above: 'Team England'. In effect they were becoming the nineteenth county, and by far the most important.

'It started off whereby players would have parallel contracts with the counties and the ECB,' says Lamb, 'but that immediately led to difficulties because there were always going to be conflicts in terms of what the counties wanted from their players. It became clear very quickly that if we were going to get this thing through, we were going to have to cross the counties' palms with silver and agree to pay the players' county salaries.

That was the tipping point. When that became clear the counties had no option but to say yes.'

This was actually an episode in which Simon Pack played a role rather than the fool, cajoling and eventually persuading the counties that English cricket needed this departure from the norm. There were, after all, going to be seven home Tests a summer from 2000 (up from six) and many more home one-day internationals (in 2000 came the first triangular series of seven matches after many years of just three home ODIs per summer), and counties were hardly going to see their star players anyway. Quite rightly Pack copped a lot of flak for his work at the ECB, but speak to anyone about his work on this issue and they have nothing but the utmost praise. He ensured that the critical mass of the counties was in favour. 'The General was absolutely fantastic,' says Brian Bolus with his usual chuckle.

So finally, on Monday, 23 August 1999, the day after the debacle at the Oval with which we began this book, the counties agreed to the introduction of central contracts. The following March twelve England players were awarded ECB contracts for the first time: Nasser Hussain (captain), Michael Atherton, Andrew Caddick, Andrew Flintoff, Darren Gough, Dean Headley, Graeme Hick, Mark Ramprakash, Chris Schofield, Alec Stewart, Michael Vaughan and Craig White.

These were only six-month contracts – twelve-month contracts were not introduced until 2002 – but crucially these players were under the management and control of the England coach, Fletcher. It was a huge step forward.

There were teething problems, of course, not least that many county fans could not and would not comprehend this new arrangement. Gough even received a poison-pen letter when he missed a Yorkshire match. The central contract was a very complicated document then; goodness knows what it is like now with its clauses regarding release to the Indian Premier League. And there was the anomaly that the contracted players were on significantly less than some county players, like Chris Adams at Sussex and Alan Mullally at Hampshire, who were earning six-figure salaries at the time. For some the ECB contract was worth less than the county contract it was replacing. Counties made up the difference in those cases. For Atherton, for example, it was a straight swap. His county contract was worth £60,000; so was his new ECB contract.

An ECB contract is worth considerably more than that these days, with match fees paid on top. There was a time when the figures, including the different bands in which various players fell, were readily available. So in 2004 we know that the contracts were graded in three bands, worth between £100,000 and £150,000, with match fees paid on top. A Test match was worth £5,500 and a one-day international £2,200. For Tests abroad there was a 40% added premium, with 20% for one-day internationals, and for global trophies 50%. So, say, a player appearing in all matches in the 2002/03 season with an Ashes tour and a World Cup would have earned a basic salary in the region of £350,000.

Now the ECB are much more careful about releasing such information, and rightly so. Nonetheless it would be a surprise were the busiest players not earning, just from the ECB, some-where near £450,000 a year. Indeed in 2011 it would be just as surprising were Test captain Andrew Strauss not earning over £1 million in total for the year: a Band A Central Contract might be worth £400,000, with bonuses for appearances and wins – which are pooled and then divided up – of maybe £150,000, and sponsorship deals with Gray Nicholls, Jaguar, etc. adding up to another £500,000. These are figures no county player can ever hope to earn. And that is how it should be; the best players should earn the biggest salaries. Mind you, there are still too many mediocre county players on or near six-figure salaries. Little wonder that the counties are in so much debt.

There was also the subject of compensation, which was not

helped by the spectacularly misguided selection of Lancashire's leg-spinner, Schofield. The search for a wrist-spinner to rival Australia's Shane Warne was at its most manic at the time, and Schofield was picked on the recommendation of Gatting, tour manager of the England A trip to New Zealand the previous winter. While he was extolling the virtues of Schofield as 'the future of English cricket', as Fletcher noted in his auto-biography, Gatting was also professing he was 'not sure about this [Marcus] Trescothick'. Thank goodness, Fletcher backed his own judgement and ensured Trescothick was on the inter-national stage by the summer of 2000. Gatting has many qualities, but, sadly, in my opinion selecting and coaching are not among them.

So while Schofield was justifiably shunted from the Test scene after two Tests against Zimbabwe, it meant his county received his services for free, while other counties like Derbyshire, who lost the non-contracted Dominic Cork for four Tests, were still paying players and not receiving too much compensation (just £12,000 in Cork's case in 2000), and were then being asked to rest him at the end of the season. Thankfully that anomaly has been satisfactorily rectified over time.

Not that contention over the issue of rest has been sorted. English cricket simply does not understand the meaning of the word. Place the lads on a treadmill in April (nearly March now, with ludicrously early starts to seasons) and make damn sure they're not allowed off it until the leaves are disappearing off the trees in autumn. Don't worry if one-day matches start immedi-ately after four-day matches so that no practice or preparation is possible, so that tired players are playing on often tired pitches. Don't worry that mental tiredness is just as debilitating as its physical comrade, meaning that just the mere sight of a cricket dressing room is too much by the end.

Fletcher always made a good point in stressing that the English summer should be viewed no differently from a winter tour. England players need rest. The county season is not sacrosanct. And once burnout takes hold it is too late. The skill of the very best coaches is being able to look over the horizon and spot not just the signs long before, but also the most dangerous periods. Fletcher was extraordinarily good at this. And at first he was pleasantly surprised by the reaction from the counties at his foresight. But then came the end of the season, when promotion and relegation were being hotly contested. The mood changed. The self-interest and short-sightedness came flooding back. One county chairman told Fletcher, 'I agree with what you're doing but there is no way I could say that in front of my constituency.'

And Graham Gooch is an interesting case. When coach of Essex he was against the resting of England players. Indeed he fell out with Hussain over that very issue. Now that he is Andy Flower's batting coach he has a very different view. He understands the demands and recognizes the need for rest.

It is rather ironic, given the (Chris) Schofield scenario, that Fletcher probably had most trouble with Lancashire as regards central contracts and the resting of players. It began with their outrage at Atherton missing some National League matches in the 2000 season and continued unabated with James Anderson and others in later years.

Take this quote from Lancashire's chairman, Jack Simmons, after Fletcher had resigned from the England job in 2007. 'The introduction of Peter Moores as replacement for Fletcher has already improved relationships with the counties,' he said. 'A player improves by being out in the middle and not sat on his backside. If Mr Fletcher is hoping to return to county cricket as a coach, I don't think he needs to contact Lancashire.'

Ah, good old 'Flat Jack', the heftily built off-spinner with a penchant for fish and chips who was still playing first-class cricket at the age of forty-eight. Simmons is actually a lovely fellow, and a loyal servant to his county as both player and administrator, but in the latter role he was as old-fashioned as he was in the former.

Simmons would do well to consider the case of Glen Chapple, a fine and persevering fast bowler for Lancashire who led his county to the championship in 2011. That he has only played once for England – and that in a one-day international against Ireland – is scant reward for his talent. But he has his own county partly to blame. In 2006 he was selected for the England one-day squad, who were meeting in Southampton on Sunday, 11 June, before flying the next day to play Ireland on the Tuesday. Fletcher did not want any players to play on the Sunday. But Lancashire wanted Chapple to play in their C&G Trophy match against Derbyshire. Fletcher refused, but Simmons got involved and went to the ECB. Chapple was allowed to play, and flew down to join the team later that night. On the Monday at practice Fletcher forgot that Chapple should not bowl as many overs as the others because he had played the previous day. He broke down against Ireland, and never played again.

Geoff Miller, the current National Selector, makes a good point about the crux of Fletcher's troubled relationship with the counties: 'Whether Duncan actually said it or not, or whether it was misquoted, the feeling amongst the counties was that he had said "The standard of county cricket is poor".'

Yes, there were undoubtedly aspects of county cricket that frustrated Fletcher. But he was hardly alone in that regard. He thoroughly enjoyed his two years at Glamorgan, even if he was distracted in the latter half of his second year, with the England job looming. Indeed he will admit now that he would have been better off joining England immediately. His greatest gripe with the county game was the volume of cricket played, leading to lazy habits. He used to be enraged with the slack running between the wickets and the lack of general intensity in the fielding, always signs of tired minds as well as tired bodies. And the excuse culture, so prevalent in county cricket, used to annoy him. For example, during slip-catching practice he would often encounter fielders pusillanimously pulling out of chances that bounced in front of them, making the excuse that fingers could easily be broken. It was the sort of attitude with which Fletcher would have no truck. 'Well done, you've saved a certain wicket,' he would say sarcastically when a catch was dropped.

Fletcher used to talk about the 'cup of tea brigade' in English cricket. In other words players who would turn up to a county ground early and be more interested in having their cup of tea than actually doing some hard graft. There is a curious habit in county cricket of players arriving ridiculously early, and then doing very little. I know that the Australians who came to Glamorgan, like Matthew Elliott, Jimmy Maher and Mike Kasprowicz, simply could not understand this behaviour. It is why it makes me laugh when county championship matches start an hour later the morning after late-finishing floodlit matches the night before. It is ludicrous that this has to happen at all, but I bet all the players are there at a similar time to usual. I know I would have been. The truth is that it is very difficult to sleep after day/night matches anyway. The brain is still racing. It cannot be calmed with the flick of a switch.

Fletcher did have respect for county cricket, but the England team was more important. And central contracts have worked – it is as simple as that. 'They were the single most important thing for the good of the England side,' says MacLaurin now. Before their implementation, England won 33.5% of its Test matches. Since their introduction in 2000 and up until the end of the 2012 Pakistan series they had won 45%. Enough said.

They worked immediately, if truth be told. One only had to consider what a threat the fast-bowling duo of Darren Gough and Andrew Caddick became. They stayed fit throughout the summer of 2000, sharing sixty-four Test wickets and only having to play three county championship matches each. This naturally evoked thoughts of what might have been. Caddick was thirty-one years old and Gough thirty by 2000.

Caddick was always over-bowled at Somerset, with the line peddled disingenuously that the more overs he bowled the better he bowled. Even though I found him a bit of a prat to play against, he could have been a great England fast bowler rather than just a very good one. His omission from the Ashes tour party in 1998/99, despite 105 first-class wickets in 1998, still counts as one of the most mutton-headed pieces of selection in recent times. He bowled 59,663 balls in first-class cricket, but only 13,558 were for England. Glenn McGrath bowled 41,759 balls all told, but 29,248 of those were for Australia. That's a difference of around 47% between the two. It is a tragedy.

With central contracts has come continuity of selection. Some have, of course, accused that of being a closed shop, but it is a far and welcoming cry from the bad old days when a player was only concerned about making the side for the next Test, regardless of the result of the one in which he was actually playing. Revolving-door selections played with players' minds, none more so, in my opinion, than Hick and Ramprakash. Had central contracts been in place at the start of their careers, I'm pretty sure we would now be considering their Test-playing days in a very different light, certainly as regards Hick, who was dropped more times in his Test career than a cockney drops his aitches.

There were other significant advancements under MacLaurin's tenure. First was the splitting of the county championship into two divisions in 2000. This was not easy, of course. It had been proposed in 1997, but a vote of the First Class Forum had decided against it 12–7.

David Morgan was still against the idea. 'Both David Acfield [chairman of the cricket advisory committee] and I were opposed to two divisions because we felt you'd have a second class of first-class county,' he says. That was a very common worry at the time, easily assuaged by the promise that every county would still receive the same ECB fee payments every year. So there was no penalty for being rubbish.

At this stage there was also no penalty for squandering the money on cheap foreigners imported through the back-door. Yes, we are talking about those delightful EU passport holders and Kolpaks who have caused me so much anguish throughout my journalistic career. Some might say that I was like a broken record, such was my persistent and vociferous opposition to these chaps from abroad. But I felt it was an issue that needed urgent and plaintive addressing.

Counties were clearly making short-term decisions in search of instant success. Because the European Court of Justice's 2003 ruling in the case of Slovakian handball player Maros Kolpak allowed a sportsman from any nation with an associate trading relationship with the EU to play freely as a professional wherever he liked, they were signing cheap South Africans by the bucketload and neglecting the much longer process of producing and nurturing homegrown players. I liked Ashley Giles's phrase at the time, likening many counties' recruitment drives to 'easy internet shopping'.

I was not, and am not, xenophobic. That much should be obvious from the thrust of this book. It is, after all, about two foreigners and the tremendous good they have done for English cricket. I have always been a huge fan of overseas players in county cricket. How couldn't I be when Viv Richards turned Glamorgan's fortunes around at the start of the nineties, teaching a talented but flabby-minded team how to win, and when Waqar Younis added the cream to a long-baked cake in the winning of the county championship in 1997? But they were top-notch overseas players; the sadness is that their ilk is rarely available any more. The huge increase in year-round international cricket, allied to the arrival of the IPL, has seen to that. The days of top foreigners playing full seasons and staying loyal to counties for years are gone, and in their place for a while came a host of jobbing, opportunistic mercenaries.

I have never blamed the individuals involved. They were, still are, just cricketers desperate to earn a living. Andy Flower signed initially for Essex in 2002 as an overseas player but then used his British passport to play as a local after retiring from international cricket; his brother Grant, who joined Essex in 2005, used the Kolpak ruling. They knew and know my feelings.

Top-quality individuals from abroad, in which category both Flowers undoubtedly fall, can add enormous value, of that there can never be any doubt. But as in life, it is a question of balance. When in May 2008 Leicestershire played Northamptonshire in a championship match and there were eleven players on the field not qualified to play for England, a tipping point had clearly been reached. Thankfully the system of performance-related fee payments, begun in 2005 by the ECB, has been strengthened, and, along with the tightening of entry qualifications by the Home Office, the problem has diminished.

The proliferation of Kolpaks has been my only regret regarding two divisions. I doubt that was troubling MacLaurin when he declared a two-divisional championship not to be his first-choice solution. As expressed in 1997 in his blueprint document for the England game 'Raising the Standard', he wanted a conference-style system, with three groups of six, and the six teams in one group playing the twelve other counties to make twelve championship matches a season. But this was rejected immediately by the counties; all the more funny then that it should arise again recently in discussion about the domestic structure.

But there is always discussion about the domestic structure. As I write, Morgan has just produced a review into the business of county cricket. It was not supposed to be specifically about the structure, but that is how it turned out, and it caused predictable uproar.

There always has been discussion about the county structure, and always will be, especially with eighteen counties, which is, of course, far too many. But to complain about that number is like complaining about old age. We need to get over it. I can't see the number being reduced during my lifetime.

What this does mean, though, is that there will always be compromise when considering the domestic structure. And so when the two-divisional championship was introduced, it came with the proviso of three up, three down. That was far too much fluidity, but that was what the counties wanted. Too many of them were fearful of being marooned in the second tier.

There was also a ridiculous early imbalance in the financial incentives available. The only prize money on offer was for the top two in each division, with the winner of division two receiving just £10,000 less than the runner-up in division one. The more materialistic cricketers quickly realized it was better to be in a yo-yo team, flitting between divisions, than a solid outfit in third or fourth in the first division.

Nowadays things are a little different, not least because of a significant upturn in the prize money available. Back in 2000 Surrey won £105,000 for securing the county championship. In 2010 the figure on offer was a very healthy £550,000, although it is spread between players (70%) and the county (30%), whereas before it was simply divided among the players. But it still beggars belief that in 2010 the division two winners received £135,000 for effectively finishing tenth, while the team third in division one received just £115,000. In 2011 it was slightly more complicated with the county's national insurance payment taken into account in the prize monies, but essentially the winners of the second division still earned £20,000 more than the third-placed county in division one.

Only in 2006 did the structure become two up, two down in terms of promotion and relegation. Me? I'd have one up, one down. Then we'd have an elite division, which must surely be the aim.

As it is, I suppose we should be grateful that the vote for change came at all. But it did come, in December 1998. Two counties abstained, but there were still fifteen counties in favour of two divisions, with one against. 'An historic decision heralding the most radical change in the structure of the first-class game since the championship was first rationalized in 1890,' wrote MacLaurin of it in his autobiography. 'This was, indeed, a quiet revolution.'

It was. And two divisions have been of enormous benefit. Intensity, competitiveness and professionalism have all increased. Even Morgan has been impressed. 'It hasn't quite worked out as I thought,' he says, 'and quite clearly when I talk to cricketers – and I always regard cricketers as extremely important people! [said with a smile and a knowing glance across the sitting-room of his Newport home] – they regard two divisions as a success. So I'm ready to admit that I was wrong.'

The other important initiative under MacLaurin's watch that helped improve England's fortunes was the setting up of a National Academy. Again, this was a long time in coming. The counties had approved its introduction by a vote of 16–2 as far back as 1995, and in June that year the former Australian leg-spinner Peter Philpott had been asked to be head coach at a proposed site in Shenley, Hertfordshire.

In October of that year Mark Nicholas, the recently retired former captain of Hampshire, was also asked by Dennis Silk, the chairman of the TCCB, to run the Academy. But by November the board's executive committee had performed an about-turn, reckoning Silk had overstepped the boundaries of his power, and an enraged Philpott, who had turned down other job offers, had received a fax stating that the idea was on hold.

It remained on hold until December 1999 when it was decided to try again. Hugh Morris, then the ECB's performance director, was the man tasked with its setting up. 'It was around the time that lottery funding became available,' recalls Morris enthusiastically of a project that was to prove the making of him as a cricket administrator, 'and Sport England [who were administering the Lottery Sports Fund] basically said, "Dream! We've got more money than we've ever had before. We need to hear your plans, and then we will sit down and assess them." I had to work with my staff to put a world-class performance structure together, of which the central part was the Academy. We spent over two years doing it. We looked at the Australian Academy. We looked at Liverpool FC's Academy. We did desk studies on academies around the world. We sent people to South Africa, and to America too.'

Morris was adamant that the Academy had to sit outside the first-class game, otherwise it would just become a county academy with a national badge on it. 'We wanted to rub shoulders with other sports and learn from them,' he says, 'so we began an open tender process, and had seventy-five expressions of interest from inside and outside the game. Then we sent out a very detailed invitation to tender, and that frightened a lot of people, so we got down to eight or nine serious bids.' Eventually Morris decided it was going to be at Loughborough, and after similar due deliberation the ECB's board agreed.

Next came the matter of funding. The centre was going to cost £4.52 million. Lottery funding would provide £4 million, but what about the other half a million? In stepped the Allan and Nesta Ferguson Trust with a generous grant. It wasn't going to cost the ECB or the counties anything, and for the first four years Sport England provided £2 million annually for its running.

In November 2003, fifteen years after Australia had opened its academy in Adelaide, the Queen formally opened the National Academy building at Loughborough. It was, and still is, the largest bespoke indoor cricket centre in the world, measuring approximately 70m by 25m, with six lanes in a hall long enough to accommodate fast bowlers off full runs with a wicketkeeper standing back.

For the two winters of 2001/02 and 2002/03 before the opening of the centre at Loughborough – renamed the National Cricket Performance Centre after the (Ken) Schofield Report in 2007 – the Academy was based in Adelaide. England were unashamedly copying Australia, and why wouldn't they, after just losing their seventh successive Ashes series at home that summer in 2001? So it also made sense for an Australian to run it. More to the point, the Australian who had been running the Australian Academy.

Step forward Rod Marsh, the legendary Australia wicket-keeper, who then ran the English equivalent for four years. 'There were a lot of Doubting Thomases about the Academy,' says Morris, 'so we needed somebody with real gravitas. Bringing Rod Marsh in was done specifically to raise eyebrows, and show we meant business.'

Among the first intake in 2001 were Strauss, Flintoff, Steve Harmison, Simon Jones, Ian Bell, Graeme Swann, Ryan Sidebottom, Chris Tremlett, Rob Key, Owais Shah, Alex Tudor and Chris Schofield. That's twelve players out of an intake of eighteen who went on to play for England. Seven of them went on to become Ashes winners, and eleven of them have either scored a century or taken five wickets in an innings for England.

It would be easy to conclude that the Academy was an instant success. It wasn't. It took years of tinkering and tailoring to arrive at the point in 2010/11 when England's Academy could be termed, without fear of contradiction, a world leader and an undoubted producer of world-class talent. They had long had the 'Merlyn' spin-bowling machine (which all eighteen counties now possess), which was so useful for England and their playing of Shane Warne during the 2005 Ashes, and the Hawk-Eye tracking system. Now everyone else in the world marvelled at their two latest technological advancements: the 'Pro-Batter', a virtual reality bowling machine where the batsman watches an opposition bowler running in on a screen before the ball is delivered, and 'TrackMan', a device that measures the revolutions a spinner is able to impart on the ball. In an instant Pro-Batter eliminates the age-old problem with bowling machines, that you could never time your pick-up and trigger movements as you would in a match situation. Indeed when I was a teenager, so much trouble did I have with synchronizing my movements on the bowling machine that I decided to stand with bat aloft, à la Graham Gooch.

The Pro-Batter, based on a device used by American baseball batters, is still not perfect, in that there is a small delay as the ball supposedly comes out of the bowler's hand, and some England batsmen have told me it is especially difficult to pick up bouncers from it, but, crucially, the length can be altered without any cue from the operator. England's batsmen undoubtedly benefited from it before the Ashes of 2010/11. 'For me, the great advantage is that you can time your trigger movements as the bowler – be it [Mitchell] Johnson, [Ben] Hilfenhaus or whoever – is coming in,' said Strauss.

As for the TrackMan, you often hear commentators talking about a spinner getting 'good revs' on the ball. Now they can be more certain of what they are talking about. Adapted from a device used by golfers, it's a small camera placed behind the bowler's arm that can measure the revolutions per minute generated by various bowlers. It should not surprise anyone that a wrist-spinner generates more than a finger-spinner, so of the England bowlers tested in 2010 Yorkshire's leg-spinner Adil Rashid recorded the highest figure (an average of 2,312), while of the finger-spinners Swann was top (2,083), with Monty Panesar (1,750), James Tredwell (1,682) and Mike Yardy (1,350) behind him.

How today's position contrasts with the Academy's beginning. I have to admit that I was never sure about Marsh.

Yes, there was certainly merit in his bark ('You overpaid Pommie bastards!' was apparently a constant scream to his quivering academicians) and his devotion to hard work, even if its implementation was sometimes crude in the extreme, but it just seemed to be a little too much about him at the Academy. It was all about how good a job he was doing. When he became an England selector in 2003, it was obvious that he was rather keen to promote those who had come under his wing. Thus his liking of wicketkeeper Chris Read, and his infamous rant in 2004, in front of the MCC players gathered at Lord's for the season's pipe-opener against Sussex, when he discovered that Read had been dropped for Geraint Jones for the final Test of the West Indies tour in Antigua. Marsh and Fletcher never got on. They got on even less after that.

I remember calling Marsh in 2005 to ask him about a piece I was doing on players who had struggled after they had left the Academy. I was thinking about the likes of Hampshire's Derek Kenway (an academician in that original intake in 2001/02), who had a shocker of a county season in 2002, averaging just 11.82 with the bat, and was out of the professional game altogether by the end of 2005, and others like Yorkshire's Matthew Wood. Marsh thought I was specifically talking about Glamorgan's David Harrison, who'd just returned to his county after a winter with the Academy with a bowling action considerably different from that with which he'd arrived there. Suddenly he was jumping extraordinarily wide on the crease. He was half the bowler he had been previously. Glamorgan were not happy, and made their feelings clear to the Academy. Marsh thought I was stirring trouble about that, and in general questioning him as much as his methods. I wasn't. I actually had some sympathy with the situation. It was obvious to me that if Harrison were to become an England bowler, he would need to increase his pace. The Academy concurred, and that was at the heart of their work with him during that winter of 2004/05. Unfortunately it resulted in a changing of action. If you don't venture, you don't discover . . .

Marsh was in charge for two years when the Academy was based in Australia, and two at the new Loughborough centre. Early on he made a prescient comment to Morris. 'We've run an Academy in Australia for thirteen years and it's changed every single year,' he said. And that is what has happened in England. It was not always necessarily for the best, but there has certainly been considerable change, not least in the name of the side representing it abroad, whether it has been the National Academy, England A or, as now, England Lions (or Elite Player Programme side – EPP), with selection now at a point where it is very nearly a second-choice England side that takes the field on most occasions.

Cock-ups are much fewer on the ground, and the selection process much further back down the line has also been revolutionized. Gone are the days of England fielding Under 15 and Under 17 sides to play international matches. Instead, at the conclusion of the annual Bunbury Festival, so enthusiastically organized for the twenty-fifth time in 2011 by David English, an England Development Programme (EDP) squad is selected with the Under 19 side as the long-term goal. Players are added and cut as the years progress.

It is no random selection process guided by vested interests and old school ties. That used to happen, believe me. My best man, Adrian Knox, a rather rough-and-ready rugby player,went to Whitecross Comprehensive School in my hometown of Lydney in Gloucestershire. When playing for the West of England in the old regional Under 15 tournament that pre-dated the Bunbury Festival, he scored more runs than anyone else. By a distance. But he didn't make the England Under 15 team selected from that tournament. A lot of public schoolboys did.

Now it is rather different. Morris had sorted the structure of the senior team, then the Lions/Academy, so in 2010 the pathways to the national Under 19 side were his last mission. And after a disappointing ICC Under 19 World Cup performance that year, it was quite a mission. But Simon Timson, the ECB's head of science and medicine, has studied NFL scouting processes in the United States, and now the ECB are using hard evidence rather than mere selectorial whim. They use tests in the four categories of technical, physical, psychological and fielding, as well as bare cricketing statistics.

That is not to say it is foolproof just yet either. I know of a young lad who only just made his regional side for the Bunbury Festival in 2011, after much persuasion from a coach who knows his onions. He then impressed so much that he only just missed out on the fourteen players selected for the EDP. Had there been fifteen he would have been in.

Research has shown that cricketers who reach the world's top ten have usually made their first-class debuts by the age of nineteen, and by twenty-three are playing international cricket. The ECB pull no punches about the function of the EDP. It is the beginning of the line 'to produce the world's best cricketers for England by the age of twenty-seven'. Some will fall by the wayside quickly. Some may reappear as late developers in county cricket. But there is now a scientific talent identification process in place. Some might even say England have managed to put in place a system that circumvents the clunky county system. It is very clever indeed.

These days more home Lions fixtures are arranged (you can't expect strong opposition abroad if you don't provide it at home), even if they enrage the counties who are reluctant to release their players. The counties need to pipe down on that issue. Those fixtures are a vital part of the England process, and the players recognize that. They know where they stand in the pecking order, and to be selected for a home Lions match is to know that a full cap is not that far away.

At the start of the 2011 season I interviewed Craig Kieswetter, the Somerset wicketkeeper/batsman who had enjoyed a successful Lions tour of the West Indies. He had just suffered a thigh muscle strain, meaning he would miss the Lions' four-day match against Sri Lanka at Derby. He was genuinely 'gutted', as he put it. This was a chap who had already played one-day and T20 cricket for the full England team (a World Cup winner no less in T20, after England's success in the Caribbean in 2010), and he was bemoaning missing his first home Lions match. There was a time during the early years of the Academy when players simply did not want to be involved. Weeks and months of perceived incarceration at Loughborough were mind-numbing and ambition-destroying. Now Kieswetter was saying, 'To be part of the Lions set-up is unbelievable. Every player has got the same ambition to play for England. In a county set-up you get some players who are quite happy to be a county player, but with the Lions the whole atmosphere changes completely because everyone has a common goal and is training the hardest, eating the healthiest, doing everything they can to play for England. The whole environment is one of pure success and enjoyment.'

I was gobsmacked by these comments. I genuinely was. He was the first player I'd heard speak so glowingly about the Academy process. I'd heard some positive things in the past, of course – indeed my former Glamorgan team-mate Mark Wallace had written in the *Wisden Cricketers' Almanack* of 2011 that 'the winters I spent at the Academy were among the most enjoyable and rewarding periods of my career' – but this was eye-opening stuff.

I had often been critical of the Academy, especially at times of the current director David Parsons, who took over in 2007 but did not play first-class cricket. I felt there was just not the technical expertise available that players close to the England side deserve. It was probably a little harsh, because Parsons is what they call in very modern parlance an excellent 'facilitator'.

In other words he is rather like a midwife overseeing the act of childbirth. He assists in the actual delivery, but is not the producer of the end result.

The shift can be traced back to Peter Moores. After a successful spell as coach of Sussex – in 2003 they won their first county championship title in a 164-year history – he was appointed director of the Academy in 2005. He made an immediate change. 'As soon as I got there I realized that it wasn't right that it was a National Academy,' he says. 'I thought, "This has got to be a Performance Centre." It wasn't servicing the England team, and it had to do that.'

Fletcher's repeated mantra as England coach was that he should be 'putting the roofs on players' techniques, not digging their foundations'. And how right that statement is. But Fletcher was astounded at the technical naivety of many of the players picked in his England Test teams. For instance, Caddick could not bowl a slower ball. So Fletcher showed him not just how to bowl it, but also where to bowl it – ideally wide of off-stump so that the batsman, having checked his shot, then has to reach for the ball.

Moores was conscious of Fletcher's mantra. 'I thought to myself, "This is where we should be building the foundations",' he says. 'But I did not have enough coaches at my disposal. So I went to see Gordon Lord [the ECB's head of elite coach development] and said, "I've got no coaches! Who are the best candidates currently on the Level Four coaching course?"'

Lord mentioned a chap by the name of Flower, then still playing at Essex. Andy, that is. 'I watched him coach,' says Moores, 'and I liked his style. He was giving simple messages, which is what I like.'

That winter Flower began the first of two winters coaching at the Academy as a specialist batting coach. Little did anyone know then where that was going to lead.

3

The Greatest Series

I still wince at the memory. I was making my way in cricket journalism in 2005, writing a weekly column on county cricket for the *Sunday Telegraph*, as well as reporting on county matches for the *Guardian* during the week. For the week beginning Monday, 8 August 2005, I was due to cover Glamorgan against Warwickshire at Colwyn Bay. The hotel and train journey had been booked, and I was rather excited. I quite like Colwyn Bay. I scored a few runs there once upon a time. A triple century even, before my braggadocio runs riot. And I'd not been back there for a long time.

But then I received a call from Ian Prior, now the *Guardian*'s sports editor. Would I fancy changing my plans and going to the third Ashes Test at Old Trafford? Though I had done some international cricket the previous summer (my international writing 'debut' was for the *Guardian* at Trent Bridge for England's game against New Zealand in 2004 when I did a piece on fielding at short leg, of all things), I had not been in the initial plans for 2005. The big guns had quite naturally been rolled out. Goodness, Gideon Haigh was even on the roster. And he is a great cricket writer, believe me.

I dallied at Prior's suggestion. I said the hotel booking might be a problem. What about the train ticket? At that moment I wanted to go to Colwyn Bay more than I wanted to go to Old Trafford. What was I thinking? The greatest Test series ever was in progress, and I was thinking I'd prefer to watch my old teammates in a county game. I do love Glamorgan, and years of underachievement, mainly due to poor off-field decision-making beginning in that year of 2005, have not diminished that (even if I have offered passionate criticism), but this was madness.

Thankfully Prior did not slam the phone down. He gently coaxed me, and off to Old Trafford I went to do what they termed some 'technical pieces'. I'm rather glad I did, not least because I witnessed at first hand the mayhem on the final morning when some twenty thousand people were locked out of the ground as they desperately sought to buy tickets for the denouement. Duncan Fletcher's wife Marina told him she thought there had been a bomb scare when she saw the crowds filing away in their thousands as she attempted to get to the ground. I was of much the same mind. The scenes were scarcely believable. The taxi ride from my hotel in the city centre was hardly worth it. You couldn't get near the place. 'I'll just get out here, thanks, driver,' I said about two miles away.

I suppose if I'd gone to Colwyn Bay I might have seen a fellow called Jonathan Trott make 152 for Warwickshire in their ten-wicket victory, but it was rather more pleasurable watching a Glamorgan bowler, Simon Jones, taking 6-53 in the first innings for England at Manchester.

The excitement was palpable. And that was just in the press box, where lack of emotion and disinterest are supposed to rule. One eminent cricket correspondent was all set to emigrate to New Zealand until this series suddenly and joyfully reignited his enthusiasm for the game. And sitting next to me there in Manchester was the man from the Press Association. When Justin Langer was dismissed, he turned to me and screamed, 'We're gonna win the Ashes!' And that was only in the first innings.

Of course, England did eventually win the Ashes that summer, but not until a thunderously memorable battle had been played out. The words upon the DVD sitting in my study describe it as 'The Greatest Series'. I have no argument with which to disagree. It truly was.

England were hammered at Lord's in the first Test, even though they had roughed up the Australians on the opening morning ('This isn't a war' remarked Langer to England's fielders after Ricky Ponting had been hit in the face by Steve Harmison and no one had enquired about his health). Then they won at Edgbaston in a synapses-shredder, decided when Mike Kasprowicz was caught down the leg-side with just three runs required for victory. There was a draw, with Australia nine wickets down, at Old Trafford, and then victory at Trent Bridge after Australia had followed on.

So it came down to the Oval, and only a draw required for England to regain the Ashes. Thanks to Kevin Pietersen's belligerent 158 on the final day they just about managed it. Cue the sort of celebrations never seen before or since in cricketing circles: an open-topped bus parade through many thousands of adoring spectators from the Mansion House to Trafalgar Square, a reception at Downing Street and MBEs all round (and OBEs for Fletcher, Michael Vaughan, chairman of selectors David Graveney and team manager Phil Neale). 'I stood there in Trafalgar Square and thought long and hard about what I had achieved in cricket,' said Fletcher. 'This was undoubtedly the pinnacle.'

It certainly was. And it was not something Fletcher necessarily foresaw. When he had asked me to write his autobiography in 2004, he had been planning ahead. It might be seen as an overly negative viewpoint, but he was worrying about the consequences of a poor tour to South Africa that winter and something similar in this Ashes series. It could have happened. Both opponents were formidable.

In case of failure he wanted his book deal in place. But at this stage in 2004 Fletcher did not want anyone knowing about these book plans. It would only increase speculation about his future. I dragged this secret around with me for some considerable time. Every time we met he stressed the importance of confidentiality. I'll admit that I was scared witless about its coming out.

We met for the first time at a Heathrow hotel prior to England's departure for South Africa. We talked about his early life. We talked a lot. Or rather he did. Once he starts, he can talk. I was so engrossed that I forgot about something. My Dictaphone. In those days I had one of those old-style cassette recorders. I'd turned it on at the start. But we seemed to have been talking for an awfully long time. I checked the cassette. The tape had snapped!

We had been talking for probably about an hour with no recording to show for it. It is any journalist's biggest nightmare. As a batsman will often wake up in a cold sweat having failed to get his pads on in time to be next to bat, so a journalist will dread this sort of situation.

I felt physically sick. What a first day as a ghost! Not only was there the unrecorded stuff, but also the recorded stuff that needed to be salvaged. Somehow the snapped tape had to be mended. Fletcher has a reputation for being intolerant of fools. Well, he was very tolerant of this fool on that day. He should have just sent me on my way with the words 'Sort it out yourself, you idiot!' Instead he spent the best part of an hour painstakingly fixing the cassette. Much of it was saved.

The next time I saw Fletcher was in Cape Town on the last

day of the third Test that winter. This was now serious undercover work. The need to keep the book project a secret had been intensified by speculation about Fletcher being in line to replace Ray Jennings as South Africa coach. He had even been approached about it, albeit remarkably clumsily via a security guard at one of the Tests.

Fletcher was on edge throughout my visit. He desperately wanted to beat South Africa, but his side had just been hammered in Cape Town; his mood was not lightened either by Marina falling ill with the first of many black-outs that were to affect her health over the following years. Fletcher, always so caring and protective of his wife, had rushed from the ground to attend to her. Interestingly, Harmison, with whom Fletcher never really got on, had arranged flowers for her from the players. It proved that, essentially, Harmison has a good heart. It is just that he can seem lazy, and easily led.

I was picked up at the airport by the team liaison officer and whisked into the ground to witness the last rites of England's only defeat in that series. I made a mistake, though, by wandering around the ground and bumping into Mike Dickson, then the *Daily Mail*'s cricket correspondent. I'm not sure he twigged the reason for my presence, but he most certainly would have done so had he seen me the following day.

Thanks to some hastily found prowess as a John Le Carré character, I just about ensured he didn't. Fletcher had agreed that Nasser Hussain, by now retired and working for Sky as a commentator and for the *Daily Mail* as a columnist, could come to conduct an interview at his house in the Claremont suburb of Cape Town, where I was also staying. But as he doesn't write his own stuff (although he did do so on occasions when employed previously by the *Sunday Telegraph* and considered doing so upon Mike Atherton's departure when he was also interviewed for the job I currently hold as columnist), he had to bring Dickson with him. As they were arriving through the front door,

I was leaving with Marina through the back door and into the garage. We were going to go for a coffee nearby and return when Fletcher called at the end of his interview.

However, when we opened the garage doors, we immediately realized there was a problem. Standing outside in the road was a photographer. And not any old photographer. There, lurking as only a waiting snapper can, was the always-chuckling Winston Bynorth, known to all as 'Muttley' and a fellow old boy of Monmouth School. It genuinely was a comedy moment.

There was no other choice. Into the back seat I went and ducked down as Marina drove out of the driveway and down the road, leaving Bynorth still waiting for the call to go inside and take some shots to go alongside Hussain's interview. Thankfully Bynorth did not see me. And I didn't tell him about that incident until 2008.

I met Fletcher regularly throughout 2005 to go through periods of his life and career, but without any fixed end-point. There seemed to be some confusion. I have a feeling that the publishers thought the autobiography was going to be finished after that 2005 Ashes series, come what may. And, of course given subsequent events, there are those who will argue that Fletcher might have been better off finishing then anyway.

But whatever the negotiations between Fletcher, his agent and those publishers, I was not ready for the phone call from Fletcher as I was driving to the annual Cricket Writers' Club dinner in Park Lane on 2 September 2005. 'We're going to do a diary of the Ashes as well as the autobiography,' he said. 'We've got three weeks to do it.'

Christ almighty.

Those were three of the busiest weeks of my life, even if the first week or so was rather frustrating with little work being done. That's because the final Test did not start until 8 September. The diary would still have gone ahead, I think, had

England lost that final Test and the series been drawn, but the title *Ashes Regained* obviously would not have stood.

As it was, of course, England drew that match to take the series and we managed to meet our deadline, and, while Fletcher was understandably keeping his most incendiary stuff for later, there were some intriguing insights into his and the England team's thinking that summer. It is not just the devil that is in the detail but, usually, the fascination.

So Fletcher revealed that it had been England's goal to win five Tests that summer, two against Bangladesh and three from five against Australia. Had they not been denied so agonizingly at Old Trafford they would have achieved that.

It was also the team's goal to make over 400 in the first innings of each Test in fewer than 130 overs. England did that on three occasions; Australia did not achieve it once.

England wanted one batsman to make over 150, and that was achieved twice through Vaughan at Old Trafford (166) and Pietersen's 158 at the Oval.

They also wanted three wickets from their fielding unit in every Test. By that they meant two catches – of the sort where the bowler knows he owes everything to the brilliance of the fielder (like Andrew Strauss's stunning telescopic slip catch to dismiss Adam Gilchrist at Trent Bridge) – and a run out. And we all know there was one very famous run out in this series, when substitute Gary Pratt hit the stumps at Trent Bridge prompting an outburst of expletives from the departing Ponting at Fletcher, who'd appeared on the England balcony having abandoned some toast-making inside.

Ponting had been furious at England's policy of frequently using substitute fielders throughout the series, reckoning they were merely allowing bowlers to change clothing, refresh and maybe even have a massage after spells. But that was palpably not the case here as Pratt was on for Simon Jones, who'd limped off with an ankle injury after bowling just four overs in

Australia's second innings, having taken five wickets in the first to ensure they followed on. And, if Ponting thought England were always making sure they had top-notch fielders on the field, he was wrong there too, because England had their best substitute fielder – the Zimbabwean Trevor Penney, who was also doing some fielding coaching – still in the dressing room.

There was also another run out attempt from another uncapped substitute fielder that is often forgotten in the analysis of this series. This was by Stephen Peters, then of Worcestershire, at Old Trafford, where in the mayhem of the final session, with barely six overs remaining and Australia eight wickets down, Peters' shy at the stumps just missed with Brett Lee not even in the picture. Ponting was out soon afterwards, but Lee was still there at the end. England could so easily have gone 2–1 up there, and the final series result might have been 3–1.

After that match I interviewed Peters. He told me that at the end of the match, after Lee had somehow blocked out Harmison's last offerings, Vaughan had called his shattered team into a huddle on the field and begged them to take a look at the Australian balcony. 'Look at those lot celebrating a draw,' the skipper had said. It was indeed a significant moment, a huge change in mindset.

Fletcher also divulged that every member of the squad had a copy of the poem 'The Man in the Glass' by Dale Wimbrow. After the diary's publication, he even found himself reciting the poem on Radio Five Live. Throughout the series England players could be heard shouting 'Look in the mirror!' At other times of stress the refrain 'Remember the Iceman!' could be heard. That referred to the visit the squad received before the series from Alan Chambers, who in 2000 along with Charlie Paton had reached the geographical North Pole without support, dragging their 250lb sledges across the ice from

Canada in horrendous conditions, the worst polar weather for twenty years. No Briton had ever achieved the feat before.

Then there were the secret, but crucial, one-on-one net sessions Fletcher had with Vaughan at the New Rover Cricket Club, home to the Yorkshire Academy near the Leeds outer ring road. They had done something similar before the 2004 Lord's Test against the West Indies when Vaughan scored twin centuries. Now, after Vaughan had failed twice in the first Test at Lord's, bowled for 3 and 4, they did so again.

Success was instant in county cricket where Vaughan scored a hundred for Yorkshire in a Totesport League match against Kent, even if for England he had to wait until Old Trafford for his reward. Speak to him now and he still looks back on those sessions with real affection. 'They were always Fletch enjoying his coaching most,' Vaughan says. 'They were really good fun. We'd try different things and different drills, but he always made sure I finished in a way he knew I'd get confidence from. I always had to end up playing on a high. Whenever I spent two days with Fletch there might not have been much of a technical change by the end of it, but I always felt better in myself. That was what he was good at. I always felt I would get runs afterwards. People will say, "Why didn't you do it every week?" But it was quite hard to get two days every week to hit balls with Duncan Fletcher.'

I know what Vaughan means. It was exactly the same at Glamorgan. Fletcher is the best batting-practice thrower I ever encountered. That may sound a little silly. But many professional cricketers cannot throw properly to a team-mate – many don't want to, if truth be told, because they don't like doing it. They'd rather just bat. But Fletcher has a strong arm and is unerringly accurate. Little wonder he has had the odd shoulder operation (as did Andy Flower, incidentally, at the end of the 2011 summer). He was always in demand.

*

Everyone has their own little story about that 2005 Ashes series, of how the series touched their lives, of missed appointments and the like. Mine is rather different. Mine comes from the last morning of that thriller at Edgbaston, which I watched from home. Alone in my lounge, I was not a journalist. I was just like any other supporter. And my advice to the England bowlers was becoming louder by the minute, as they appeared to be allowing the last pair of Lee and Kasprowicz to secure a victory, after having come together still with 62 required. Just as my sledging of the Australian batsmen became louder too.

At this point my six-year-old daughter Bethan entered the room. Looking at the television, she said, 'Isn't that Michael? He's your friend, isn't he? Why are you saying nasty things to him?'

As captain of Glamorgan I had signed Kasprowicz as an overseas player in 2002, and our families had become close. I can say without fear of contradiction that he is one of the nicest blokes I have come across in cricket. But here I was screaming at him. Or rather at pictures of him on the TV. Bethan was, quite naturally, rather perplexed.

When it was all over, she said, 'You'd better say sorry to him. Phone him now.'

It was, of course, no time to phone, not least because the Anti-Corruption Unit of the ICC does not permit phones to be used in the dressing room. But I did text. 'Bad luck, mate' I typed.

As it happens, it was bad luck, because the glove that deflected Harmison's delivery into wicketkeeper Geraint Jones's gloves was not actually on the bat handle at the time. Kasprowicz should not have been given out. Under today's Decision Review System, he probably would not have been given out.

But, once the initial despondency subsided, it has not done him that much harm. He now has a rather good theme for his after-dinner speeches. I emailed him some time afterwards to organize an interview on the subject. 'I would love to have a chat to you re. Edgbaston and my role in assisting the promoting of cricket for the benefit of all,' he wrote in reply, referring to the effect that the England victory had there.

So this is how that after-dinner speech now goes. 'I was approached by an Indian gentleman some time afterwards and asked whether I was Michael Kasprowicz,' he says. 'He was delighted when I replied that I was, and he immediately thanked me and said that I had single-handedly saved Test cricket. He pointed out that if we had successfully chased down the runs and won that second Test, Australia would have gone to a 2–0 series lead and, as he said, "on to win the series, leading to the slow death of Test cricket". I politely thanked him, but did feel the need to point out that the single hand he spoke of was actually off the bat at the time!' Ah, good stuff.

For many, the enduring image of the whole series occurred just after Kasprowicz was out, when Andrew Flintoff was seen with a consoling arm around the distraught non-striker Lee. 'No one came to comfort me, did they?' joked Kasprowicz. 'I was left on my own.' Crouched down, trying to bury his head in his bat handle.

Dismissing Kasprowicz was not England's only piece of fortune. There was Glenn McGrath standing on a stray ball before that game had even started, putting him out of that Test and the next one at Trent Bridge. And then soon after that there was skipper Ponting astonishingly opting to bowl, even after McGrath's injury. 'I could not believe my ears,' said Vaughan. And as Fletcher later said, 'What was he thinking? There was no doubt in our minds that we were going to bat first.'

But more than anything this was triumph for Fletcher and Vaughan, and their meticulous planning. Beforehand they had resolved to 'get into the space' of the Australians, in other words never to stand back in any confrontation. This was first manifested in a one-day international at Edgbaston in the series that preceded the Tests, when Simon Jones hurled a ball at Matthew Hayden and it hit him in the chest. Hayden was enraged and, with chest pumped out, Buzz (to his England opponents, after Buzz Lightyear) flew back at Jones.

In earlier years, and indeed sadly in the later Ashes of 2006/07, Jones might have found himself fighting a lone battle. Here he was backed as the likes of Collingwood, Strauss and Vaughan ran in to support their team-mate. The throw had accidentally hit Hayden, and Jones was about to apologize before Hayden reacted so strongly.

The truth is that Australian cricketers love to trade on their macho, aggressive on-field attitude, but once an opponent reacts in similar fashion it is as if some terribly heinous crime has been committed. They like to dish it out, but . . .

So they bristled throughout this series, with Ponting often demonstrating the Tasmanian Devil that lurks within him. His greatest frustration must have been that he was comprehensively out-captained by Vaughan. The England skipper's field placings took planning and preparation to new levels, often befuddling the Australians in the process. For instance, Hayden had a poor series that was only partially rescued by his 138 in the final Test at the Oval, as he was shackled by a series of men placed strategically 'on the drive' (in other words, in a stationary catching position much closer to the bat than they would be when saving the single), often one of them standing on the very edge of the cut strip on the off-side.

Then there was England's mastery of reverse swing. Australia had simply not reckoned with that, and in Flintoff and Jones England suddenly had two magnificent proponents of the art. Given Australia's disgruntlement with England's unexpected success, it was little surprise that there were dark mutterings over the reasons behind England's propensity to achieve this. There always are where reverse swing is concerned. But it was wide of the mark when it was suggested that Murray Mint sweets had been the reason behind its regular appearance. As illegal as it is, those sweets are used in the game, certainly in the county game. But they are used to cultivate conventional swing. The essence of reverse swing is keeping the ball dry; applying sticky sweet-laden saliva does not quite fit into that theory.

Previously in the world game reverse swing had mainly been achieved into right-handed batsmen, although Pakistan's Waqar Younis and Imran Khan could take it away a little. Now Flintoff and Jones were reversing it both ways, and a considerable distance too. Flintoff was quite superb, and not just with the ball. His century at Trent Bridge was undoubtedly his finest international innings. And, of many bewitching spells, his first over of the Australian second innings at Edgbaston will always rank as one of the greatest in Ashes history. With its first ball he bowled Langer, and with its last he dismissed Ponting caught behind. In between Ponting suffered hell on earth. It was an over that exists only in a batsman's worst nightmare.

But Jones, so shrewdly picked by Fletcher, was the real surprise. To me too. I'd seen him as the wild and woolly fast bowler of his youth. But I'd always liked him and tried to back him. In my brief stint as Glamorgan captain I only capped two players: Jones in 2002 when it was announced that he was to win his first England cap, and Mark Wallace, the wicketkeeper/ batsman with whom I've become close friends as I have tried to help him on his desired path to becoming a journalist. I capped Wallace just before I announced in 2003 that I was about to enter hospital for a major knee operation, effectively ending my first-class career. 'Can I have your bats?' Wallace remarked cheekily, as I finished what was quite an emotional speech.

It was assumed that Jones learnt reverse swing from Waqar, who was at Glamorgan in 1997 and briefly in 1998. But he didn't. It is just another of those urban myths. The 'Racehorse', as Jones is known, was only a colt then. He probably only had a couple of nets in total with Waqar. Jones taught himself reverse swing while out in Australia with the National Academy in the winter of 2001/02. 'I was messing around in the nets at Adelaide with an old ball, and it was going big,' Jones says. 'That's when I did it for the first time; I hadn't really tried it before. The boys were in a bit of trouble when I was bowling it. Straussy wasn't too happy at a net session, was he?'

Indeed he wasn't, and Strauss could still recall that session some time later. 'I didn't know which way he [Jones] was swinging it,' he said. 'He bowled me a couple which swung away, and the next one started yards wide and just missed my off-stump.'

Nets are one thing, though; match situations quite another. So when it worked for Jones, firstly in a middle practice when he tied Chris Schofield in knots, and then in a match between the Academy and the Western Australia Second XI at Abbett Park in Scarborough, Perth in March 2002, he knew he was on to something. Western Australia were going along nicely at 106-1 when Jones changed the game and probably his career, quickly plunging his opponents to 146-6 on his way to 6-48, reverse-swinging the ball both ways for the first time. The Academy's manager Nigel Laughton was there. 'They couldn't get a bat on him,' he said. 'Our boys came off in disbelief; they'd never seen anything like it. It was boomeranging.'

Jones was back in Australia the following winter, this time with the full England squad, but his tour was cut as tragically short as his Test career later was, carried off on the first day of the first Test at Brisbane with a snapped anterior cruciate ligament in his right knee. Injury has bedevilled his career ever since. He never played another Test after Trent Bridge in 2005. But he was still due to play county cricket in 2012, having returned permanently to Glamorgan from Hampshire, whom he'd joined from Worcestershire.

England's bowling coach in 2005 was an Australian, Troy Cooley. He received much praise for his work that summer, not least from his bowlers, with whom he formed a close bond, as much a kindred spirit as a coach. And there was little doubt that Fletcher rated him. Fletcher did not credit Rod Marsh with much, but bringing Cooley to the National Academy was undoubtedly one move he was happy to endorse. It took just one practice session with Cooley for Fletcher to realize this was 'one quality individual', as Fletcher has said. Their views on reverse swing were similar, and Fletcher was incandescent with rage when the ECB allowed Cooley to leave in 2006. Cooley merely wanted a contract extension to take him up to the World Cup in 2007, but the ECB dithered and Cooley returned to Australia sooner than he had planned. Although, interestingly, late in the writing of this book I had a chance conversation with an ECB official who told me that he thought Cooley wanted to go home all along, whatever the length of contract that would have been offered.

But it was Fletcher, not Cooley, who initiated the plan of bowling around the wicket to Australia's left-handers during this 2005 Ashes campaign, with the reverse swing of Flintoff and Jones for the first time neutering the threat of Adam Gilchrist down the order. For years there had been a question mark next to Gilchrist's name on the whiteboard in England's dressing room detailing opposing batsmen's weaknesses.

One player involved in that series who wished to remain anonymous said, 'Troy got a lot of the credit for the bowlers in 2005, but I reckon it was more down to Fletch. For Gilchrist, the plan was not just to bowl around the wicket but to use Flintoff straight away. Fletch had seen something that meant Gilchrist struggled facing someone so close from around the wicket. It wouldn't have worked with Harmy [Steve Harmison] or Hoggy [Matthew Hoggard] because of the angle they created from wider on the crease. I know that Fletch was so confident beforehand that he said to Vaughany something along the lines of: "He [Gilchrist] won't get a run if Fred gets it right."' And

Gilchrist didn't get a fifty, averaging just 22 and being dismissed four times in the prophesied manner.

So the regaining of the Ashes in 2005 came down to the simple-looking but always-tricky-in-reality task of batting long enough on the final day of the series, Monday, 12 September, to ensure Australia could not chase down the remaining runs. It was so tense a day that even Fletcher admitted to nerves beforehand, revealing in *Ashes Regained* that he retched on the way from breakfast to his room. It was certainly no ordinary day. Not least because England had to abandon their usual plan of driving to the ground in their own cars and use a team bus because of impending celebrations. That might, of course, be the norm on tours abroad, but this was a deviation from normal practice that could easily upset the superstitious. And the leaked news that Trafalgar Square had already been booked did not help.

To tell the story of the pressure involved one needs only to consider the early stages of Pietersen's innings of 158. He would undoubtedly be the hero later in the day, but he could so easily have been given out first ball to give McGrath a hat-trick (the ball brushed shirt amid the most vociferous of appeals in those times before the DRS), then he was dropped on 0 and, probably most memorably, dropped again on 15 by Shane Warne at slip. 'Warney's dropped the Ashes' they said. And they were probably right, harsh as it might sound on the great leg-spinner who, amid a mountain of personal problems, took forty wickets in the series at an average of 19.92.

England were eventually all out for 335, leaving Australia an impossible 342 to win. They faced just four balls before bad light intervened, and at 6.15 p.m. the umpires Billy Bowden and Rudi Koertzen walked to the middle and removed the bails to spark the sort of celebrations that English cricket had long since forgotten. The Ashes had been Australia's – not physically, of course, but that is another matter – for a long sixteen years and forty-two days. At last they were England's again.

Those celebrations went on all night, and all the next day from Trafalgar Square to 10 Downing Street and on to Lord's where the symbolic gesture of handing back the Ashes to the MCC took place. The tales are legion, encapsulated by Flintoff's response to David Gower on live television that Tuesday morning: 'To be honest with you, David, I'm struggling. I've not been to bed yet and the eyes behind these glasses tell a thousand stories.'

Ah, the utter saintliness of victory. Flintoff's considerable and public inebriation – he was about as steady on his feet as Long John Silver after more than one bottle of rum – was to become the stuff of legend, the people's champion in all his glory. But really it was gory crapulence. For me this was the moment the 'Freddie' story began to spiral out of control. The reaction a couple of years later, when he drunkenly boarded a pedalo after a World Cup defeat in St Lucia, was rather different, and rightly so. Then he was pilloried and suspended.

Such behaviour in Trafalgar Square and thereafter should never have been so publicly acclaimed and glorified. But then the open-top bus parade should not have been the day after the Test finished. That was a mistake. 'It was a shambles,' said Harmison some time afterwards. 'We'd worked so hard for so long, so to tell us at the end of the game that we had to be ready to get on the bus at nine the next morning . . . I'd defy any sports team to be bright-eyed and bushy-tailed after what we'd just gone through. They should have let us sit in the hotel for two days, then we would have turned up clean-shaven, suited and booted, but too many people wanted to make a photo-opportunity out of us, especially the Prime Minister [Tony Blair] and the Mayor of London [Ken Livingstone]. Actually, I didn't think we got as rough a ride as we should have done. We got off scot-free, really. I was embarrassed. We had to celebrate it, but certain people bowed to pressure and put us straight on that bus.'

It was not the only mistake. The subsequent awarding of MBEs and OBEs was misguided. In my opinion only Vaughan, Flintoff, Trescothick, Strauss and Fletcher should have been rewarded. Bell's and Collingwood's could have come later.

And why did it take this victory for Fletcher to be granted the British passport he'd first applied for way back in 1991? He'd been coach of England for six years. His parents, his two younger brothers and sister all had British passports, but not him and his two older brothers. Apparently it was all to do with dates of birth, and whether they'd been born before 1 January 1949. Anyway, he received the good news via text during the Trafalgar Square celebrations.

Not that the rationale behind the celebrations was necessarily wrong. At the time tens of thousands filled London to acclaim their cricketing heroes. Two years later such antics were being described as those of unjustified jingoism and triumphalism, the beginning of the end for that England team. Nothing, of course, to do with an injury list containing Vaughan, Giles, Jones (S.) and Trescothick that could have prompted a souvenir issue of the *Lancet*.

Speak to Hugh Morris, now the ECB's managing director, and you discover the true impact of those Trafalgar Square celebrations. 'I remember being there at 6.30 that morning,' he says. 'There was obviously nobody around, except a few men putting some scaffolding up. And I did worry, "What if no one turns up here today?" But they did turn up, and it was an awesome sight. I remember thinking, "It's incredible how victory in international sport can inspire the nation." From that moment our every move at the ECB has been to inspire the nation. That is our vision. I thought that day was a really good thing. It showed that we'd made a lot of progress.'

Indeed they had made a lot of progress. That 2005 Ashes victory had been a long time in its planning, and its coming. It was actually the sixth Test series England had won in succession.

They had won thirteen and lost only five of the twenty-two series since Fletcher took over in 1999. To compare: in the previous twenty-two series before Fletcher arrived, they had won just six. That is some turnaround. To think that in the Schofield Report of 2007, commissioned after the 5–0 humbling at the hands of a great, bent-on-revenge Australia side, it was said there had been 'steady progress' in this period. It was just a little more than that, let me tell you.

4

Forward Press

If one Test can be pinpointed as the turning point under Fletcher, then it is surely the Lord's Test of 2000 against a West Indies side that still contained the legendary pace duo of Curtly Ambrose and Courtney Walsh. Having beaten Zimbabwe 1–0 (a draw against them at Trent Bridge betrayed the uncertainty still evident in England's cricket), England had lost the first Test at Edgbaston by an innings and 93 runs.

By the start of day three of the next Test at Lord's, having dismissed the West Indies for just 54 in their second innings the previous evening, they were chasing 188 to win on an increasingly uneven pitch. No matter that Andrew Caddick, Darren Gough and Dominic Cork had done to a decent West Indian batting line-up – including Brian Lara, Shivnarine Chanderpaul and Jimmy Adams – what West Indian attacks had been doing to England's batsmen for years: that is, roughed them up with pace and steep bounce. It would mean nothing were these runs not knocked off.

Somehow, amid agonizing tension and drama, England just

scraped home by two wickets, with that wonderful competitor Cork hitting the winning runs. The sight of the last man, the debutant Hoggard, nervously sitting just inside from the dressing-room balcony, waiting with helmet on and chinstrap in mouth, was a snapshot of the nation's cricket team at the time. It was unsure of its quality and its ability.

This was the victory that sent belief coursing through the team's veins, as well as confirming that Vaughan, with a calm second-innings 41, was a batsman of rare character. Thereafter the series result was almost a formality. The Wisden Trophy was England's after being in the West Indies' possession for twenty-seven long and painful years (many England batsmen of those times still bear the scars). A squad containing the experience and class of players like Hussain, Atherton, Stewart, Thorpe, Gough and Caddick should have been able to compete healthily on the world stage. But the complexity, sometimes selfishness, of some of these characters had been holding England back.

To take a small example from this Lord's Test. Neither Gough nor Caddick had before taken a five-wicket haul at Lord's. Neither, therefore, had his name on the famed honours board. In the first innings Gough came mighty close with 4-72. Then in the second innings Caddick at last achieved his goal with stunning figures of 13-8-16-5, offering easy evidence of the discrepancy between his bowling average in the first innings of Tests (37.06) and the second (20.81). The differential is too large to ignore; there was undoubtedly something within his mental make-up that predisposed him to react to situations rather than go out and create them himself. As Atherton observed later, he was definitely 'more sheep than shepherd'.

Anyway, Caddick entered the Lord's dressing room in un-surprisingly high spirits. 'I'm on the honours board!' he exclaimed joyfully right in front of Gough, who never did make it on to that hallowed timber. It was a miracle there wasn't a bust-up there and then. But Gough just about managed to keep his cool with his gauche New Zealand-born colleague. Watching from the corner of his eye was the all-seeing Fletcher. He recognized the playing talents of this unlikely pair – Gough short, skiddy and bustling, Caddick tall, loping and bouncy – but also the need to harness some sort of professional relationship between them. They were never going to be close mates, the heart-on-the-sleeve extroverted Gough and the introverted, insecure Caddick, but they could be as close to a world-class opening pair of bowlers as England had had for some time.

Later in the day Fletcher took Caddick out on to the balcony and advised him, among other things, on the follies of insensitivity. It was one of Fletcher's sternest lectures. Caddick had mocked Gough during the Zimbabwe Test earlier in the season when again Gough had finished with four wickets.

To me that was typical Caddick: he just speaks before he thinks. In word and deed he always seemed to lack maturity as a cricketer. His sledging was simply inane most of the time. Those who went on the 1997/98 tour of the West Indies still tell the tale of Caddick professing to know more about seam movement than both Ambrose and Walsh. Caddick, though, listened to Fletcher and later apologized to Gough. From there their partnership flourished.

'I often sit back and wonder what might have been if we had lost that Test,' says Fletcher. Indeed. Ironically the captain Hussain wasn't actually playing at Lord's, having broken his thumb in Birmingham, with Stewart deputizing. But had they lost that match England would surely have lost the series and then Hussain would have lost three out of his first four series in charge. He couldn't score a run that summer anyway, finishing with a pair at the Oval, and even in victory told Gough that he was considering quitting. He would surely have gone, with Vaughan obviously not ready to take over as he was to be in 2003, central contracts might easily have been rubbished, and Fletcher might not have been signing the two-year extension to his contract that he did sign, in October 2000.

Thankfully, none of that happened. And Fletcher could take England to the sub-continent that winter for their first tour there since 1992/93, and truly show his worth.

Whatever the reasons for England's prolonged absence from Asia, unequivocal success was certainly not among them. Since 1980 England had played twenty-three Tests in India, Pakistan and Sri Lanka, and won just four of them. They played spin as if it were spoken in a different dialect.

Fletcher was to change all that. He had been a good player of spin himself, as many Zimbabweans seem to be. Andy Flower might come to be regarded as one of the best to grace the game in that respect. Another Zimbabwean, Dave Houghton, was an excellent player of the twirlies too.

If Fletcher is famous for one particular piece of coaching advice then it is surely his urging of his batsmen to use the 'forward press'. Apologies for becoming technical here, but I do feel it is an important part of the story.

Fletcher especially advocated this trigger movement against spinners, but liked it to be used at all times if possible. It is basically a small step forward – not a lunge, because it is important that the head is kept behind the front leg – to ready the batsman before the ball is bowled.

This is how Fletcher used to explain its use to his charges. 'This is the deal, guys,' he would say. 'You have a million-pound job, but the only snag is that you can only get to work each day by bus. And there is only one bus. It arrives punctually every day at eight o'clock. If you are late for work, you lose your job. So you have a decision to make: do you get to the bus stop early, on time, or late?'

The answer, of course, is that you want to get there early – the 'there' in this case being the pitch of the ball. Ideally you would want to arrive there bang on time, but then you would run the risk of getting there late.

Trigger movements are a very modern phenomenon. Or at least the attention paid to them certainly is. In the old days batsmen were taught to stand still before the ball was bowled. And there are some players who still do that. But the truth is, however unpalatable it may be for the old-timers, that was advice dispensed in an age when all play was conducted at a slower pace. It is a dangerous policy having to make a decision so early as to where the ball will pitch when you have no idea about the degree to which the ball might swing or seam. It is much better to make small initial movements (ensuring you are momentarily still at the point of delivery, of course: a moving head means that the camera that is your eyes takes fuzzy pictures) and then another smaller movement.

That is at the heart of Fletcher's advocacy of the forward press. On turning pitches against wily spinners many wickets are often taken at the close-catching positions of silly point and short leg. If you do not move before the ball is bowled, you are taking a big stride towards the ball and therefore creating considerable momentum towards it. It is often hard in such circumstances to stop the ball deflecting to those close fielders. Fletcher's 'forward press' makes it much easier to kill the ball stone-dead in defence. How I wish I could have 'pressed' against the spinners (I think I naturally did so against the seamers). Fletcher tried to get me to do it, but I was too long in the tooth.

In the wet early summer of 2011 during yet another rain delay at one of the Tests against Sri Lanka, Sky Sports showed a re-run of the 1998 Sri Lanka Test at the Oval, my second and last Test. There I was, for my very last act in international cricket, lunging forward without a 'press' to Muttiah Muralitharan, caught at silly point off the glove. QED.

The 'forward press' also makes the sweep shot much easier. And Fletcher was hugely keen on the sweep, and indeed the sweep/slog. He was adamant that, especially on sub-continental pitches, they were the safest shots to play. Again the old-timers might advise to advance down the pitch and hit the ball straight, which is clearly sound counsel if you can get to the pitch of the ball and negate any spin. But what if you don't quite get to the pitch, and the ball is spinning sharply? By still trying to hit down the ground with a straight bat, you are actually playing across the line of the ball. By sweeping you can smother that spin and you don't need to know which way the ball is turning.

Fletcher worked out that it is better to crouch in your stance against spinners (as you naturally do in the 'forward press'). Again this went against traditional theory. Young spin bowlers are told to flight the ball above the batsman's eye-line, but Fletcher reckons it is best for the batsman to be underneath that line of the ball. He thinks it is easier to pick up its length from there, with its reference points simpler to spot.

Euclid would have been proud of Fletcher. Just like the Greek mathematician who was known as the 'father of geometry', Fletcher loves his angles. He was constantly reminding his players of the sort of alignment required to 'hit the ball back where it comes from', as the old adage goes. But that adage could be nebulous in its meaning. Fletcher made sure he was always much more specific in his advice. For example, for a left-arm seamer bowling over the wicket, the right-hander was told to try to hit the leg-stump at the far end. Not the stumps, but specifically the leg-stump. Or for the South African Makhaya Ntini, who bowls from very wide on the crease, to try to drill the ball straight back at his body.

With spinners, especially those who turn the ball prodigiously, it is more difficult. The old advice was always 'play with the spin'. Say for a right-handed batsman facing a sharp-turning off-break, that would usually mean his going across his stumps to play to leg. Or for a left-hander facing the same bowler from over the wicket to close himself off and play everything through the off-side. Well, Fletcher revealed this to be tosh. 'Try and play a straight ball with a straight bat' were always his words. So for the right-hander to the off-spinner, it would be best to stay leg-side of the ball and, if the length was right, to play through the off-side with a straight bat, even if a dozy commentator might say 'He's playing against the spin there!'

It's easier said than done, however. Marcus Trescothick had all sorts of problems understanding it, so much so that Fletcher playfully went out and bought a protractor to slip under his bedroom door on tour in Sri Lanka.

I could rarely work it out either. I recall one match in particular when I incurred Fletcher's wrath. It was at Sophia Gardens, Cardiff, in 1999, the second and last of Fletcher's summers at Glamorgan, and Durham were the visitors. In their ranks they had Simon Brown, the once-capped England left-arm swing bowler and a fine county practitioner. Bowling from the River Taff End he created such a mess in his follow-through that a huge crater appeared on a length. Consequently the ball spun from that end more than I'd ever experienced in my entire career at that ground. And off-spinner Nicky Phillips had the match of his life, taking twelve wickets.

Fletcher talked to us about how to counter this, as we chased 247 to win in the last innings, how we should stay on leg-stump to the off-spinner. I didn't get it. I felt as if I was exposing my stumps; just like when I couldn't sweep/slog, which, if played properly (think of the late Hansie Cronje hitting Warne over mid-wicket), is executed with the front leg thrown out of the way so that the arms can be freed. I got bowled around my legs trying to sweep Phillips with my body way outside off-stump. It would be wrong to say that Fletcher was fuming. Outwardly anyway. Because that was not how he operated. He merely gave me a look that told me everything I needed to know, and probably knew already.

Fletcher applied his geometry to bowlers too. Ashley Giles achieved notoriety for bowling his left-arm spinners over the wicket to right-handers. 'I still get remembered for that as much as anything else,' laments Giles now, 'even though I've gone back and counted my wickets, and it's about half and half bowling over and around the wicket to right-handers!' It was Fletcher's idea. He quite rightly reasoned that there was no difference between Giles bowling over the wicket to right-handers and any right-arm off-spinner bowling over the wicket to a left-handed batsman. The angle was exactly the same, with turn created naturally by that angle. And Fletcher had realized that Giles's bowling action involved significant crossing of his right leg across his body. If he bowled around the wicket, he would need to turn the ball an awful long way just to counteract the angle caused by his action.

So the trip to Pakistan and Sri Lanka in the winter of 2000/01 was Fletcher's chance to put all these methods and theories into practice. This was new stuff to the England players, and, while Fletcher was making it quite plain that he thought this to be the best method, he wasn't forcing it on anyone. Talk of the 'forward press', though, and two names immediately spring to mind: Trescothick and Vaughan.

Vaughan was undoubtedly the quickest of the England players to adapt to it. 'He didn't speak to me about it for a year or so,' says Vaughan, which is unsurprising since his debut had come in South Africa in the winter of 1999/2000 and before their Asian adventure England had not been faced with too much spin thereafter, 'but I think he felt I was a quick learner so he was never afraid of giving me new ideas. My thought when playing the forward press was that you were basically playing a forward defensive before the ball got there. That was Fletch's theory so that you had so much more time to decide what attacking shot to play.'

Trescothick had made his international debut the previous summer, and, as already mentioned, was very much a Fletcher pick. He hung on Fletcher's word and was very soon earning himself the nickname 'Fletcher's Son'. 'The forward press changed my game really,' he says now. 'I started learning it in Pakistan, came home and did loads of work on it over Christmas, and then went back to Sri Lanka and it clicked. I got a hundred in a warm-up match [against Sri Lanka Colts], and then my first Test hundred in the first Test at Galle.'

He had a different way of thinking about it from Vaughan. Trescothick would fake as if going down the pitch to the spinner. 'I found it really hard to get used to,' he admits. 'I got stuck at first, so I just practised. Learning the timing was key for me. When am I going to "press"?' You can 'press' too early ('fall asleep at the bus stop' as Fletcher says, going back to his original analogy).

Alastair Cook would never be termed a Fletcher acolyte – he was very friendly with Flintoff and Harmison, playing darts with them regularly on tour – but he knew the importance of the 'forward press' (as well as moving his hands lower on the bat handle, which, as Fletcher suggested, gave him more control against the spinners, and, as I mentioned, was a feature of Andy Flower's batting style too) and worked hard on its implementation into his game. It took him eight months, but he cracked it and still uses it now. It is pretty useful these days where the DRS is concerned, because spinners receive so many more favourable lbw decisions and so you must try and play them with your bat rather than your pad, and that is so much easier having 'pressed' first. Not that England 'pressed' at all well against Pakistan in the United Arab Emirates in early 2012 when they were whitewashed by Pakistan 3–0.

Andrew Strauss, who was not to make his Test debut until 2004, did not take to Fletcher's methods of playing spin immediately. He preferred to play as he'd always done. Then he embarrassingly padded up to Warne at Edgbaston in 2005 and was bowled. Having turned a huge amount out of the rough outside Strauss's off-stump, it was heralded as a ball to match Warne's first in Ashes cricket, the one that bamboozled Mike Gatting at Old Trafford in 1993, but in truth Strauss, having gone way across his stumps, had played it poorly. He went to Fletcher afterwards and admitted that he needed to change his method against spin. Hours of work on the Merlyn machine followed.

Of course, there were others who couldn't pick it up at all. Flintoff was one. Asked by reporters after scoring a hundred in a warm-up match in India in 2008 whether he had been confused by the 'forward press', he answered with another question, 'What did you think?', and laughed uproariously. But then Flintoff never was a technical cricketer, even if Flower did admit surprise to me about some degrees of subtlety in his batting when he first worked with him.

Wicketkeeper Geraint Jones, who controversially replaced Chris Read at the end of the 2004 West Indies tour, is an interesting case. 'I tried it but it never really clicked for me,' Jones says. 'I could understand the theory behind it, and I tried hard because I'd seen Tres and Vaughany play so well using it, but I struggled to do it properly. I think I probably do it naturally now, but with not as big a "press" as Fletch wanted.'

There were some players who knew what Fletcher wanted and would try everything to impress him. I remember interviewing Kent's Rob Key once, and he seemed rather keen to keep mentioning that he was using the 'forward press'. Unsurprisingly he was out of the England side at the time. Afterwards another Kent player told me he thought the interview 'embarrassing' in the way Key gave a fawning message to Fletcher. It is said that Ian Bell only employed the 'press' to satisfy Fletcher. I've never been able to confirm that, but what I will say is that Bell uses it today to spinners, and it worked pretty damned well. Until he was bamboozled by Saeed Ajmal's 'doosra' in the UAE in 2012.

It is, though, easier as a coach to destroy a player than improve him. Fletcher would never dive in and advocate radical changes to a player's technique immediately. He would always watch and observe, bide his time before making judgements and considering alterations. When he arrived in 1997 at Glamorgan he barely said a word for two weeks, standing at the back of the nets, thoroughly inscrutable. It was as if the Sphinx herself was sitting there. Skipper Matthew Maynard said to me, 'I think we've signed a mute!' But we hadn't. Only the strongest and best coaches behave in that manner. Lesser coaches feel the need to justify their position immediately.

Fletcher improved England dramatically that winter in Asia. It was not merely the playing of spin and Giles's emergence as a spinner/batsman/reliable fielder just as Fletcher wanted, but also the clever plans among the seam bowlers, with the instant abandonment of English-type plans on English pitches in favour of the modern Asian way in the use of reverse swing and cutters. Gough and Craig White were vital in that respect.

England had not won a Test in Pakistan since their very first Test in the country in 1961, yet they won the third Test at Karachi, where Pakistan had never lost any Test before, to take the series 1–0. It may have been pitch black when England triumphed, but England had shown the sort of bottle too often absent in such tense run chases in years gone by.

Crucially England had then to prove it was no fluke. They did that by winning 2–1 in Sri Lanka in a spectacularly ill-tempered but highly significant series. Not least among the positives (of which Thorpe's mastery of Muralitharan was pivotal) to come from it was the return to form of Hussain with a courageous century in Kandy. Since taking the captaincy he had made just one century, 146 not out against South Africa in Durban, and since returning from that tour up until the start of the Kandy Test he had averaged just 12.53 in eighteen innings. Throughout this time he had captained the side astutely, but even the best captains have to justify their position in the side some time, so Hussain was near to despair with his batting. He could not sleep in Sri Lanka. Team-mates recall seeing him wandering the hotel corridors at all hours of the night. Then, after more personal failure and an innings loss for the team at Galle, he went to Atherton and admitted that he was close to resignation. He wanted to know what the mood was among the players about his continuing as leader. Atherton reassured him that the team was behind him, and also reminded him of the England Young Cricketers tour they had undertaken together to Sri Lanka in 1987 and of the 170 Hussain had scored at the Asgiriya Stadium, Kandy, scene of the next Test.

It worked. Hussain made a horrible-looking and indeed downright fortunate 109 (escaping with one 'catch' to silly point), but he was back. Upon reaching the milestone Hussain 'went berserk', as he later wrote. 'I ran towards the pavilion, towards my boys,' he said. 'The hundred wasn't for me, it was for them. For ten months they had carried me with their performances. They had made me look like this great captain with the results they were earning for England and they had not said a bad thing against me or questioned my place at any time.'

Not only were England transformed as a Test team, having won four series on the trot, but so was Hussain. Selfish? Selfless, more like. A remarkable transmogrification.

But that did not mean, of course, that England could conquer the world. Between 1987 and 2005 there was always a rather large and weighty albatross on their shoulder, a bird going by the name of Australia. They arrived in 2001 and promptly thrashed England 4–1. It was a summer in which the toughness of English cricket was questioned. Australia's captain Steve Waugh pulled a calf muscle badly in the third Test at Trent Bridge, yet still managed to score a century on one leg in the final Test at the Oval.

In contrast, England's players missed Tests as a truant child does classes. Hussain was absent for two, Thorpe for four, Vaughan for the whole series and Giles for four. I too missed much of the county season that year, Caddick having broken my hand at Taunton. I'd already been out for a month with that injury when I chanced upon Fletcher in the gym at Sophia Gardens. 'How long have you been out for?' he asked. I told him, and he did not respond. He did not need to. He shook his head solemnly and walked off. He may as well have just said it: 'You English are soft cocks.' And, though he will not like Marina reading such things, that is the sort of language he sometimes uses in the dressing room, just like the word for his favourite characteristic in a cricketer: 'dogfuck'.

Of course, injuries can happen, but different people deal with them in different ways. Just after Fletcher arrived at Glamorgan he was hit on the finger while giving slip-catching practice (he always wore a batting glove on his bottom [left] hand but nothing on his top hand), and blood was pouring from it. He just carried on with the practice. We pleaded with him to get it seen to. He refused.

Fletcher was always keen on fitness, but with England he felt he rarely had the time required to supervise or instigate it. As captain of Zimbabwe he had led from the front in that regard. Macky Dudhia, a seam bowler of Indian descent who played under Fletcher in the early eighties and eventually went into cricket administration when spending time as the Bangladesh Cricket Board's chief executive, tells a wonderful story of Fletcher's maniacal attitude. 'I recall an arduous fitness session at Alexandra Sports Club nets where we had been divided into groups to undertake certain fitness training drills in rotation,' says Dudhia, who was manager of the black team Bionics in Harare whom I appeared for in the early nineties, first along with Glamorgan team-mate Adrian Dale, then with Surrey and Durham off-spinner James Boiling. 'The group I was in were not pushing themselves hard enough and as a consequence, at the end of the fitness session, we were told by Duncan that we would need to do fifteen minutes extra. We all groaned, muttered and sulked. For me who had very little air left in the lungs this was going to be very difficult indeed! As we all, most grudgingly, lined up to do these shuttle runs, Duncan, to our astonishment, joined us in the "punishment" and did the shuttle runs for the full time. To me, that spoke volumes of the man and his leadership qualities.'

With England, though, Fletcher often had to leave players to their own devices, especially between tours. And this invariably led to trouble where, say, Harmison was concerned. Sometimes he would turn up to a tour barely having bowled a ball, and certainly not having acquainted himself too regularly with his local gym. It was little coincidence that Harmison's apogee in 2004, when he became the number one ranked bowler in the world (taking sixty-seven Test wickets in thirteen Tests that year, including the remarkable 7-12 in the first Test of the West Indies tour in Jamaica), came after spending considerable time doing fitness work with the footballers at Newcastle United's training ground early that year.

Harmison was also not awarded a central contract at the beginning of that winter in 2003, and had not then impressed in Bangladesh in the first tour of three (Sri Lanka followed before the Caribbean), whence he had returned home early with a back injury. That Bangladesh trip was another important staging post in Fletcher's regime, a chance at long last to implement, in conjunction with his trusted physiologist Nigel Stockill, the sort of fitness standards he had demanded when captain of Zimbabwe.

It had not been easy under Hussain, whose attitude to fitness was not exactly enthusiastic. He almost delighted at being at the back when there was any kind of team run, even if just during a warm-up. This irked Fletcher a little, who wanted his captain to set an example (as he had advised Hussain upon first meeting him when talking of his body language). But in fairness Hussain's response was that he had been doing that for so long that to change then would have looked rather too manufactured. Ironically Hussain spends more time in the gym now as a commentator than he did when he played. He looks a lot trimmer.

Hussain had been precisely the right captain at the time, but in his successor, Vaughan, Fletcher found someone who could advance the team in other areas. During the summer of 2003 Vaughan had been to the British Grand Prix at Silverstone and had marvelled at the smartness of the Ferrari team. Just like Lord MacLaurin previously, Vaughan vowed to smarten up England again. It was not that they had returned to the sort of scruffiness MacLaurin had encountered, because Fletcher was always pretty strict on dress code. He had certainly transformed us at Glamorgan in that respect. It was just that some of the older sweats had become a little lax in their application of Fletcher's principles. So between them Vaughan and Fletcher vowed to sharpen up the England team in every respect in Bangladesh.

They trained their socks off, morning and night when they were playing, and morning, noon and night when they were not. It was an exhausting regime, but it was certainly worth it. In 2004 England did not lose a Test, drawing just two and winning the other eleven, with their eight on the bounce – the summer's seven plus the first in South Africa that winter – being a record. Their 3–0 win in the West Indies was the first series victory there since 1967/68.

It was a shame England were not that fit when they went to Australia in 2002/03. They were actually in worse shape than for that home series in 2001. They travelled with concerns over Flintoff, Gough and Simon Jones, and soon lost Jones after his horrific knee injury in the first Test at Brisbane. Giles's tour was over after one Test when he broke his wrist in the nets, John Crawley missed two Tests with a hip injury, Stewart missed one as did Caddick and Harmison. Then some replacements arrived, and they got injured too. Chris Silverwood, Craig White, Alex Tudor and Jeremy Snape were all called up for some part of the tour including the one-dayers, and all were injured.

You felt for Dean Conway. He copped some stick, some of which still rankles today. But for too long he had been asked to do too much, even if he had by now split his physiotherapist's role with Kirk Russell, who was doing the Tests while Conway did the one-dayers. He needed help. And if any good was to come out of the winter of 2002/03, it was that early in it Peter Gregory was appointed as the ECB's full-time medical officer. Now, since the appointment of science and medicine manager Simon Timson in May 2006 and Nick Pierce's replacing of Gregory later that year, England can probably boast the best cricketing medical set-up in the world.

The other significant positive to come from that winter was the fact that Vaughan was clearly a world-class batsman. Three centuries and 633 runs at 63.30 said so very loudly. But even he had his own injury worries with his knee. And he could not have known that his ascension to the captaincy would come so soon. Hussain resigned the one-day captaincy after the 2003 World Cup, and then lasted only three Tests that summer before resigning after the first Test against South Africa at Edgbaston.

In truth it was little surprise when you look back now. Hussain admitted that once Vaughan became one-day captain the situation became 'strange'. Crucially his relationship with Fletcher changed. Fletcher realized that too. Whenever he spoke to Hussain, Fletcher found himself mentioning Vaughan and what had happened with the one-day side. He felt conscious of being seen to be talking to Vaughan in Hussain's presence, so actually made a conscious decision not to do so. That's how bad things became. It was no longer just the Fletcher and Hussain show. Hussain didn't like that. I remember him saying, jokingly of course, to Fletcher, who was a consultant to the home team during the England tour of South Africa in 2009/10, 'What you doing going for dinner with Jamo? I thought I was your best mate!' He clearly felt like that about Vaughan.

So, all in a rush at Edgbaston, Hussain resigned. After four years in the job they said he was the best England captain since Mike Brearley. Simon Barnes of *The Times* went further.

'Nasser Hussain is the most significant cricketer to have played for England since the war and perhaps the finest captain to have held the office,' he wrote. 'Hussain took on an England side that was hopeless. He fought not cricketing opponents but the enemy within – the sneaking, insidious culture of defeatism, the weasel in the heart of the English pro.'

When he finished as captain, Hussain wrote to Fletcher, saying, 'Thanks for making me look a better captain than I was.' That is a little too self-deprecating. Yes, Fletcher's remarkable technical know-how dovetailed perfectly with his passion ('Hussain generated heat, Fletcher light' wrote Scyld Berry), but as Barnes writes so eloquently, Hussain fought so many important battles that were not just on the cricket field. He fought the authorities and helped alter the way of thinking in English cricket. He toughened it up.

His acme as captain was definitely the 2000/01 tours in Asia, with the series wins over Pakistan and Sri Lanka. If one session lingers longest in the memory it was when Sri Lanka were dismissed in the third Test in Colombo in only 28.1 overs. Hussain had pulled his hip flexor muscle early in the match and could barely walk by the end of it, but his unrelenting passion and desire drove his side home in blistering heat.

After a productive start with the bat in his first away series in South Africa, Hussain had lost his way with his own game. He eventually realized that more attention was required personally, and so came to string together an impressive list of tone-setting innings in series. In his last five series as skipper before the three Tests against Zimbabwe and South Africa in 2003, he scored at least a half-century in his first innings of every series. The gutsy 106 at Christchurch in March 2002 was undoubtedly a highlight, but all were incontrovertible evidence of a captain leading from the front.

Hussain acted with hugely impressive dignity and sensitivity when confronted with the tragic death of Ben Hollioake during that tour of New Zealand – Fletcher was almost in tears when recounting the details of that episode to me for his auto-biography – and, at the other end of his character traits, won plaudits for the moral victories he secured during the tour of India in late 2001. There he demonstrated the more inventive side of his captaincy. England, with a weakened team, lost the series 1–0, but they frustrated the Indian batsmen, especially the great Sachin Tendulkar, who became so flummoxed by Giles's over-the-wicket leg-stump line in the third Test in Bangalore that he was stumped for the first time in his Test career. It attracted many critics, but as Hussain says, 'I can't believe people expected me to just stand back and admire him [Tendulkar]. No, mate, you're the best player in the world and you're going to have to work for your runs.'

Hussain said it was 'the peak of my captaincy'. And if the nadir had been that day at the Oval in 1999 with which we began, he is also easily recalled as the captain who inserted Australia at Brisbane in 2002. As Australia racked up 492 he is easily pilloried, but he was hardly alone in thinking it best to bowl first. Fletcher agreed, as did many senior players. And England had sought Marsh's advice on all the Australian pitches beforehand. Of Brisbane he'd written 'if there is to be any lateral movement off the seam it will be on day one'. Waugh later admitted he would have inserted England. What is also forgotten is that Simon Jones suffered that nasty injury of his on the first day, leaving Hussain a bowler short.

Of course, Hussain was not quite finished as a player in 2003. He would play on, and play some significant innings as the senior batsman, until the summer of 2004 when he called time after making a match-winning century against New Zealand at Lord's. It might have only been the first Test of the summer, but Hussain's timing was impeccable.

Farewells in professional sport are rarely fairy tales – mine came at a dank Derby after being lbw to probably my least favourite opponent, Cork, for not very many – but Hussain's was a joyous exception. Vaughan had twisted a knee before the match and in his stead had arrived a chap named Strauss, who'd made 112 and 83 (run out by Hussain in the second innings!). Selection might have been mighty difficult for the next Test, so Hussain scored his runs and left in the grandest of manners.

5

Black Armbands

The country of Zimbabwe might háve provided the England cricket team with two perspicacious coaches, but it has also provided it with untold anguish and heartache. The Cullinan Hotel on Cape Town's Waterfront describes itself as 'stylishly grand and perfectly majestic', and, having visited it myself, that is no idle boast from one of South Africa's better hotels. But for a weekend in February 2003, it became nothing less than a hellhole for England's cricketers.

It was here that meeting after meeting was held to discuss whether England should travel from Cape Town, where the opening ceremony of the World Cup was being held, to Harare to play Zimbabwe in their opening match of the tournament. Politics engulfed sport to the extent that sport was forgotten, a mood summed up neatly, if rather crudely, by Michael Vaughan at the time. 'I'm sick of fucking meetings,' he said in a rare break from them. 'I've been in there so long I've forgotten what a cricket bat looks like.'

Zimbabwe had altered horrifically from the country I had

rushed eagerly back to during my cricketing winters in the early nineties. Robert Mugabe had begun his awful land redistribution policies in 2000, and as a result the country had begun to fall into the sharpest of declines. The economy collapsed and riots ensued. It was a social and political disaster – a word never to be used lightly, but one wholly applicable here. In a sickeningly short space of time, Africa's 'bread basket' had become a basket case.

The 2003 World Cup had been awarded to South Africa as long before as 1993, and they in turn had decided to allocate some of the ties to Zimbabwe and Kenya. That decision had been taken before Mugabe began those land policies. But given this sudden turn of events, there was considerable apprehension about the staging of matches – in Kenya as well, where there had been terrorist attacks. However, a delegation from the ICC had visited both countries and, while recognizing some deep concerns over security, deemed them safe enough to host their scheduled World Cup matches.

New Zealand declared their hand early and asked for their match to be moved from Kenya. That request was refused, so they declined to play, and forfeited the four points on offer. England too asked the ICC to move their match from Zimbabwe, citing worries over the security of all involved, spectators included. And they too forfeited four points when they eventually refused to play in Harare. But what a horrible, snaking road it was to reach that decision.

A clearly vexed Nasser Hussain devoted the first chapter of his autobiography to the issue, and in talking now to some of the other chief movers in the episode, like Tim Lamb and David Morgan, it is easy to detect their angst with a situation which could, and should, so easily have been resolved by politicians rather than by cricket administrators and, even more ridiculously, by cricketers themselves. Had it occurred five years later the government would simply have forbidden the England cricket team from going to Zimbabwe, as it did when banning Zimbabwe's tour of England in 2009, thus preventing their participation in the ICC World Twenty20 here in the same year. But in 2003 the government merely advised England not to play in Zimbabwe, even though Zimbabwe had been suspended from the Commonwealth in March 2002. They contended that they couldn't insist on England's withdrawal.

The previous December the Cabinet minister Clare Short had been outspoken in her opposition to England visiting Zimbabwe. 'I think it is deplorable and shocking,' she said. 'I think they should not go. It is like pretending everything is OK in Zimbabwe and it is not.' Pressure was added when it was made clear that the Prime Minister, Tony Blair, and the Foreign Secretary, Jack Straw, were against the fixture. Downing Street called on England's cricketers to 'reflect' on the 'humanitarian and political crisis' inside Zimbabwe. 'Seven million people are already in need of food assistance,' a Number 10 spokesman said. 'We ask them to reflect on this but ultimately it is a decision that can only be taken by the ICC and ECB. It is not for Government to tell the cricketing authorities what to do.'

What poppycock! This was Secretary of State for Culture, Media and Sport Andy Burnham in 2008 when announcing that Zimbabwe's tour should be cancelled: 'It was quite unfair to leave individual players in the position of having to make a moral judgement in the context of an awkward and un-comfortable position. The right thing to do was to provide clarity. We made the decision after giving it the longest possible time for the situation to change in Zimbabwe. The Zimbabwean Government has ceased to observe the principle of the rule of law: it has terrorized its own citizens, including the ruthless and violent suppression of legitimate political opposition. Accordingly, the UK Government has responded with a measured approach which seeks to isolate Zimbabwe inter-nationally and bring pressure to bear on supranational institutions such as the United Nations and European Union to take yet firmer action against the despotic regime, whilst ensuring that its humanitarian life-saving mission to Zimbabwean citizens continues. The UK Government considers it would be contrary to this general approach for the English cricket team to participate in bilateral fixtures with Zimbabwe. The close ties of the Zimbabwe cricket team to the Mugabe regime have also had a bearing on our decision.'

Sadly there was no such *force majeure* in 2003. And so the saga began. 'It was one of those intractable issues,' sighs the then ECB chief executive Lamb now, as we sit in a restaurant close to the London office of the Sport and Recreation Alliance, where he has been chief executive since 2005. 'We didn't get any help from the government, and there were so many dynamics and conflicting influences that contributed to make this an absolute rock-and-hard-place issue.'

England had been in Australia before the World Cup, and there in their penultimate one-day international of the tour, in Sydney, the whole squad received letters and pamphlets from a protest group called the 'Organized Resistance', outlining the situation in Zimbabwe. There were no death threats, but there was some strong propaganda, warning especially of serious unrest should the team travel to and play in Zimbabwe.

The squad travelled straight from Australia to South Africa – a source of some irritation to the players who had hoped to pop home first, particularly as the best-of-three finals of the VB one-day series against Australia had not lasted three matches. Some, like Andrew Flintoff and Ashley Giles, had been at home recovering from injuries before the World Cup. They had seen and heard that the public mood was very much against going to Zimbabwe, and they had also seen a Channel 4 documentary about some of the terrible happenings in the country. They had made up their minds that they were not going to Zimbabwe, come what may.

This was not a topic that could be dismissed easily, especially as it was likely that, if England didn't go to Harare, they would lose vital qualifying points. By not going many players would be waving goodbye to their last tilt at a World Cup. Upon arriving in South Africa, the first of the many interminable meetings took place, and at it Hussain said to his players, 'Some of you are going to have to take some serious growing-up pills and take this issue very seriously indeed. It's looking as though everyone is going to leave us to make some pretty big decisions here.'

Duncan Fletcher was in an awkward situation. On the surface it seemed ideal for England to have a Zimbabwean coach at this time. But in truth it was not. It was more complicated than it appeared for him, thus the reason why he did not make one public pronouncement on the issue, frustrating many observers in the process. The crucial thing was that, although Fletcher left Zimbabwe in 1984, he was still travelling on a Zimbabwean passport. Once inside Zimbabwe the authorities could have done what they liked with him. They were doing this on a regular basis. Imagine if he had said something the government did not like. Also, many of his wife's family still lived in Zimbabwe. In no way did he want to endanger them.

Privately Fletcher thought the game should go ahead. Although he abhorred the decline in the country he loved (in a way he had seen it coming, though, deciding to leave in 1984 when, after dislocating his shoulder, the local hospital did not have a safety pin for his sling), he thought Zimbabwe to be safe, and he was wary of cricketers making moral judgements. He thought there were many countries that England visited to play cricket you could make a case for not visiting on moral grounds. But there again he felt his view was biased. He had helped announce Zimbabwe itself as some sort of international cricketing force with his own performances at the 1983 World Cup, and he feared boycotting the match could now help destroy Zimbabwean cricket. He hardly wanted that to happen.

Fletcher offered advice to Hussain and the players – 'At no stage did he let me down,' said Hussain later – but suggested that the Professional Cricketers' Association would be of more help. So stepped forward their group chief executive Richard Bevan for a starring role. He enjoyed that. Bevan, who as I write is football's League Managers' Association chief executive, has never been one to shirk the limelight. But he is good at what he does. He took over the PCA in 1996, at a time when it had little influence or power. By the time he left eleven years later he had transformed it commercially, and begun to ask questions of the game's administrators that needed asking. He gave the players a sense of professionalism, and he gave them a proper voice.

Bevan certainly ensured the England players possessed the latter on this issue. And so on Monday, 27 January they issued this statement: 'The England players urgently request the Zimbabwe match on February 13 to be moved to South Africa. As concern has grown over the current political situation in Zimbabwe, the players request an urgent review of the World Cup schedule. Without doubt the (moral and political) issues have been weighing heavily on players' minds. Concerns are increasing daily and it is clear the situation in Zimbabwe is highly volatile. The players are greatly concerned for the welfare of the people of Zimbabwe . . . it is very important that no one comes to any harm because of a cricket match in Harare.'

It fell on deaf ears. This was, though, a period when players and administrators clashed as rarely before. It was not Lamb's finest hour, or long hours as they were, especially when he was waking Fletcher up at 3.30 a.m. (as he did one morning) to talk about the issue. He is a charming man, but his approach was a little too patrician. The 'them and us' attitude that Lord MacLaurin had been shocked to encounter when he went on the Zimbabwe tour of 1996/97 was still very much Lamb's default position. He annoyed the players on this issue with his constant references to the damage that their not playing in Harare could do to the English game as a whole.

Lamb just did not empathize enough with the players, even if his reasons for England playing the match were sound. 'I was very conscious of the consequences of not fulfilling the commitment to play the match in Harare,' Lamb says now, 'unless we had a bloody good reason which was robust and defensible. My consistent view was the same as the ICC's. At a time when British Airways was still flying into Harare, when three hundred-plus companies were still trading with Zimbabwe, when we hadn't broken off diplomatic relations with Zimbabwe, why should cricket suddenly have to be upholding the moral stance of the nation? Of course we abhorred what was happening in Zimbabwe, but is it right for cricket to make value judgements about the morality of political regimes around the world? I would contend not. Just because you carry a cricket bat, does that make you any different from a banker, insurance provider or airline pilot?'

But it was Malcolm Speed, the ICC's chief executive, who irked the England players most. Speed began a chapter of his recently published autobiography *Sticky Wicket* with the words 'Nasser Hussain does not like me'. And he is right. Hussain was enraged by Speed's perfunctory manner when he appeared at a meeting with the England players. 'No respect. No appreciation that England were in a difficult position regarding Zimbabwe,' as Hussain later wrote of him.

It was in this meeting that the England players were made aware of a letter received by Lamb back in England. It was from an organization calling themselves 'The Sons and Daughters of Zimbabwe'. In it they warned 'COME TO ZIMBABWE AND YOU WILL GO BACK TO BRITAIN IN WOODEN COFFINS!' It continued, 'Anyway, we know your Team. Come to Harare and you will die. And how safe are your families back there in the UK?' It finished with the message: 'DON'T COME

TO ZIMBABWE OR YOUR PLAYERS WILL BE LIVING IN FEAR FOR THE REST OF YOUR LIVES.'

It was dated 6 January 2003. The letter was post-marked London, sent to the ECB and received by Lamb on 20 January. He had been concealing it for nearly three weeks. 'What was the point of worrying the players? We didn't want to let it out too early,' explains Lamb, none too convincingly. 'There were one or two sensitive souls with young families, and it didn't seem sensible to share it.'

Now it did, though. Security was the only reason England could give for not going to Zimbabwe. Not that Lamb believed the threat for one minute. 'I never took that threat seriously,' he says. 'Maybe I should have burned it and put it in the bin. Why didn't I just shred that bloody letter, because I knew it was a hoax?'

Into this mess had stepped Morgan, newly appointed as ECB chairman. As a Welshman, Morgan will probably appreciate the analogy that it was like a hospital pass as first touch on debut for an international rugby fly-half. But Morgan managed to avoid the oncoming forwards pretty well. That is because naturally he seeks to avoid confrontation. Diplomacy and conciliation are his constant allies. They were good friends to him here. Without Morgan the consequences of this situation don't bear thinking about.

Call me biased, if you like, as Morgan was, of course, chairman of Glamorgan before he went on to become ECB chairman and then ICC president, but I will refer you to my father on this matter. He is an exceptional judge of character and he reckons that the two best people he has ever met in cricket are Morgan and Geraint Jones, whose first season playing cricket in England was at my own Lydney CC. The club had a habit for a number of years of employing professionals from Australia (or rather putting them up wherever they could and finding them some part-time work) and for a while Jones stayed with my parents. Jones was the only player about whom my father, as president of the club, felt moved to write a letter (to Jones's father) to pay a compliment on his behaviour and attitude.

Morgan took control. 'In the early stages all the meetings were chaired by officials of the PCA – by Richard Bevan with his lawyer – but I decided that I would chair all further meetings,' he says. 'I felt sure that if it was safe and secure for the team they should go. I interviewed players one-to-one on the importance of the match taking place. But I was persuaded by Nasser that I should not insist on one or two of the younger players coming in one-on-one, so I spoke to them as a group of three. I remember Ronnie Irani standing out as somebody who really wanted to go and play. He set a great example. He was a substantial figure in all of this.'

England also had some visitors to their Cullinan Hotel. Secret visitors, smuggled in. The first was a member of Zimbabwe's opposition party, the MDC (Movement for Democratic Change). For a long time afterwards his name was not revealed ('he must remain anonymous for his own safety,' said Hussain). But it has since emerged that it was David Coltart, now Zimbabwe's Minister of Education, Sport, Arts and Culture. He spoke to Fletcher and Hussain about the fact that he was working with two of Zimbabwe's players, Andy Flower and Henry Olonga, on making some sort of protest at the death of democracy in their country and wondered whether England might do the same if they were to play in Zimbabwe. He then led Fletcher and Hussain into another room of the hotel, and standing there were Flower and Olonga. Two England coaches, present and future! What irony. Not that the situation was laced with it then. Rather it was fear that pervaded the room, as Flower and Olonga outlined their plans. 'There go two incredibly brave people,' said Fletcher solemnly to Hussain as the pair left the room.

The idea to make such a stand had been first suggested to Flower by a chap called Nigel Hough, although Coltart's influence should never be underestimated. 'He [Flower] rates Coltart as a human being,' says Alistair Campbell, the former Zimbabwe captain. 'He rates him as one of the bravest okes he knows in fact.' 'Oke' is South African slang for bloke, if you're wondering.

Like Coltart's, Hough's was a name that had remained anonymous for a long time, indeed until Olonga revealed it in his autobiography *Blood, Sweat and Treason*, although he spelt his surname 'Huff', which may or may not have been some kind of cover-up. Flower has been careful never to mention Hough's name in public.

I knew Hough from my time playing cricket in Zimbabwe. He was a decent batsman, who occasionally bowled some leg-spin. I recall him scoring a double-hundred against the touring Durham county side for a Manicaland Select XI in 1992. I also recall him having an eccentric sense of humour. He was always saying something on the field. And for some reason I remember him once saying, 'Come on, boys, let's be alert.' There was a silence as his team-mates looked at him, as if to say 'Come on, you can do better than that'. And then Hough said, 'Yes, Manicaland needs lots of Lerts today.' Bizarre.

Hough is better known for him and his white family being the subjects of Christina Lamb's excellent book *House of Stone*, the true story of their terrible troubles during Mugabe's land redistribution policies and especially of their complicated relationship with their black maid, Aqui.

I'll allow Flower to take up the protest story, as related in a subsequent interview with the *Guardian*:

About a month before the World Cup started in South Africa I met a friend with whom I'd played Zimbabwean cricket. He'd just been thrown off his farm at the dead of night. He had lost this magnificent farm where he'd employed hundreds of people and had set up a school and clinic. He said, 'We'll take a drive and I'll show you what's happened to this once thriving community.' And he took me around and it was very sad to see. He was quite religious and he said, 'I believe you guys have an obligation to bring this to the world's attention.'

On the same day I opened a newspaper – it was the only independent paper at the time and was constantly harried by the Government. On the inside page was an article about an MP who had been arrested and tortured in police custody. It was a tiny article, hardly any space at all. And suddenly I was struck, as if for the first time, by the sheer horror of living in a nation where torture is so widespread it does not even make front page news.

He [Hough] wanted us to boycott the World Cup but I wasn't comfortable with that. We came up with a different plan. It changed my life because it was, I guess, a little scary. But once the principle had been planted in my mind, and I planted it in Henry's mind, there was no other way to go. Without sounding pious we knew it was the right thing to do. We had to do it, regardless of the consequences. I've never been able to go back to Zimbabwe – and neither has Henry. The sacrifice he made was huge.

I'll be honest and say that I was surprised when I heard Flower and Olonga were doing something together. They were not close. Flower, so I reckoned, was not alone among the Zimbabwean team in considering Olonga a little soft. Olonga seemed to succumb rather too easily to niggling injuries. If there was one thing I had learnt during my time in Zimbabwe it was that Flower, like Fletcher, abhorred any sign of softness in a sportsperson.

When Flower first asked to speak to Olonga, the black fast bowler was surprised too. 'I couldn't figure out why this guy who hadn't been prepared to give me the time of day for so long would want to talk to me now,' Olonga wrote.

'I wouldn't say Andy was my best friend, but he was my captain for years and I respected him as a player,' said Olonga later. 'How he knew I had the aptitude to make this protest, I don't know. He needed a black person, and a black person with some influence. I certainly had that: I'd sung a song and people loved it, I was the first black player to play for Zimbabwe, and if I said something it had some weight. Andy is world class, I'm not, but we'd got a combination of sport and music – Posh and Becks, if you like.'

Flower's brother Grant wanted to be part of it too. 'I asked if I could be involved,' Grant admits now, 'but they said they'd rather not. They wanted one white and one black guy and did not want it to be seen as a racist thing. None of the other black guys would have done it. One other white player, Brian Murphy, showed some interest, but no one else really knew about it.'

Indeed they didn't. It was all very secretive. It had to be. And it was not a case of Olonga being persuaded to do something he didn't want to do. He too felt strongly about the mess into which his country had descended. He made up his own mind. 'My motivation was that, two years ago, I had been handed a dossier of human rights abuses that occurred in Zimbabwe, notably the early 1980s Matabeleland massacres,' he said. 'Up to that point, I'd thought Robert Mugabe was a very fair, true, honest president.'

He and Flower thought long and hard about how they could best make a stand before coming up with the idea of a black armband protest at their first World Cup match, against Namibia in Harare on 10 February, accompanied by a statement detailing their feelings. Coltart, a lawyer by trade, helped them draw it up.

An English journalist, Geoff Dean of *The Times*, was involved too. 'Andy took me aside at nets the day before the game,' recalls Dean, 'and asked if I could do him a favour. I said, "Sure. What is it?" He said he couldn't tell me. I just laughed. But he said that if I was willing to do it, I should wait outside the entrance to the Harare Sports Club half an hour before the game was due to start the next day, and there someone whom I would know would meet me. It was all very cloak and dagger!'

The following morning Flower put about fifty pieces of paper into his cricket case. On each was printed the following statement:

Issued 9.30 a.m. February 10, 2003, at the start of Zimbabwe's opening World Cup match against Namibia.

It is a great honour for us to take the field today to play for Zimbabwe in the World Cup. We feel privileged and proud to have been able to represent our country. We are however deeply distressed about what is taking place in Zimbabwe in the midst of the World Cup and do not feel that we can take the field without indicating our feelings in a dignified manner and in keeping with the spirit of cricket.

We cannot in good conscience take to the field and ignore the fact that millions of our compatriots are starving, unemployed and oppressed. We are aware that hundreds of thousands of Zimbabweans may even die in the coming months through a combination of starvation, poverty and Aids. We are aware that many people have been unjustly imprisoned and tortured simply for expressing their opinions about what is happening in the country. We have heard a torrent of racist hate speech directed at minority groups. We are aware that thousands of Zimbabweans are routinely denied their right to freedom of expression. We are aware that people have been murdered, raped, beaten and had their homes destroyed because of their beliefs and that many of those responsible have not been prosecuted. We are also aware that many patriotic Zimbabweans oppose us even playing in the WC because of what is happening.

It is impossible to ignore what is happening in Zimbabwe. Although we are just professional cricketers, we do have a conscience and feelings. We believe that if we remain silent that will be taken as a sign that either we do not care or we condone what is happening in Zimbabwe. We believe that it is important to stand up for what is right.

We have struggled to think of an action that would be appropriate and that would not demean the game we love so much. We have decided that we should act alone without other members of the team being involved because our decision is deeply personal and we did not want to use our senior status to unfairly influence more junior members of the squad. We would like to stress that we greatly respect the ICC and are grateful for all the hard work it has done in bringing the World Cup to Zimbabwe.

In all the circumstances we have decided that we will each wear a black armband for the duration of the World Cup. In doing so we are mourning the death of democracy in our beloved Zimbabwe. In doing so we are making a silent plea to those responsible to stop the abuse of human rights in Zimbabwe. In doing so we pray that our small action may help to restore sanity and dignity to our Nation.

Andrew Flower – Henry Olonga

Once inside the ground, Flower met his father Bill. He was the man Dean would know. Dean had known the Flowers and most of the other Zimbabwean cricketers for some time, having covered their inaugural Test series against India in 1992 and having played some cricket in Zimbabwe on various tours. 'The instruction I was given was to distribute these statements to everyone in the media present that day,' says Dean, who still has a couple of the statements at home as mementos. 'I read it and straight away knew it was going to be dynamite.'

So it was. And that was just within the Zimbabwe Cricket Union. Coach Geoff Marsh, team manager Babu Meman and

CEO Vince Hogg were all shocked, pleading with Flower and Olonga not to go through with their protest. But, as the pair emphasized, it was too late. The world already knew.

Flower has obviously gone on to achieve greater fame, but for Olonga it was his defining moment. 'Did I change the world?' he asked later. 'Probably not. Did I change Zimbabwe? Probably not – but I played my part. And if I hadn't embraced the moment, I could have been a nobody, had a mediocre World Cup, and no one would have remembered. Now I'm remembered as the guy who wore a black armband.'

Not that Olonga was particularly prepared. Flower had always planned to retire from international cricket after this event, and leave Zimbabwe to play in England for Essex (and in Australia, although his stint with South Australia lasted only one of its three intended years). Olonga thought maybe he could still live in Zimbabwe. As the days passed after his protest that looked more and more unlikely. There was a vicious campaign against him in the local press and he was followed by state security agents. A few days before Zimbabwe's last qualifying match against Pakistan in Bulawayo, he knew for certain he couldn't stay. His father had received a message from someone high up in the secret police: 'Tell your son to get out of Zimbabwe now!'

Had Zimbabwe lost to Pakistan in Bulawayo they would have been out of the World Cup and Olonga would not have had a ready-made escape route. As it was, it rained, allowing Zimbabwe to progress to the Super Sixes in South Africa. 'I believe in God, and in a way I believe God sent the rain that day,' said Olonga.

That Pakistan match was on 4 March, so there had been nearly a month since the protest, time enough for Flower's father Bill to confirm that it was time to leave. 'We had been planning a withdrawal for a few years,' he says. 'The signs had been there. Then Andrew visited us one day and explained what he was going to do. One thing I was adamant about was that he should not boycott the World Cup, as Nigel Hough would have liked to have seen. But after the protest, we definitely had our phone tapped. Several times we picked up the phone to dial and we could hear them chattering at their listening posts. We always felt someone was listening in. Then when we went down to Bulawayo to watch the matches down there, we stayed with my sister-in-law and she got a phone message from an anonymous African to say something along the lines of "You are part of the Flower family and you'd better watch your back!" Then when we were watching one of the games, some Africans dressed in sharp suits came and sat either side of me and Jean [his wife]. They knew nothing about cricket and were trying to pick up what we were saying. They were from the CIA [Zimbabwe's version of the Central Intelligence Agency]. We drove back to Harare after that last match against Pakistan and packed up Andy's household with Becky [his wife], and then we all left together.'

Andy Flower still owns that house in Harare. Indeed he went back there after the World Cup had finished, much to the consternation of family and friends. 'What could they do?' he asked me later. 'Kill me?' Well, yes, they could have done.

The last I heard his house was being rented by Chris Harris, the former New Zealand all-rounder, who was out in Zimbabwe coaching the national Under 19 side and playing in the domestic Twenty20 competition. Surprise, surprise, Zimbabwe Cricket (as the ZCU became in 2004) was a little slow in paying the rent for Harris.

Of course, Zimbabwe should have played another match in Harare in their qualifying rounds. That was against England on 13 February. 'We took the decision that the England team should not get on the plane to Zimbabwe,' says Morgan. 'We took it on the basis of duty and care to our employees, the England cricketers and their support staff. The letter had been submitted to the World Cup organizing committee. And they sent it to the security unit. And on the morning of the day of the opening ceremony, Mark Roper-Drimie, our in-house lawyer, came to Tim Lamb and myself with a response from Interpol in Pretoria. The response is something I shall never forget. It said "The Sons and Daughters of Zimbabwe is an organization known to us and any threat that they pose should be taken seriously". Once we had that, we decided that all efforts to persuade the players to go should cease and we instructed them that they wouldn't be going. It was a surprise because we didn't even know it had gone to Interpol and I thought it would be declared as of no significance. It should have been plain sailing from there. But I then ran into Dr Ali Bacher [the tournament director], Malcolm Speed [ICC chief executive], Malcolm Gray [ICC president] and Percy Sonn [president of the United Cricket Board of South Africa]. They took a lot of convincing that we were right to exercise that duty of care.'

The ICC may not have been happy, but England did not go to Zimbabwe. Morgan did, though. 'As the World Cup was approaching its end,' he says, 'I was asked by Justice Ebrahim [ZCU's vice-chairman] if I would go to Zimbabwe to address their board. So I went and explained that the only reasons that we didn't turn up were safety and security. And they were the only reasons. I remember Ozias Bvute [now ZC's managing director], whom I met there for the first time, in the course of that meeting attacking Tim Lamb verbally [even though he wasn't there!]. I was unprepared to let the attack go, and I responded in a way I remain proud about. Tim Lamb is a thoroughly decent man and administrator.'

The problem was that Zimbabwe were due to tour England that summer, and South Africa, who were visiting afterwards, were threatening not to tour because of the no-show in Harare. 'That would have been a financial disaster for the ECB,' says Morgan. 'In world cricket you make your money when you host.

You don't make any money when you go away. So I had the task of making sure Zimbabwe came, because if they wouldn't come, then it was likely that South Africa would stay at home as well. In explaining that safety and security were the only reasons, they [Zimbabwe] agreed to tour. It was often said that there was another side to this, that I agreed that we would make the scheduled tour to Zimbabwe in 2004. But there was no talk about that. That was in the Future Tours Programme [FTP] and everyone knew that, short of a safety or security issue, or government intervention, England would have to fulfil those commitments.'

Yes, even though Zimbabwe did tour England without serious incident in 2003, the issue just would not go away. It had been said that there would be no repeat of the World Cup fiasco, but as the proposed tour in November 2004 approached it began to look, as many masters of malapropism have observed over the years, like déjà vu all over again. The only difference was that it was a tour rather than a one-off match, with its FTP implications as outlined by Morgan above, but all the same questions and issues remained.

The beginnings of this second Zimbabwe crisis for the ECB can be traced to the moment in June 2003 when Des Wilson was elected to the ECB's management board as chairman of the corporate affairs and marketing advisory committee. Wilson had formerly been a director of Shelter and Sport England and, among other things, had campaigned for lead-free petrol, so his appointment was always likely to be both interesting and a little dangerous. Having seen the World Cup farrago from the outside, Wilson offered his assistance to Morgan this time. He was not explicitly asked by Morgan to compile a detailed report on Zimbabwe and whether England should tour there, but was asked to maintain 'an overview of the issue'.

The result was a detailed seventeen-page report entitled 'Reviewing overseas cricket tours – a framework for rational decision-making'. It argued that 'to seek to isolate sport as an activity that stands alone in human affairs, untouched by "politics" or "moral considerations" and unconcerned for the fate of those deprived of human rights, is as unrealistic as it is (self-destructively) self-serving . . .'

There was no specific mention of Zimbabwe in it; that was to come in a second report, in the form of a letter to Morgan, in which it was argued, in Wilson's words, that 'the tour could only strengthen Robert Mugabe's regime by allowing him to claim international respectability; that it would undermine UK foreign policy in the region; that it would be contrary to the wishes of the cricket world and deeply damaging to the game's image in the UK; and that it was morally wrong to play cricket at an oasis within a country suffering such repression and hunger'.

Wilson's framework report, however, was leaked to the press before the ECB management board saw it. He was not particularly popular on the board before that; he was even less so afterwards. And the board did face a problem in that to adopt Wilson's proposals would be to perform a U-turn, after distancing itself from moral considerations during the World Cup deliberations. So they never really discussed it.

There was additional pressure exerted by the ZCU, who emailed every first-class county warning them of the financial implications should England cancel the tour. 'A claim for damages and compensation would run to millions of pounds,' said its chairman Peter Chingoka. And there was concern over the Champions Trophy, which was to be held in England in September 2004, and for which the contract had yet to be signed. The three counties responsible for holding that tournament – Hampshire, Surrey and Warwickshire – were all well represented on the management board. Guess what they wanted? They wanted England to go, of course. Self-interest and loot. They are a potent mix in the shires.

Then there was the position of Foreign Secretary Straw. Some thought he might give an instruction to the ECB not to go. Indeed when he wrote a letter to them in January 2004 Lamb announced that it was 'tantamount to an instruction' to cancel the trip. But it was not really. It said nothing new about Mugabe's regime, and concluded with the claim that the UK was 'taking a leading role' internationally against Zimbabwe, and that 'you may wish to consider whether a high-profile England cricket tour at this time is consistent with that approach'.

Morgan knew that there would be no *force majeure* from the government. 'We had various meetings with the government – known as positioning meetings,' he says. 'And finally Tim Lamb and I went to the Foreign and Commonwealth Office to meet with Jack Straw and Tessa Jowell [then Secretary of State for Culture, Media and Sport]. Both ministers knew we would have to go unless they could instruct us not to go, and Mr Straw said to us: "We do not have the legal powers to instruct you not to go. If we stop and think about it, I don't think any sport in this country would wish the government of the UK to have such powers." And so we ended that meeting with a joint media conference, where the government understood the ECB's position and the ECB understood the government's position.'

Pressure was brought upon the ECB by the ICC, who had been emphasizing the financial penalties that might be incurred if the tour were to be cancelled, that they should defer a decision on the tour until after the ICC's board meeting in Auckland in March 2004. And there a bombshell was dropped that blew any escape route for the ECB to pieces. 'Out of the blue,' says Morgan, 'it was proposed and accepted by the board by a substantial majority that the FTP should become a regulation of the ICC. And then once it became a regulation, any failure to fulfil that regulation would result in suspension.'

The suspension, in addition to already agreed financial penalties, would be for a short period. It would be long enough, though. Morgan did his maths. There would have been no 2005 Ashes. England's decision to tour Zimbabwe became as inevitable as Wilson's resignation.

But, of course, that was not the end of the matter. In May 2004 Australia toured Zimbabwe, but they went without leg-spinner Stuart MacGill, who made himself unavailable for selection. 'Whilst I fully support the ICC future tours policy that requires all member nations to play each other on a regular basis,' he said, 'and understand Cricket Australia's obligation to tour, I told them that I was uncomfortable about touring Zimbabwe at this point in time and maintaining a clear conscience.'

MacGill's stance clearly set some of the England players thinking. By then they had a new captain in Vaughan. All along he had emphasized that it was for the ECB to make a decision, and that whatever was determined, he and his players would abide by that decision. During the final Test of that summer the team met at their Grange City Hotel in London and decided that they would stick together as a team whatever decision was made.

However, during the subsequent Champions Trophy it became clear that some players were wavering. So Fletcher and Vaughan decided that it might be better to rest some of the more senior players ahead of a hard tour of South Africa and then the Ashes the following summer, as the visit to Zimbabwe was hardly likely to be taxing in terms of the opposition en-countered. That was because the whole situation had been complicated by a row: captain Heath Streak had been sacked and in all fifteen rebel white cricketers had had their contracts terminated when they expressed their displeasure at selection methods clearly designed to rid the side of whites and fill it with blacks.

England had beaten Zimbabwe easily, by 152 runs, in their first match in the Champions Trophy, so resting seemed a sensible idea to Fletcher, who was still not making any public pronouncements on Zimbabwe, but was feeling much more relaxed privately as he had just received a South African passport (his mother was born in Kimberley).

Fletcher was scuppered in his plans, however, when Steve Harmison used his newspaper column to announce that he was not going to Zimbabwe. 'In all honesty my decision was made in Cape Town over eighteen months ago when England's World Cup squad spent a horrendous four days before finally deciding not to go to Harare,' Harmison told the *News of the World*. 'Nothing has changed for me. The situation there is worse now – that's what the official reports say – and Zimbabwe's top players have been sacked. Being a personal decision, I realize I could be the only player who does not go. I'll respect what everyone else decides but I hope my refusal is not held against me.'

Both Fletcher and Vaughan were furious. So much for the team agreement earlier. This was becoming messy. Fletcher now let the ECB know of his intention to rest players. 'Duncan let me know through John Carr [ECB director of cricket],' says Morgan, 'that he wanted to rest some players for the tour, including Vaughan and Trescothick. But I decided that the tour had to be led by one of those two players. It was up to Duncan and the selectors to decide which one. I said, "You can't leave both behind. It is an extremely important tour." And it was. There were protocols in place from the government in the event of Robert Mugabe coming to the match.'

So Vaughan did lead the team. Trescothick and Flintoff were rested, while Giles went in support of his captain even though he had the option of being rested. Flintoff later admitted that he would not have gone anyway on moral grounds. Sadly it was little surprise that he should make such a public announcement when he did not need to; even less surprising that he and Harmison should be the two reluctant tourists. It was to become a familiar theme.

Originally the team were to acclimatize for the five-match Zimbabwe one-day international series in South Africa, but negotiations with the United Cricket Board of South Africa broke down, so England instead went to Namibia to play two one-day matches.

Morgan was on his way to Heathrow airport to fly to Zimbabwe when he received a call on his mobile phone (he had a driver). 'I'm on the Severn Bridge,' says Morgan, 'and the mobile goes, and it's Peter Chingoka [ZC chairman]. He said, "I'm pleased to tell you that we have clearance for visas to be issued to all your journalists with the exception of . . ." And I think the number was about fifteen. I said, "What do you mean with the exception of fifteen?" They all have to be allowed in, unless you can demonstrate good reason for them not to be allowed in.'

Morgan's phone did not stop all the way to Heathrow. The BBC were among those banned. That seemed deliberate, but the others, including my own *Sunday Telegraph* (Scyld Berry was travelling), appeared random choices.

The team heard this news just as they were leaving Namibia on a flight to Johannesburg, from where their connection to Harare had always been planned. Their initial reaction was 'We're not going', which I've always found rather amusing as most of the time they would much rather have journalists nowhere near them. But they went to Johannesburg, where they were met by Bevan. Meanwhile Morgan was flying to Zimbabwe with his deputy Mike Soper, and Carr.

The England team were in both limbo and transit. Where to have a team meeting? The smoking lounge in Johannesburg airport, of course. If that seemed bizarre – and there might have been an element of rudeness in ejecting some passengers desperately craving their nicotine fix – then some humour was soon to enter that glass-panelled lounge. This was Matthew Maynard's first tour as an assistant coach (he was still a player with Glamorgan), and Fletcher decided this was the time for him to make his first speech to the troops. He gestured to Maynard, who collected his thoughts and tried to speak. He tried again, and again. But there was not so much a frog as a cane toad stuck in the back of his throat. Nothing would come out. The room dissolved into fits of laughter. Thankfully Maynard has a remarkable ability to laugh at himself, and was soon laughing with them. Most grown men would have been mortified. I'd have simply booked a flight back to London. Not Maynard. He'd forgotten about it instantly, too. Luckily one of his management colleagues reminded me about it for the purposes of this book.

Then Morgan sent the instruction that the team should stay in Johannesburg and not fly to Harare. That was simple enough for everyone apart from team manager Phil Neale, the former Worcestershire captain who has been a willing and wonderfully diligent ever-present throughout the regimes of Fletcher and Flower up to the present day, who had to haul the mountain of bags already on the plane off again. He did so uncomplainingly, and off the team went to the nearby Caesar's Palace Hotel. It might just as well have been the Cullinan Hotel in Cape Town again. And the players were just as militant, so much so that Morgan sent Carr from Harare to speak to them.

Up in Harare, Morgan was negotiating with ZC and via the British Embassy through to Whitehall. Some thought the tour should be called off immediately, and the ICC president Ehsan Mani had indicated there might be some sympathy towards England should they take such a course of action. But Morgan was ever-mindful of the implications, and especially the 2005 Ashes.

He had, however, told the players that they would be going home unless the journalists were allowed in. ZC knew that too. So it wasn't long before the call came from Chingoka: 'David, I'm pleased to tell you that we've opened the can and all the journalists are allowed in.' 'The BBC were astonished,' admits Morgan. 'They never thought they would be let in.'

It was too late for all five ODIs to be played, even if Zimbabwe tried their hardest to do just that, as well as attempting to make sure England's accommodation in Bulawayo was as spartan as possible. But go to Zimbabwe England did, even if, since the last of those four ODIs there, England have played Zimbabwe on only one other occasion, during the ICC World Twenty20 in South Africa in 2007. In going to Zimbabwe and winning 4–0, however, England did derive one significant benefit: they gave a debut to a promising young batsman called Kevin Pietersen.

He was to prove a decent pick.

6

The Brains of Cricket

I've been called a Duncan Fletcher apologist. But I make no apology. Fletcher is quite simply the sharpest mind I have ever encountered in cricket. I learn something new from him every time we talk cricket. And I reckon I know a little bit about the game, having played it professionally for nearly twenty years. As Ashley Giles says of Fletcher, 'He is the brains of cricket.'

Fletcher is indeed that good. It is why former England charges like Nasser Hussain, Michael Vaughan, Marcus Trescothick, Andrew Strauss, Paul Collingwood and Kevin Pietersen swear by him. So too the South Africans like Jacques Kallis, Herschelle Gibbs and Gary Kirsten whom Fletcher coached at Western Province. Gibbs called him a 'legend' in his recent autobiography and Pietersen could easily have been charged with harassment, so frequent were his text messages begging Fletcher to work with him prior to England's tour of South Africa in 2009/10. There was, though, the small matter of Fletcher actually being employed by South Africa as a consultant at the time!

Hussain tells a good story of how technically sharp Fletcher is. It came on his first tour with England to South Africa in 1999/2000, where he was lumbered with a squad many of whom he hadn't seen before. 'He saw Chris Adams once in a net,' says Hussain, 'and said, "With his hands as they are, this lad might struggle outside off-stump against Allan Donald."' And twice in the first Test that's what happened – Adams was caught behind off Donald.

Interestingly, all the players mentioned in that second paragraph are batsmen. Indeed as an analyst of opposition batsmen Fletcher has few peers. 'I haven't met a coach who is as good at that or as quick at doing it,' says Geraint Jones. 'The plans he came up with were always spot on. I've never known a coach get it right as regularly as he did. Take Jacques Rudolph in South Africa in 2004/05. Fletch thought he was a massive candidate for being bowled, whereas everyone else had been saying to push the ball across him. So Fletch got us to bowl a straighter line and Rudolph hardly scored in that series [just two fifties in ten innings].'

There is a commonly held perception that Fletcher did not get on with his bowlers. It is an easy generalization, though. As England coach Fletcher always had a specific bowling coach, through whom most ideas were filtered so that the bowlers trusted that man, whether it was Bob Cottam, the late Graham Dilley, Troy Cooley or Kevin Shine. Fletcher mostly had a batting coach too, but always ensured that he himself was in charge of coaching the batsmen. That was undoubtedly his forte, but as a cricketer he was a genuine all-rounder. His finest playing hour demonstrates that amply: 69 not out and 4-42 as captain to defeat Australia in the 1983 World Cup at Trent Bridge.

Maybe it is more a matter of the characters involved. Bowlers like Andrew Flintoff, Steve Harmison and Matthew Hoggard disliked discipline. So they eventually disliked Fletcher.

Although I suspect there is more respect on both sides than is often revealed. Flintoff was as upset as the other players when Fletcher announced his resignation in the West Indies in 2007 and he resisted criticizing him heavily in his autobiography, despite Fletcher's obvious dismay with him and the revelation about his drinking exploits in his own autobiography. Mind you, maybe Flintoff was mindful of other drinking and disciplinary tales Fletcher could easily have divulged. I could have added Eric Simons to the list of devotees above. As I write he is now India's bowling coach under Fletcher. He is undoubtedly a confirmed Fletcher protégé from his time at Western Province. By way of further example, Simon Jones admits that Fletcher's advice on lengthening his run-up and grip on the ball (spreading his fingers wider) was significant in his remarkable transformation from raw fast bowler to world-class performer in the 2005 Ashes. 'He was brilliant with me,' says Jones. 'I always found him really approachable, and I remember when he changed my grip on the tour to Zimbabwe in 2004 that my control went up massively from there.'

'He had a great relationship with the bowlers,' says Matthew Maynard. 'I didn't ever see a clash – and I'm not just saying that to protect Fletch. But he had two very different characters there in Harmy and Fred. Harmy is one of the nicest blokes you could wish to meet, and he is very close with Fred, and Fred could be a pain in the arse to handle at times, but that was Fred. That was what probably made him such a good player. He wasn't quite wired the same way as everyone else. Fletch loved his bowlers because he knew they would win him matches. Batters set the game up; bowlers win it.'

Indeed when Fletcher was handed the list of potential names for the first intake of the National Academy in 2001/02, he noticed two glaring omissions: Simon Jones and Harmison. He said one thing to Rod Marsh: 'I don't care who you take, but those two must go.'

When consultant to South Africa in Australia in 2008/09 Fletcher reiterated his advice to England's bowlers in 2005 about bowling around the wicket to Australia's left-handers. The raw Morne Morkel in particular benefited, and South Africa won the Test series 2–1.

There is also little doubt in my mind that the two players who made the most noticeable technical advancements upon Fletcher's arrival at Glamorgan in 1997 were fast bowling all-rounder Darren Thomas and left-arm spinner Dean Cosker.

So Fletcher is much more than just a batting expert. Indeed his initial impact at Glamorgan was on our fielding. On a pre-season trip to Christ College, Brecon he organized the most enjoyable yet lung-bursting fielding session I or any of the other players had encountered. It was as if a new coach had arrived from a different planet such was the intensity, precision and variety of his drills. His ten-catches routine became legendary. It sounds simple but it tested even the fittest, because every catch, ten in a row without a drop, was taken at full stretch, the victim probably having run a considerable distance to try and take it. On his first England tour Vaughan was sick behind a tree having only just managed to complete the exercise, and Phil Tufnell began throwing returns over Fletcher's head in the vain hope that he would run out of balls.

The selection of wicketkeepers became a highly controversial part of his regime, especially when Geraint Jones was preferred to Chris Read, but Fletcher helped his keepers too. He talked to Alec Stewart about taking the ball standing back with his fingers pointing skywards, and to Jones about taking the ball in front of the stumps for run outs, now a trendy and highly effective tactic to save frames in television replays.

None of this, however, is to say that Fletcher does not have his faults. Of course he does. We all do. Even as a coach Fletcher had his faults. But then coaching is not an exact science. Fletcher could help players in all facets of the game, but one man's mentor can easily be another man's tormentor. Even at Glamorgan there were those who were not overly enamoured of some of Fletcher's ways, those who felt neglected. Mind you, they were usually not very good. Often those who complain about the coach are those who are not in the side.

There is a perception that Fletcher wanted yes-men around him, whether players or assistant coaches. Maynard is seen as a classic example. It is simply not true, and I will vouch for that. They were always arguing at Glamorgan. As Maynard says, 'My wife Sue always used to say when he was coming round for dinner, "You're not going to row with Fletch again tonight are you?"'

Maynard also has some interesting thoughts on Fletcher's attitude to difficult characters within the team environment. 'He used to talk about the terrorists within a team,' he says. 'You need them in your side but you know they will cause some problems too, and that you have to bring them into the circle. You can't isolate them because then they might be more destructive. It was about getting the balance right – the critical mass, as he always said. He wanted eight good characters who could drag the weaker ones through, one who might be a quieter lad and two who were tougher to handle.'

Fletcher can appear dour and grumpy and many of the other adjectives that are often bandied before his name. But, like Mike Atherton as England captain, Fletcher often played up to this part. The image had been cast early, and he was not going to alter it just to please the media. Often when I phone him he will answer mockingly with a voice as gruff as possible: 'What do you want?' And then later he'll suddenly say 'Right, you're boring me now. Time to go, Sidney from Lydney [his nickname for me, combining the actor Sid James and my hometown]' and will chuckle and hang up.

Fletcher has a lighter, more humorous side. Inside he is a happy, contented man. But because of his public image I'd need to provide examples of his successfully auditioning as a stand-up comedian to convince some of as much. I was never part of his dressing room with England, but I was at Glamorgan, and it was not the sour-faced morgue many would think. It was a wonderfully happy place, full of fun as well as hard work. I'm told it was very similar with England.

Fletcher would socialize with the team, but not for long. He knew to keep his distance, and it helped that he was forty-nine when he took the England job. His was a different generation. Only once did I see him inebriated at Glamorgan, and he still mentions it today. It was in 1999 when a lunch was held at Sophia Gardens for the Australia team who were based in Cardiff for the World Cup. He began the lunch by talking in hushed tones about the Australians who had just told us they were on an alcohol ban for the two weeks up to their opening match in the tournament. We were under no such ban, though. Every time I turned my head away Fletcher would fill my glass to the brim with red wine. Naturally I began returning the favour. It proved to be an interesting afternoon. By the time we adjourned to the nearby Beverley Hotel it was, as Dean Conway would put it, 'carnage'. I am pleased to report that Fletcher was seen eating some petunias outside the hotel later on. Pleased because it shows a side of his character few have seen. And I'm sure Fletcher will not be displeased, even if when I mentioned the incident in my autobiography he did say 'I hope Marina doesn't read that!' She knows he has got a slightly wild side. He's Zimbabwean after all.

'People only saw him on the media side and there he was stern-faced and a closed shop,' says Marcus Trescothick, 'but behind closed doors he was a completely different character. If you get to know the guy he is very jovial with a sort of sly sense of humour. He enjoys his golf, but he always got distracted if you started talking about cricket because it would mess him up. He hated it if he'd had a phone call from Grav [David Graveney] and had a bit of a disagreement about selection because he couldn't switch off then. He was completely different from what was seen in the media.'

Fletcher was strict on dress code and punctuality, and collated any misdemeanours so that they could form part of subsequent fines meetings. Fletcher loved such gatherings. At Glamorgan he would giggle when, for example, announcing that so-and-so had been fined for a PDA – a 'public display of affection' for his partner.

Such events could become rather raucous. On his first tour with England, to South Africa in 1999/2000, Fletcher asked Conway, his entertainments manager as well as physiotherapist, to organize a team meal at a restaurant in Sandton's Nelson Mandela Square in Johannesburg. It became such a riotous affair that no less a rabble-rouser than Phil Tufnell was calling for calm. Maybe he'd noticed that the press corps were dining nearby, to a man astonished to be witnessing such revelry. No one reported it, though.

This did not prevent another evening of high-jinks later in the tour, namely after the now infamous Test victory at Centurion. Nobody knew then what Hansie Cronje had been up to. There was celebrating to do, even if Atherton did observe later in his autobiography *Opening Up*, 'For the first time in my life I felt completely flat at the moment of a Test victory. It wasn't that I suspected match-fixing, but a Test match victory is a thing that has to be earned; you need to put in the hard work.' England hadn't done that really, with Cronje's generous and deviously minded declaration setting up a game.

A fines meeting ensued after the Test. As Conway relates, 'The manager of the Sandton Sun Hotel had sorted a lot of things for us: we had two sheep's heads and a pig's head on silver salvers, live birds flying around and chickens running around. I'm not really sure why we had such things, but it had been a funny tour for that sort of thing. I'd been having a running battle with Jacques Kallis [whom Conway knew from Kallis's season at Glamorgan the previous summer] and his room-mate Mark Boucher. One afternoon I'd found a snake in my bed, so as revenge I'd got into their room [both teams were staying in the same hotel] and put a [dead] chicken on their washing line in the bath and then put a meat cleaver through it so that there was blood all over their bath. I drew the shower curtain and left. Kallis told me that Boucher went for a shower later in the day and the screams could be heard on more than one floor of the hotel.'

Conway and Giles were chairmen of the meeting, in which Fletcher, all the players and management staff took a full part. For some reason everyone was asked to kiss one of the sheep's heads. 'Kiss the sheep, kiss the sheep!' was the chant that rang out as the miscreant went up to the chairmen's table. But Tufnell could not do it. 'I can't do it, Phys,' he said to Conway, which was clearly not true given his later exploits on *I'm a Celebrity Get Me Out of Here!* 'You're going to have to talk to him then,' said Conway. So, with fag dutifully at the side of his mouth, Tufnell said, 'Awright, sheep?'

In stitches with the rest of them was Fletcher. The trouble is that judgements about Fletcher's character are made about his demeanour in public, and in particular at press conferences. Those are not situations in which he is comfortable. Essentially he is a shy man. He takes some getting to know. And he will take his time getting to know you.

Speaking in public is not an easy exercise for him. Indeed I never felt he was truly at ease when speaking to the Glamorgan team as a whole. He certainly betrayed some nervousness when ending his opening address to us in 1997 with a humorous 'Let's get this road on the show then'.

He was often lambasted for his infamous 'Duncan Days', as the media labelled his press conferences, but the truth was that Fletcher would mostly be wheeled out after a poor performance.

He did not enjoy them, clearly, but he thought he should protect his players in such circumstances.

Not that he really worked out the media game. 'He was highly protective and supportive of his team,' says Giles, 'and they are great attributes as coach. Yes, to a degree you have to try and manage the media and keep them on-side, but the important stuff is to win games. Managing the media isn't going to win you games. If you can only do one or the other, he got the right one.'

At the crux of Fletcher's philosophy in life is loyalty. That was drummed into him from his schooldays at Prince Edward, Salisbury (now Harare). And he always perceived most of the media criticism as being disloyal, especially when he considered his words had been twisted. And sometimes they were, partly because that's what happens in journalism occasionally, but also because Fletcher's cricketing ruminations could be so deep that either he struggled to get his point across in such a formal forum or some journalists simply could not comprehend it.

Fletcher knew that playing the media game might help him, and that not doing so might precipitate his exit should results turn ugly, as indeed was the eventual case after the calamitous winter of 2006/07 when the Ashes were lost 5–0. And there were times when he considered a change of attitude. Jonathan Agnew, the BBC's cricket correspondent and a former team-mate of Fletcher's at the Alexandra club in Harare, often spoke to him about this. So in Bangladesh in 2003 he resolved to do something about it.

The trouble was that by the end of that short two-Test tour he had already changed his mind, upset by what he considered a 'stitch-up'. England had been hit by injuries to their bowlers on that trip, with Harmison returning home after the first Test and both Flintoff and James Anderson missing out. In their stead Hoggard won man of the series, and when Fletcher was asked afterwards by Angus Fraser, then correspondent of the *Independent*, whether England should now base their bowling attack around Hoggard, he made the mistake of not wholly endorsing that viewpoint. The headlines the next day were predictable. 'Hoggard the hero slated by Fletcher' was the general gist when all Fletcher had really said was 'I wouldn't say Hoggy is the guy we're going to build the bowling around. He bowled well yesterday and got some nice rhythm. But he's got to make the batsmen play a bit more early in the innings. That goes for all the quick bowlers. They've got to know what their roles are.'

Hoggard was no leader, as he himself explained in his auto-biography *Hoggy: Welcome to My World*, describing how his captain Vaughan saw his role: 'It was my job to keep sweeping the shop floor, grafting away at the menial work while the other bowlers were grabbing the glory upstairs in the office. I wasn't to get ahead of myself and try to show the office workers how to do their job.'

Even though Fletcher did not necessarily rate Hoggard that highly, what miffed him was that it appeared that he was criticizing one of his players in public. As Giles said, in Fletcher's scheme of things that was as forbidden as the consumption of pork in Islam. Fletcher had to phone Hoggard, who had already flown home because he was not involved in the one-day series that followed the Tests, to explain.

But there was another problem. Fletcher is never wrong. He may not like my saying that, but it is meant in the nicest possible way. He has his strong views, and, by and large, he sticks by them. And the thing is that, on cricketing matters, they are mostly right. In reality he rarely is wrong.

Early in the writing of his autobiography I often questioned him on points he was making. Always he would respond immediately with a cogent argument. I soon learnt to shut up and listen. It was his book, not mine. And he did know what he was talking about. It was always worth listening.

The book whipped up considerable controversy, not least

because its serialization was quite naturally centred upon a revelation that Flintoff, then the England captain, was still drunk at practice the day before a one-day international in Australia in 2007. I still wonder to this day whether I might have written things differently, whether I could have protected and advised Fletcher more wisely on this.

Often during the book's composition Fletcher would say things like 'I am worried that I am having too much of a go'. Because of this, many incidents (especially involving Flintoff) and observations were removed from draft versions. 'I need some advice. You're the expert,' he would often say, and I'd sometimes think to myself, 'I'm not sure if I am the expert!' The truth is that this was not a straightforward assignment. Fletcher wanted to demonstrate how difficult a job it was to coach England, and he wanted to get a considerable number of gripes off his chest. He felt his seven years in charge had been a constant battle, not just against opposition teams but against the ECB, the media, the dinosaurs still roaming county cricket and even members of his own team. He wanted to express some strong words about some supposed sacred cows of English cricket, like Flintoff, Ian Botham and Geoffrey Boycott. That was always bound to generate a strong public reaction.

And not all of it was complimentary for sure. By far the most withering book review came from Patrick Collins, an award-winning columnist for the *Mail on Sunday* and both a writer and a person whom I like and respect. But he penned an extraordinarily acerbic piece for *Wisden*. He cleverly picked out a number of instances where Fletcher mentioned that various people had apologized to him, but then let fly with this: 'But it is the tone of this ill-judged book which will linger longest in the memory: vindictive, self-justifying and relentlessly mean-spirited. In time, Duncan Fletcher may come to realize this dreadful book was his greatest mistake. And the one by which posterity will judge him.'

The book was not a mistake. Even if I say so myself, it was a damned good read. It was an honest reflection of Fletcher's life and his struggles, as well as his successes. So many sporting autobiographies are anodyne pap; here was a book full of strong opinions, one shorn of the usual flouncing platitudes towards colleagues and opponents, and one with some outstanding technical analysis. Yet it attracted some contemptuous condemnation.

It always amuses me when reviewers describe a book as self-justifying. Isn't that part of the point of an autobiography? If you don't get your point across there, when are you ever going to do so? It's your side of the story. And it hardly scuppered all future job prospects for Fletcher. Being appointed coach of the World Cup champions India in 2011, for all its initial difficulties, rather demonstrates that. And between that appointment and the publication of his book, Fletcher had worked for South Africa, New Zealand and Hampshire on a consultancy basis, while also being approached by the West Indies, Glamorgan (again) and various South African provinces. He was not exactly in coaching purdah.

To me, Fletcher has expressed only one regret about the book: the treatment of Chris Read, which might have been more sympathetic. He did not rate Read as an international keeper; a very good county cricketer, yes, but not an international. He felt his catching channel was too narrow, that he was too quiet and that his batting lacked the necessary defensive technique. But that is not to say that Fletcher disliked him as a person. 'He's a good kid,' Fletcher said to me afterwards. Between us we should have worded his faults more sensitively. After some deliberation Read, whom I know reasonably well and like, decided that he would not respond to Fletcher's comments for this book.

There was the accusation that Fletcher had betrayed Trescothick's trust by revealing details of his breakdowns in India and Australia. 'I chatted to Tres about it,' says Fletcher.

'There was a phone call that took place long before the book was completed and I said I'd mentioned some of the incidents in the book. At no stage did he say "No, I don't want it in". Whatever has been written has been out there, has been basically covered before. I said "Is that all right?" and he said "OK" and left it at that.' These are points reiterated by Trescothick himself. 'We'd had a conversation,' he says. 'I wasn't bothered. He didn't tell anything that hadn't been told before.'

Should we have included the Flintoff stuff? I still think it was right to do so. It was hardly something that happened in private; it happened at a public training session. It was the perfect example of the problems Fletcher was facing. Flintoff was out of control that winter in his off-field behaviour. In making him captain Fletcher had placed a huge amount of trust in him. He had let Fletcher down, and basically cost him the job he loved and cherished.

As Fletcher said afterwards, 'People have turned round and said, should I have brought it up? From my point of view the two [the revelation in the book and the "Fredalo" affair during the 2007 World Cup in the West Indies] were directly linked. You had a situation where an incident took place and rightly or wrongly I kept it in-house, then in three or four weeks' time we had a similar affair. I just thought it was important it was brought out in the open. If the pedalo affair hadn't happened I wouldn't have revealed it [the story of England's abandoned practice in Australia]. Having had a chat with him, if nothing had happened, I definitely wouldn't have revealed it. But they were so directly linked I was taken aback by it – enough is enough, sort of thing.'

Predictably, Flintoff's great mate Harmison was outraged when the book serialization appeared. 'The code states that what goes on in the dressing room stays in the dressing room,' Harmison said. 'It was a code very dear to Duncan Fletcher's heart and, sadly, Duncan Fletcher has broken it. For someone to be able to justify doing what Fletcher has done they would have to have a very good reason. If not, it's just telling tales out of school. Fletcher took me from a young player to someone who has won fifty-odd Test caps. And I admit I've given him a lot of problems to deal with. So it's disappointing that my relationship with him should end on such a sour note. The sadness is that Fletcher was a very good coach who did a lot for our game. But the picture he paints of Freddie is unfair and one-sided. He's said nothing about what a positive force Fred is within the dressing room, which to me, says it all.'

Well, Fletcher did actually, but not in the serialization of course. I do not think Fletcher will mind my saying that he did not contribute much to the actual writing of his two books. That's what ghosts are for. He spoke, I listened, and then I wrote. But when I wrote 'Flintoff bowled with the heart of a lion' with regard to his superhuman performance in the final Test of the 2005 Ashes at the Oval, Fletcher read it and said, 'No, that should be "the heart of three lions".' Fletcher knew all about Flintoff's talent, that is for sure.

But they were very different characters. As Simon Jones says, 'Fletch and Fred just didn't see eye to eye. Fred always respected him because he was such a good coach. I just don't think they liked each other as people. Fred is a bit of a piss taker and joker, and he'd have a laugh with most people, but I never saw him and Fletch having a giggle once.'

Flintoff himself admits as much in his book *Ashes to Ashes*: 'As far as Duncan and I are concerned, it was a case of two people who didn't get on being thrown together for eight months of the year as part of the England cricket team. We had completely different views on life, the relationship didn't work, and it came to an abrupt end after the World Cup, so it was clear he was not going to be very complimentary about me, although I've lost count of the number of times I was injured, or had jabs, while he was England coach and played to help the team. I had an inkling he was going to have a go at me, even though he once said, when the press were on his back, that the weakest way to have a go at someone was in print.'

There are and were some journalists Fletcher quite liked during his time with England. It is probably best not to name any names, but there were many he simply had no time for. He had a particular problem with many of the newspapers' number twos, who, more often than not, are promoted to pole position during the one-day series that follow Tests. Fletcher felt they understood cricket much less than their seniors. And, with the tiredness and general problems that always followed England's one-day cricket, this made for some tricky times during press conferences at the end of many tours.

Before returning to the international game with India, there were also some other awkward moments because Fletcher had to spend time in various press boxes while waiting to do summarizing stints on radio with *Test Match Special*. He did not enjoy his first experience during a one-day game at Cape Town in late November 2009. And I was not surprised. On radio you often just have to talk. Fletcher doesn't just talk. As I said earlier about the early writing of his autobiography, he can talk at length, but it has to be about a subject that is really engaging him. It is a consequence of his upbringing as much as anything. At Carswell Farm the spaces were wide and open. It was a place where very few words were required. It was a place for action and thought, not for lots of words.

But by the time of the Test there later in that tour, and the arrival of his former captain Vaughan alongside him, he was much more relaxed and comfortable on air, with his ever-so-sharp technical expertise being gently coaxed out of him. Indeed there was one lunchtime filler that the pair did about the 2005 Ashes that received much acclaim. I saw Fletcher in the Cape Town press box just afterwards. He was in unusually high spirits. 'That was so enjoyable,' he beamed.

The obvious downside for Fletcher in the *TMS* box was the

presence of Boycott. It goes without saying that never once did they exchange words; never once did Fletcher even look at the former England opener. Fletcher simply cannot stand the man. Boycott was a critic from the very moment Fletcher was appointed, questioning how he could take the job without any Test match experience. Early on in his tenure Fletcher even wrote a ghosted piece (not by me but by Mark Hodgson, then the ECB's media liaison officer) in the *Daily Telegraph* in response to some of Boycott's criticisms, especially of his resting of players from county cricket.

After the 2005 Ashes win, Boycott phoned Fletcher at his Cape Town home. Boycott has a place in a golf estate in the Western Cape and wanted to play a round on the course with Fletcher and the late Bob Woolmer, then Pakistan's coach, whose side England were about to face that winter. Fletcher was having none of it, letting rip, swearing loudly, and asking Boycott how he could try to be so friendly when he had been so vitriolic in his broadcasting and ghosted observations. Boycott realized that the golf was not going to happen, so downgraded his offer to a cup of tea somewhere. Fletcher refused and slammed the phone down.

He felt better for having stuck to his principles, but he also knew there might be further criticisms in store. Marina even mentioned this to him the minute he had put the phone down. Fletcher was sufficiently worried to phone Hussain to seek his advice. 'I'd have that cup of tea if I were you,' said Hussain. Of course Fletcher did not do that, and there was an inevitable consequence, because even before England had set off on what would be a calamitous Ashes tour in 2006/07 Boycott was calling for Fletcher's head as coach. And this while England still held the Ashes! But a bandwagon had begun its journey, and its passengers became many, varied and more and more vociferous as the winter progressed.

With some journalists, Fletcher's stance will simply never

soften. In September 2010 I was with him and a couple of other friends outside the Mochyn Du pub next to the Swalec Stadium, Cardiff when a journalist extended his hand to Fletcher, who promptly looked the other way. Now, I've had the odd difference of opinion with this journalist, but I still shake his hand.

Later that evening I spoke to Fletcher about the incident. I related a story of my own, in which my father had given me one of my biggest bollockings after a rugby match when I was playing for Lydney against Cheltenham. It had been a niggly, sometimes violent match in which I felt I'd been targeted. So when it came to a conclusion and the opposition formed their traditional tunnel to clap us off and shake hands, I skirted around it and rushed to the changing rooms in a huff. My father caught up with me in the bar afterwards. He was not happy. 'Whatever happens you still shake their hands afterwards,' he growled. 'You need to grow up.'

With my father's advice returning after all those years I told Fletcher he should have shaken the journalist's hand. 'No, no, it's different,' he replied. 'On a sports field there is a natural respect for each other. I don't respect that man. I don't see why I should shake his hand.'

The relationship between journalists and players and coaches is an interesting one. Gone are the days when they were close friends on tour. I still can't get over reading that John Woodcock, the cricket correspondent of *The Times* from 1954 to 1988, once shared a room with Brian Statham the night before a Test on tour, because Statham's room-mate Peter Loader had flu. Imagine that today.

Now there is mainly distrust. Even when Fletcher is telling me something important he will presage it with something like 'Now, Sidney, how confidential are you?' He's never been upset that I leaked something (I haven't) but he was upset with a piece I did about Matt Prior in the West Indies in 2009.

'Where has that journalist with vision I once knew gone?' he asked.

He was unhappy that, in praising Peter Moores for his promotion of Prior to the Test team in 2007, I had forgotten something: that Fletcher had wanted Prior to replace the out-of-form Geraint Jones midway through the Pakistan home series in 2006. But the selectors wanted Read, and got their wish. All the fuss about Read or Jones for the Ashes that winter might have been avoided. Prior actually played twelve one-day internationals under Fletcher, opening in ten of them, and was – still is of course – Fletcher's type of combative cricketer. Fletcher wanted him for the one-day series in Australia and the subsequent World Cup in 2007, but was persuaded to go with the veteran Paul Nixon by skipper Vaughan.

As Fletcher said of Prior in 2009, 'It seems to have taken them [the selectors] three years to realize just how good this guy is. To have found a bloke who can bat at number seven is a huge plus. People who criticize his keeping should remember that most keepers struggle when they first come on the international scene: Alec Stewart, Brendon McCullum, Mark Boucher, even Kumar Sangakkara. All keepers miss chances, it's just that a guy like Adam Gilchrist could get away with it because Australia had an attack that covered up any mistakes he made. Prior should be cut some slack.'

Even after the calamitous 3–0 series defeat by Pakistan early in 2012, Prior still averaged 44.24 in his fifty Tests, higher than any other England keeper (Les Ames averaged 43.40) and with only his coach Andy Flower (53.70) and Gilchrist (48.60) above him among those keepers who have played ten innings. Fletcher would have liked working with Prior the Test batsman/keeper.

Being an ex-player in the media brings with it its own challenges. Players quite naturally look to you for more sympathy, and seem especially enraged when that is not necessarily forthcoming. And, of course, they may know you a little better than some other journalists. In that regard I learnt an important early lesson as a journalist. It was at Headingley in 2006, and Ian Bell had just scored his third Test century in four innings. I did a piece for the *Sunday Telegraph*, which was generally full of praise but did contain some light-hearted negativity, suggesting Bell had had a bit of fortune in reaching that century on the Saturday morning.

Twelfth man for England on the Sunday was Mike Powell, a Glamorgan player and good friend. After England had finished their pre-match practice I wandered down to the entrance from which the players used to emerge on to the ground at Headingley, where there was a curious arrangement whereby players and press could easily mingle as the press had to pass the dressing rooms to go to the toilet. I spoke to Powell to arrange dinner for that evening. He was keen and mentioned that Bell wanted to have dinner with him too.

Just a few minutes later Bell came past having finished his practice. I said hello chirpily but received only a grunt in response as Bell quickly walked past me. I was a little shocked, if the truth be told. I thought my piece had been pretty complimentary!

By lunchtime I'd spoken to Powell again. The dinner was off. Bell was unhappy with my piece and certainly did not want to have dinner with me.

The lesson I learnt was not that players are sensitive – of course they are – but that a journalist should never expect a player to speak to him. From that moment I have always made sure that if I encounter a player in a hotel or wherever I allow him to do the greeting first. If he does not want to, then I have no problem. If he feels he has been criticized unfairly, that is his prerogative. That's probably why, were I not so close to him, I wouldn't try to shake the hand of someone like Fletcher without the nod first.

7

The Terrorists Take Charge

Duncan Fletcher's reign as England coach ended after the World Cup match against the West Indies in Barbados on 21 April 2007. Two days earlier at the Police ground on the island where England were practising, Fletcher had announced to the team that he was to end his seven-year tenure. The night before that he had called captain Michael Vaughan and met him at the bar of the Hilton Hotel. He told Vaughan that he had already met with ECB chairman David Morgan to agree his terms of departure, and that the West Indies match was to be his last in charge. They reminisced for a good few hours. 'We probably had about twelve rum and Cokes,' says Vaughan with a smile now.

But the following day Vaughan was in tears as he thanked Fletcher for his work. 'I can't believe I just cried in front of grown men,' he later told Dean Conway by text. It was certainly emotional. Even Fletcher, the inscrutable 'Silver Fox', wiped a tear from his eye.

If there was sadness that Fletcher's departure from the top

job was rather inevitable, there should also have been sadness that such vast cricketing knowledge was being tossed so insouciantly out of the English game. Conway is clearly a close ally of Fletcher's but he does have a point when he says, 'Say a business institution had had a CEO like Fletch for so many years. Would they just say "Thanks for coming"? No. The ECB should have dovetailed Peter Moores in. Fletch would have been a perfect number two. He wanted a six-month handover [and India, one of the visitors in the following summer of 2007, were the only country he did not beat in a Test series]. How could the ECB presume that Moores' philosophies could take them forward from day one? Why invest so much time in one man and then do this? There is an energy you need at the top, and maybe it had dipped a bit, but you couldn't lose somebody like that with their bank of knowledge.'

One influential player told me, 'He should be at the Academy now. Imagine if he were a selector too. He'd be brilliant. There were signs at the end of the India tour the previous winter that he was tiring. The ECB should have started making moves then.'

Fletcher, of course, resigned in the West Indies, and woe betide anyone who writes that he was sacked. But the ECB hardly supported him. He had challenged too many people there. Morgan was a strong supporter, but so many others weren't. They were glad to see Fletcher go, despite the monumental task he had managed. Fletcher cared little for what others thought of him, and he paid for it in the end. He tried hard to change anachronistic English ideals, with some people more worried about keeping their jobs than actually doing them properly.

Chairman of selectors David Graveney was a classic example. He's a decent bloke. And not just because he picked me for England, even if he did phone after one Test to announce 'They [supposedly meaning the other selectors Graham Gooch and Mike Gatting] want to go with a right-hand/left-hand opening partnership' in justifying Nick Knight's inclusion ahead of me for the next Test after I'd been called up as a late replacement for the injured Mark Butcher for the Lord's Test against South Africa in 1998. Graveney was always looking to tomorrow and next week. Fletcher was looking years ahead. He viewed selection as an investment, and anyone who knows him knows how careful he is with his money! So when he said things like 'I want to know what my returns are going to be in five years' time and not next week' you knew he was thinking long and hard about that investment.

Not that Fletcher ever forced a selection upon his captain. Both Hussain and Vaughan have confirmed to me that Fletcher never did this to them once. For example, at Lord's in 2000 against Zimbabwe, Fletcher wanted Harmison to play instead of Ed Giddins. He saw Harmison as the investment, while Hussain was very much in Graveney's world then, thinking only of the horse for the course. Fletcher knew Giddins' swing might be too much for the callow Zimbabweans, but he worried that he would then have to be picked in the following series against the West Indies and get exposed. Giddins did take wickets against Zimbabwe at Lord's (7-42 in the match) and did reasonably well in the next Test at Trent Bridge, but when he was thoroughly ineffective against the West Indies at Edgbaston (0-73 from eighteen overs), Hussain had to admit that Fletcher might have been right. Giddins never played for England again.

Hussain and Fletcher rarely disagreed after that. The captain/coach bond that Fletcher preached saw to that. 'He said very early on "I want your trust. We've got to trust each other completely,"' says Hussain. And Hussain can only remember one occasion when Fletcher was upset with him. It was at a dinner in Port Elizabeth during the World Cup of 2003 after all the problems about Zimbabwe when Hussain had had too much to drink. There were others present and Hussain began bringing up private conversations that he and Fletcher had had over the issue. Fletcher gave him an icy stare and said, 'Right, that's enough of that.' And Hussain shut up immediately. 'When Fletcher said boo, I jumped,' Hussain admits now. 'If you cross him, you cross him for life. He is a very, very stubborn man.'

The commissioning of the Schofield Report was the final straw for Fletcher. He felt it thoroughly undermined him. He was right to point out that England were actually still number two in the Test rankings at the time. They'd been hammered by the number one team. The report was really all about the jerking of a number of knees.

Not that it can be denied that the winter of 2006/07 was anything other than a 'Winter from Hell', as I entitled the thirteenth chapter of his autobiography. It certainly was unlucky. England had lost the Ashes 5–0, and even though they surprisingly won the subsequent Commonwealth Bank series one-day trophy, Fletcher came in for unprecedented criticism. It wore him down. 'He defended the team a lot,' says Geraint Jones, 'but I think he got to the point in Australia where in a way he got sick of defending us and that was the first time I'd seen him in that frame of mind. I think he changed a bit on that tour. He got worn down by all the media pressure and that changed his outlook on people. I felt that approachability between the two of us had gone a bit.'

Fletcher was not the same man, or the same coach, on that trip. But it was little surprise. He'd been let down, and he was tired, as he later admitted to me when I wrote after the Ashes triumph of 2010/11 that the ECB should be careful about how they handle Andy Flower and his workload. 'You might be on to something there,' said Fletcher. 'I never realized how tired I was when I was doing the job.'

The fun, such a vital part of every dressing room in which Fletcher had been involved, disappeared a little on that Ashes trip of 2006/07. The social committee waned in its activities, and by the one-day series the tour had descended into bacchanalia, with Vaughan, returned from injury, deciding against exerting the sort of discipline he might usually have brought to bear. 'We were like a throwback to the 1970s,' wrote Vaughan. 'And we just about managed to keep it from Duncan.'

I was not on that tour. But plenty of journalists were, of course. And back home Peter Preston of the *Observer* reckoned they should have said something. 'The cosy inner circle of travelling journalists and retired England stars didn't exactly fulfil the most basic requirement their audience demands: that is, breaking a totally valid news story,' Preston wrote. Was it that bad? Some say it was, some say it wasn't. The very fact that one player was heard to joke 'This drinking team has got a cricket problem' is probably sufficient evidence.

Should Fletcher have done something? He had never imposed a curfew on any side he had coached, from the University of Cape Town upwards. He wasn't going to start in Australia. His view was that international cricketers get paid a lot of money in this day and age. With that comes responsibility. It should be obvious to any sensible person what those responsibilities are. Banning alcohol from cricket would be like taking Yorkshire pudding from a plate of roast beef.

Under Flower and Andrew Strauss England make sure the whole team celebrates personal milestones of a century or five wickets in an innings with a beer in the dressing room at the end of the day's play. 'Fitness trainers and physiologists will say that beer might make you feel more stiff the next day, but I think that's a small price to pay for genuinely celebrating one of your team-mates' successes. I brought it in pretty much straight after I became captain,' writes Strauss in his diary *Winning the Ashes Down Under*. It certainly seems better than Peter Moores' handing out of big cigars after a victory. 'It always seemed a bit forced to me,' wrote Vaughan of that.

When I met Fletcher at the team's Gatwick hotel before they left for the World Cup, he was more uptight than he had been in

South Africa in 2005. I knew it was over then. In fact I thought it best that it was over soon. This was not about the much-quoted 'coach's shelf life'. This was about a man for whom the very worst of British sport, with its passion for scapegoats and blood-letting, had become too much. He was fighting too many battles; against selectors, administrators and the media. I knew then that news of the Schofield Report had finished him off.

It was a sad day for me. I went home to my wife later that day and said, 'The book will be out this year.' And so it was. I'd finished it by the summer's end, and it was in the bookshops in time for Christmas, preceded by days of serialization that rocked the sport with their ferocity.

So where did it all go wrong? Well, the simple answer is that England were never going to win that Ashes series away to a great Australian side – and they were still great in 2006/07 – who were hell-bent on revenge after the loss in 2005, and with England missing three key players in Vaughan, Marcus Trescothick (who left the tour before the Tests) and Simon Jones. As Trescothick said to me, 'The reason we lost 5–0? We didn't have our best side out.' To emphasize: not one of England's top seven for the first Test had played a Test in Australia before.

Crucially, England did not have their captain. They had had two captains in that year, neither of whom had made a cast-iron case for the job. There was Andrew Flintoff, who'd led the side to a remarkable Test victory in Mumbai the previous winter, but then had suffered injury during the English summer. Then there was Strauss, who'd taken over in Flintoff's absence. He'd lost his first one-day series 5–0 to Sri Lanka, but had shown signs of growing into the role during the Test series against Pakistan that is always rather better remembered for an alleged ball-tampering incident that forced the abandonment of the Test at the Oval.

Flintoff was, of course, appointed for the Ashes. With the

benefit of hindsight it is a decision that has been lambasted. But I do not recall such opprobrium at the time. That Mumbai victory was enough for most observers; enough evidence of an inspirational leader.

It clearly was a tricky decision. It was certainly one which exercised Fletcher's mind throughout the summer. I remember being in his car, having done some book stuff, when he asked my opinion. In reply I asked him whether he thought Strauss could cope with the big characters in the team, in other words Flintoff and Harmison. 'He can cope with anything,' said Fletcher then.

He'd obviously changed his mind by the time the decision was made, but I could actually see why. The only way England could beat Australia was if Flintoff was firing, and if Harmison was too. There might have been the thought that Flintoff could run rampant off the field (as happened anyway) if he were not captain, but it was mainly on-field considerations that held sway.

Fletcher still stands by the decision today, even though his assistant Matthew Maynard says, 'I know that he spoke to a lot of people about that, but I haven't spoken to one person who said it should be Flintoff. I said Strauss.'

Well, the chairman of selectors, Graveney, did say Flintoff, while fellow selector Geoff Miller said Strauss.

It is here that I will ask one very important question: did Strauss really want the job then? It is my understanding that in private he was showing quite a lot of negativity towards it. He was worried about the public's support for Flintoff, their champion after all, who was making it all-clear that he wanted to be captain. And he was worried that he would not be able to control a disgruntled Flintoff and his mate Harmison. 'There was a story in the *Sun* saying Fred wanted to be captain,' says one player. 'Straussy knew then that he could not get the public on his side.'

After every tour the ECB writes a detailed report, and I have seen a copy of the report for that 2006/07 Ashes tour. This was its summation of the captaincy debate (with due apology for some over-excited use of capitals):

> It was clearly a close call between Andrew Flintoff and Andrew Strauss for the Ashes Captaincy. On balance the Selectors favoured the former as with Andrew Flintoff having his heart set on the Captaincy they felt it was the most likely way to get the best performances out of him and his close friend Steve Harmison, and they hoped that he would prove to be a talismanic leader.

Much was made of the revelation in Fletcher's book that he was swayed finally by a DVD shown at Loughborough at the end of the 2006 summer by Colin Gibson, then the ECB's head of corporate communications, with the words 'The team has to be together to beat Australia'. I'm not sure I wrote that too well. 'That was it. It had to be Flintoff,' I continued in Fletcher's voice. It left Fletcher open to easy criticism, the tale of a decision made on a whim. It was not like that. Fletcher does not do whimsy. He'd agonized over that call.

He said to Strauss 'You might thank me for this one day', although Strauss has admitted privately that he is unsure whether they were the exact words. But they were the gist. And Strauss does indeed have cause to thank Fletcher. Had he been captain in 2006/07, he would not have been captain in 2009 and in 2010/11. He would not have been an Ashes-winning captain, of that I am pretty sure.

It soon became clear that Flintoff as captain was a huge mistake, not least for Fletcher because the 'critical mass' he so often talked about was skewed against him. Flintoff was always a very persuasive voice in the dressing room, especially with the younger players coming into the side (they were easily won over by his huge presence and friendliness). His group of followers meant that Fletcher's desired number of eight good characters was seriously diminished. The terrorists were in charge.

These words from the aforementioned ECB tour report tell the story succinctly:

An off-field 'leadership vacuum' was allowed to develop on the Tour. Duncan Fletcher has always favoured empowering the captain as 'leader' whilst he plays a 'consultancy' role. Andrew Flintoff has proved not to be as natural a leader as Nasser Hussain or Michael Vaughan and not to have had as close a working relationship with Duncan Fletcher. It does not appear that sufficient time and effort was spent building team unity off the field. Andrew Flintoff has been a player who has needed 'managing' – it does not appear that the award of the Captaincy has led to him moderating his behaviour or to this situation changing. In the preparatory work prior to and at the start of the tour, the Team had agreed to take on a challenging, aggressive persona rather than a non-confrontational, friendly one that had the danger of setting a submissive tone and of isolating any England player targeted for sledging by the opposition. The Captain clearly did/does not believe in this approach and this issue was not properly ironed out in advance of the tour. The end result appears to have been a degree of disillusion and frustration for those players who believed in and aimed to carry out the original policy.

That is all so true. Only Kevin Pietersen and Paul Collingwood initially challenged the Australians verbally, but even Pietersen relented a little once he made up with Shane Warne after a spat, leaving Collingwood fighting a lone battle. There was an awful moment in Sydney when Collingwood and Warne (who was batting) were going hard at each other, with Chris Read standing between them in silence.

In Fletcher's book we used the words 'I was soon to discover he [Flintoff] was unsure of what true leadership is'. Fletcher should have been stronger, and at one stage did want to be so.

England simply had to do well in the first Test in Brisbane. Otherwise Flintoff would run away from the problem, as I believe is his wont. That is in his character. He dislikes confrontation, as well as making decisions that might prove unpopular. I'll give you a little example of something that has happened since he finished playing. Myles Hodgson is a respected cricket writer who ghosted all of Flintoff's books and has always been loyal and helpful to him. He considered himself a friend of Flintoff's. In 2009 he began working part-time for Flintoff's management company, ISM (International Sports Management). About a year later Hodgson was sacked suddenly by the company, but, as I write, he has not heard a word from Flintoff since.

England did badly in that first Test, and so Flintoff ran to the bar. He subsequently revealed that he may have been suffering from depression at the time, worsening his tendency to heavy drinking. The 'Fredalo' incident later in the winter was almost inevitable. It was also another problem that the embattled Fletcher could have done without.

The incident occurred on 16 March 2007, the night after England had lost to New Zealand in St Lucia in their opening match of the World Cup. Two days later they were to face Canada, also in St Lucia. The performance against New Zealand had been disappointing, a loss by six wickets, so when Flintoff saw a group of journalists at the Rex Resorts Hotel bar later, he told them he was not drinking that night. With laptop under arm, he was talking excitedly about 'Skyping' his family.

Flintoff, however, is easily persuaded, and did have a drink. He was soon joined by Jeremy Snape, the former England one-day spin bowler who'd been employed by Fletcher as a psychologist. Together they went to the local Lime bar, and from there to the Rumours nightclub. With them were five other players – James Anderson, Jon Lewis, Ian Bell, Paul Nixon and Liam Plunkett (although I gather one other senior player may have been there and therefore been a little fortunate to escape the flak that followed) – as well as the bowling coach Kevin Shine, who was mightily unfortunate to be caught up in all of this as it was his first night out on tour, having met up with his holidaying brother.

Flintoff can take up the story. 'Not long after I arrived at the club, I realized I'd had enough to drink and slipped out – intending to walk back to the hotel,' he wrote in his book *Ashes to Ashes*. 'Instead of walking down the road, I decided it would be nicer down the beach and come into the hotel from the back. A row of kayaks caught my eye, but none of them had any oars. Next to them were some pedalos, and I remember dragging one to the edge of the water – presumably because I fancied a ride. But for the life of me, I couldn't work out how to get on it – or my legs into it – so I let go of it, and it quickly drifted away from the shore. I think I slipped and fell over in a few inches of water, but nothing more.'

By the next morning it was obvious that the incident had not gone unnoticed. The *News of the World* had the story. How they came about it remains something of a mystery, and it was rather strange that the story appeared under the byline of David Norrie, a close friend of Flintoff's who had been on his stag 'do' to Budapest in early 2005.

The source is not important. The story was valid, and embarrassing, even if the physiotherapist Conway could extract some humour from Flintoff the next morning.

'Where were you going, Fred?' he asked.

'Preston, I think,' replied Flintoff.

In fact all Flintoff did that weekend was go back to his room. He was banned for the Canada match.

Up until 'Fredalo' there had been no greater fuss that winter than that made over England's selection for the first Test in Brisbane. England chose Geraint Jones as wicketkeeper ahead of Read, and Ashley Giles as spinner over Monty Panesar. They were seen as contentious picks because Read and Panesar had finished the English season in possession of those places. Giles had been injured for some considerable time.

Jones was also put on the team management group that Fletcher always used to help with decision-making. This was seen as ridiculous Fletcher favouritism. But I will quote that ECB report again:

> The Cricket Management Group for the Ashes comprised Andrew Flintoff, Andrew Strauss, Paul Collingwood and Geraint Jones and played just the same consultative/advisory role to Coach and captain that it has played since Duncan Fletcher established the concept when he was first appointed. The media seized on the inclusion of Geraint Jones on this group seeing it as a sign of DF's strong support for Geraint Jones. DF explains in his report the reasons Geraint Jones was on the Group – Andrew Flintoff was very keen to have him there, he is a good contributor to the group and it was felt that it would be a good move to boost his confidence.

Jones himself wishes it had not happened. 'In hindsight I wish I'd said no,' he says. 'It put a lot of pressure on me early on. I'd gone into that tour with the mindset that Readie would have the gloves and maybe I'd get a chance come Boxing Day. I just wanted to play my cricket and not worry about all the extra stuff.'

Giles was also unsure of his elevation. 'It was a bit of a surprise to me that I got the call,' he says. 'Even up to the last first-class game before the Test I didn't play. The first Test was my first first-class game in twelve months. It was quite a big ask. And just by getting picked for the first Test everyone was against me.'

In truth there were bigger issues than these two selections, which Flintoff not only agreed with, by the way, but positively pushed for. Little wonder that Fletcher eventually cracked and said 'I am not the sole selector' after the second Test in Adelaide in which he had wanted to play two spinners in Giles and Panesar, but had been thoroughly outvoted, with everyone on the management team disagreeing.

I do not think the supposed under-preparation of the team was an issue either. 'Undercooked' quickly became a cliché, but it was an easy line. There was the Champions Trophy in India just beforehand, so preparation time was limited, especially as, against Fletcher's wishes, there had to be a one-day match against a Prime Minister's XI at the start of the tour. Quite how a fifty-over match was supposed to aid Test-match preparation has never been made clear.

England did play two three-day matches, against New South Wales and South Australia. They faced some rather decent players in the shapes of bowlers Glenn McGrath, Brett Lee, Stuart Clark, Jason Gillespie and Shaun Tait, and batsmen like Phil Jaques, Simon Katich, Michael Clarke, Matthew Elliott and Darren Lehmann. Mischievously a Cricket Australia (CA) official told journalists that England had turned down the opportunity to play four first-class matches before the first Test. It was not true. In fact CA made the ECB pay for their first two days on tour, because they were two more days than England had hosted Australia for before the first Test in 2005. So this rather silences those who criticized England for going home for four days after the Champions Trophy rather than travelling straight to Australia. It would have cost more money, and Fletcher said he would have given the players four days off even if they had gone to Australia.

Another major gripe among observers was that the NSW match was a fourteen-a-side affair. But that had always been Fletcher's way. He viewed such matches as no more than practice. He preferred his players to be a little underdone going into a Test series. But it was never a popular policy, and now in Australia the brickbats flew.

When in 2010/11 England played three first-class matches

(two of them lasting three days and one four) and won two and drew the other, much was made of the preparation, but I reckon England were a little lucky. They played the same top six batsmen in all three games, therefore depriving the reserve batsman Eoin Morgan of a match before the first Test. Imagine if one of the chosen six had broken a finger the day before that first Test. Yes, Morgan showed at the start of the 2011 season that he could play first-class cricket with little preparation, returning from the Indian Premier League to score 193 for the Lions against Sri Lanka to secure a place for the first Test, but this was different. It was a gamble.

It worked, though. But there was no such luck in 2006/07. With the 5–0 drubbing completed in Sydney, at the city's Sheraton on the Park Hotel the ECB called an emergency board meeting of the seven of its twelve members present at the Test. 'The board were united on the need for a review,' says Morgan, 'and came to the conclusion that it should have a ring of independence about it. A shortlist of potential independent review leaders was drawn up and after running it past Ian Jones, a trusted Mayfair-based head-hunter, I decided to opt for Ken Schofield. And the rest is history.'

That Test in Sydney had finished on 5 January. By 11 January Schofield was receiving a call from ECB chief executive David Collier asking him to head the review. 'It came as much of a surprise to me as to all those who were equally surprised that an ageing Scotsman of doubtful cricketing pedigree could play any meaningful [part in a] review of the disappointing winter that had unfolded in Australia in terms of the Ashes defence,' Schofield wrote in his introduction to the eventual report, the full version of which I have seen, and just about waded through without falling asleep.

No matter. The Scot Schofield, the former director of the PGA European tour, was actually a decent choice. He was going to be in Australia during the one-day series anyway, having previously arranged to go there with his wife to visit their son who was on a two-year work secondment. He was given a six-man committee of Nasser Hussain, Angus Fraser, Nick Knight, Mickey Stewart, Hugh Morris and Brian Rose, all former England cricketers.

Mike Atherton declined to be on the committee, citing a conflict of interest with his media duties. And good on him for doing so. He still spoke to Schofield, as did 'between 80 and 100' other cricketing people according to the author of the report, to air some of his views. But Atherton's desire to remain on one side of the fence is depressingly rare in English cricket, indeed in cricket in general. Too many want to wear too many hats. Fraser was still cricket correspondent of the *Independent* when sitting on this report committee. Not without justification did he at the time have the nickname 'Martini', as in 'any time, any place, anywhere'. He could certainly keep a number of plates spinning at the same time. He would say that he was helping the game, and it might be partly true, but a conflict of interest is never a good thing. I have been asked to stand for the Glamorgan committee, asked to sit on Review Groups there, but have always declined. To undertake any official position brings instant compromise. I gladly offer opinion and help, but never on an official basis.

At one stage Alec Stewart managed to be a coach (at Surrey), broadcaster and an agent/mentor all at the same time, while running, alongside Alan Smith, the former manager of Crystal Palace, his sports management firm Arundel Promotions (now taken over by Essentially Group Limited). I'm not sure Stewart was actually involving himself in deals concerning players under his wing, but that can't have been right when he was looking after cricketers such as Bell, Prior and Collingwood. As I write now the likes of Warwickshire's Chris Woakes and Surrey's Jade Dernbach, two promising young bowlers for England, are in Essentially's stable where Stewart acts mostly as an ambassador, as well as offering guidance to players. Once in 2008 Stewart was particularly scathing about the performances of Bell and Collingwood. 'I call it as I see it,' he said, 'and I don't ever let any agency connections get in the way when my role is to comment on performances. The players understand that you have to be hard sometimes.'

In 2011 Surrey's director of cricket, Chris Adams, spent four days at Hove commentating for Sky Sports when his team, complete with Pietersen returning from injury amid an inevitable welter of publicity, were playing at Cambridge University. How does that work? Surrey lost too. While at Hove Adams was asked whether he thought the Surrey fast bowler Chris Tremlett should be in the side for the first Test of the summer. What was he going to say?

Away from media conflicts of interest, the case of Ashley Giles is interesting. He is Warwickshire's director of cricket, as well as an England selector. To add to the mix, after the Moores/Pietersen double sacking in early 2009, he applied to take over as England team director. Amid suggestions that he was too close to too many of the players, he was not interviewed for the role. 'With hindsight it is the best thing that could have happened to me,' he says. 'I needed more time. I felt I could do it. And I never felt the relationships with the players would have affected that. I had similar relationships with the Warwickshire players when I took over there. We all know where the line stands.'

It is a fair point, but, with Warwickshire always on the lookout to sign new players, there have been complaints from other counties that his position as a selector might attract players to his county. Some have even suggested privately that Giles might be using that position to lure players. That is ridiculous, maybe even slanderous. Giles is an unimpeachable character. But he does not take kindly to criticism. He has been one of the more sensitive England cricketers of recent times.

'You read one bad line in a newspaper and it kills you,' he says. 'You think "Shit, why do I bother?"' Mind you, when Dave Houghton said that England were better off playing with ten men after the first Ashes Test in 2005 than including him, that was pretty harsh criticism.

Less harsh was a flippant ironic throwaway line from David Hopps in the *Guardian* in 2007, which is barely worth mentioning because it was so inoffensive. But, prompted by the man from Radio Five Live with whom he was working during the Test against India, the then-retired Giles came to the press box and began what we journos love to term a PBI (press box incident). Hopps, who had ghosted Giles's *Guardian* column in 2005, reckons he's never been more angry and had to leave the box to calm down. Somehow, probably because at the time I was working for the *Guardian* too and because I think Hopps said something like 'You tell him, Jamo' as he left, I got involved. I'm not sure I told him, as Hopps asked. Indeed I'm not sure I said anything. It was all rather silly.

Giles appears a shrewd selector. We can be thankful to him for the discovery of Jonathan Trott as a Test batsman. Trott made his sensational Test debut (scoring 41 and 119) in the deciding Ashes match at the Oval in 2009, after the whole of England had seemingly given their opinion as to who should replace the out-of-form Ravi Bopara. I'm sure W. G. Grace was mentioned at one point. Or was it Mark Ramprakash?

But the truth is that decision had already been made for the previous Test at Headingley, in which England were thrashed. The batsman they had called into the squad and discarded on the morning of the match was Trott. I happened to see him leaving the ground with his pregnant wife. He was genuinely distraught. I know a few English cricketers who wouldn't have been. The pressure would have been postponed.

But as Giles said to me on a later occasion, he knew that if Trott was playing well, which he was at the time, 'he could block out all the external pressures and just bat'. And that he did rather well at the Oval. So well done to Giles.

Picking selectors is a curious business. It's not exactly a sage career choice. You can't really say 'I want to be a selector, sir' to your careers master. For Giles and James Whitaker, it is not paid well enough to be a full-time job. Poor old Graveney spent ten years as chairman of selectors on modest pay, and then the moment the role was made important after the Schofield Report and given the grander title of 'National Selector' as well as considerably more dosh, he was sacked. As I mentioned earlier, I'm not sure that Graveney was that good, but he was not that bad either. Selection definitely improved in some areas during his time, in terms of consistency and logic for sure, although I suspect Fletcher had much to do with that.

But Fletcher had nothing to do with the setting up of the Schofield Report, and that angered him. He felt it was designed solely to get rid of him. As the then team analyst Mark Garaway says, 'I've only been involved in two official reviews, and in both those the outcome was already decided and it seemed they were trying to find a way to get to that end point. One was with Somerset [where Garaway was promoted to be head coach instead of Shine, who was demoted to the Academy], and this one with England. Fletch didn't deserve this.'

Was it all about sacking Fletcher? 'I remember speaking to Mickey Stewart and us saying "If this is purely about sacking the England coach, then we don't want to be part of it",' says Hugh Morris. 'The driver was to identify key areas that had gone wrong and make sure they didn't happen again. If it was meant to sack Duncan I wasn't going to do that, nor was Mickey or Nasser for that matter.'

As Schofield himself says, 'It was the first question Nasser asked me in Melbourne. He immediately nailed his colours to Duncan Fletcher's mast, and I said to him, "We're not a hiring and firing agency." That heartened Nasser. There wasn't an overall running down of the coach during the report.'

You sense Hussain had mixed feelings about being part of the report. 'Duncan was cross,' he says, 'but he only told me that afterwards. I just got a phone call asking if I would sit on the group. I have always thought that I should help if I can, so I said yes. Hugh was on it and he was not anti-Duncan. We just went through everything that people had been critical of.'

On 24 May 2007, ECB chief executive David Collier announced the following nineteen recommendations from the Schofield Report:

Focusing on the Individual

1. Central Contracts To ensure the system of Central Contracts is maintained and developed by establishing challenging individually tailored training and preparation programmes which are closely monitored through the Performance Centre at Loughborough University, and reflect the 'needs' rather than the 'wants' of the players.

2. England Performance Squad Players outside the system of Central Contracts but selected for the England Performance Squad should have an individually tailored 12-month training and preparation programme closely monitored through the Performance Centre.

3. Skills Sets Skills Sets of players up to the age of Under 19 should be established, and have individually tailored 12-month training and preparation programmes closely monitored through the Performance Centre.

4. International Exchanges Maintain and develop links with Academies and teams throughout the World in order to provide players in England squads with the opportunity to spend time overseas developing their technical and tactical skills at appropriate times during their development.

5. Fitness and Conditioning The introduction of individually tailored strength and conditioning programmes for players within England programmes at all levels.

6. Medical Support and Screening To implement the recommendations within the ECB Science and Medicine Review, enhance the medical screening of all senior players, particularly fast bowlers, and provide 'World Class' medical support for Centrally Contracted players.

7. Player Personal Development To provide individual personal development programmes for each player in the England Performance Squad programme including media training in order to ensure the development of 'well-rounded' individuals.

8. Captaincy and Leadership Development The establishment of mentoring and development programmes for players who are in, or have the potential to be in, Captaincy and leadership roles within England cricket.

9. Coaching and Support Staff Professional Development The establishment of professional development programmes for England coaches and support staff in order for them to remain leading-edge practitioners.

10. Skill Development Supplement the coaching resources at the Performance Centre by appointing a Fielding Coach responsible for raising the standards of this discipline throughout the game.

11. Succession Planning Maintain a succession plan for all key positions within the England programme.

Focusing on the Team

12. International Programme To provide more opportunities for players to prepare, perform, repair and regenerate by reducing the amount of International cricket.

13. Establishing the National Cricket Centre as the 'Performance Centre' Refurbishment and rebranding the National Cricket Centre at Loughborough as the ECB Performance Centre, and establish the Centre as the focal point for all England player monitoring and development.

14. Domestic Competition Structure To reduce the amount of cricket played at First Class level to enable players to maintain and develop their cricket skills and fitness levels during the season, and provide competition formats and regulations which as far as possible mirror the international game.

15. Improving the Quality of Coaching A review and continual updating of the Level 4 Coaching and CPD programme to ensure the top coaches are equipped with the necessary skills and knowledge to develop 'World Class' players.

16. Improve Links/Communications with Counties Establish within a management structure, executive responsibility for promoting engagement and communication between England programmes and Counties, and raising the standards of First Class cricket.

Focusing on ECB

17. England Management Structure The establishment of a new management structure within the ECB with full accountability and responsibility for the selection and performance of the England cricket team.

18. Player Tracking Database The establishment of a player tracking database with the ability to monitor the development of every player in an England Squad.

19. Ongoing Planning Process Establish a robust biannual review process including all stakeholders and designed to take the game to the next level.

Sixteen of these were adopted immediately, and another, the 'establishment of a new management structure', was resolved in due course, but two other recommendations – 'reducing the amount of International cricket' and 'to reduce the amount of cricket played at First Class level . . . and provide competition formats and regulations which as far as possible mirror the international game' – remain on the mantelpiece, like unwanted wedding presents; gaudy-looking vases gathering dust. The volume of cricket internationally and domestically just isn't decreasing, and doesn't look as if it will by any great measure, even if Morgan's Report of 2012 suggests a reduction to 14 county championship matches. That review also proposes fifty-over county cricket, but as of 2012, county cricketers still don't play fifty-over one-day matches, as they do at World Cups. 'If I have one real regret,' says Schofield, 'it is that the counties still don't play fifty overs.'

For me the best thing to come out of the Schofield Report was the appointment of Hugh Morris as the managing director of England cricket, to fill the 'vacuum of accountability at the heart of the England set-up', as Morris has said since, and to rectify 'a distinct lack of communication between the England set-up and the ECB', and to be 'accountable for everything that comes under the broad remit of England cricket'.

I'm not just saying this because of my obvious links to Morris. It was not necessarily an appointment that was received with widespread favour. There were some who questioned how a man on the report committee could then claim the lucrative job that it recommended. 'Jobs for the boys!' screamed Hussain at the time, but his ire was probably more directed at Gatting, who was appointed managing director of cricket partnerships. They've never got on, ever since a match at the Parks in 1989 actually, a match I played in for the Combined Universities against Middlesex, when Gatting took exception to the young Hussain not walking.

Morris was deputy chief executive at the time of the report. He had first been technical director upon retiring from first-class cricket in 1997, then performance director and even acting chief executive in between the reigns of Tim Lamb and David Collier. As soon as the report was adopted, the role of deputy chief executive became redundant. He was one of fifty people to apply for the new role, with only six being interviewed. He was a worried man. Clearly had he known that a managing director would be recommended in the report, he would have had reservations about sitting on it in the first place. But he was very well qualified for the job. He'd played international cricket, he'd been heavily involved in elite coaching, he has a sports science degree and he has an MBA. And as he says, 'It's not unusual for top companies to promote from within.'

The recommendation of a managing director only came late in the Schofield Report's discussions, but it should have been one of the first. Fletcher might still be England coach today had he had such a buffer between himself and the administrators at the ECB. I asked him during the course of writing this book whether he would have liked such a person to help, and he agreed instantly. Ask those in the ECB and they will say that the increasingly autocratic Fletcher would not have entertained such a thought; indeed that it was mentioned but Fletcher refused. But it is surely more a matter of personnel. At the time of the Schofield Report Fletcher was angry with Morris, and indeed with Schofield, because they were staying in the same hotel as the team in Melbourne, and neither went to see him. Morris says there was no time, and that Stewart was due to speak to him before his departure to the Caribbean for the World Cup.

Morris as managing director and Fletcher as team director, as Flower is now titled, would have made an excellent combination. Many of the stresses that eventually dragged Fletcher down could have been taken from his shoulders. Fletcher has never openly criticized Morris to me. Deep down I think he knows he is a good man. It's just that, as already mentioned, if you cross Fletcher once, the road back is a long one.

But Morris is a good man, and a mate, even if the administrator/journalist relationship cannot be as open as most friendships are. It can be tricky at times because the easy assumption is, especially among fellow journalists, that he feeds me information, stories even. I can assure you that never once has he been the source of any 'story' I have obtained.

We shared some good times opening together for Glamorgan. Over the courses of our careers we made a hundred first-class centuries between us (forty-seven for me, fifty-three for him) and underwent twelve knee operations (seven for me, five for him). We had some ups and downs (the bastard dropped me!), but he was undoubtedly the better player. I also thought him the bravest of all the batsmen I batted with, although Atherton clearly ran him close. Quite how brave I didn't fully realize. For in August 2002 Morris suddenly discovered an opponent that was to prove tougher than anything he had ever faced on a cricket field.

One morning Morris cut himself shaving, and as he tended to the blood, he felt a lump on his neck. Three weeks later the lump was removed, and he was advised to return to see the surgeon in ten days' time. But the next evening Morris was told to return the following morning, and to bring his wife Debbie with him.

I remember in 2007 talking to Morris about Fletcher's book and excitedly telling him that I thought some of Fletcher's early life had been interesting, especially during the war years. 'He's faced death, and not many of us have done that,' I said. Immediately I realized what I had said. Morris smiled. 'I have,' he said.

He began retelling the story of that day with the surgeon, a man called Rogan Corbridge, when he was told he had a secondary cancer. Biopsies were taken from his tonsils, throat, tongue and nose, and the primary cancer was found in the tonsils. In early 2003 he underwent a seven-hour operation, called a bilateral neck dissection, and then had six weeks of radiotherapy treatment.

Morris has always enjoyed a healthy appetite, and I don't think he will mind my saying that he was never the most svelte of cricketers. Lunch was never ready unless Morris was at the front of its queue. There was one famous occasion at Sophia Gardens when such were his stomach's desires after a hard morning session in the field that he hurtled across the outfield, hurdled the advertising hoardings and was in that queue seemingly with the umpires still lifting the bails from their grooves.

But in early 2003 Morris lost nearly four stone in weight. That summer he came to Sophia Gardens to watch a game. I chanced upon him in the car park. I fully admit that I nearly burst into tears. The sight before my eyes was quite shocking. He looked like a man of seventy years rather than thirty-nine.

Words are not easy in such circumstances. But you know what? As soon as I spoke to him, I was convinced that he'd win his battle. For a man so clearly in such a bad way, he was remarkably upbeat. Cancer had chosen the wrong person. He was going to beat it.

And he did. On 14 May 2008, five years after he'd completed his radiotherapy treatment, Morris was given the all-clear. 'It is a date indelibly marked in my mind,' he says, with plenty of justification. English cricket has a special man overseeing its work. He gives it a perspective sport too often lacks.

8

Respect No Moores

Peter Moores' first Test as the new England coach was at Lord's against the West Indies in May 2007. The visitors won the toss and elected to field. As England's openers Andrew Strauss and Alastair Cook began their innings, I decided to take a stroll down from the Media Centre to one of the many food outlets at the Nursery End, searching ostensibly for a stronger cup of coffee than was available upstairs (yes, my name is Steve and I am a coffee addict), but also mindful that a player or coach or both might still be lurking around the net areas.

What I didn't expect to see was the head coach there. Moores was in the nets throwing to Liam Plunkett, the Durham bowler playing in his seventh Test. My heart sank. It is the kind of scenario you see every day at a county ground, and good on the coaches at that level for being so industrious. But at international level, you just cannot do that sort of thing. You have days in advance in which to do such work, and plenty of assistants to do it during the match if need be. When the Test starts you must be watching every ball. The media might be quizzing you about any aspect of the day's play later.

England had hastily installed a county coach, an extremely good county coach admittedly, in charge of the national team. At that moment I knew they'd made a mistake. I wish I'd had the courage to write as much. But I'd have looked pretty silly. Even now it seems such a petty crime on which to hang a man. But I do think it was a loud and early indication of the perils of hasty over-promotion. Moores was trying to be a county coach in the international game. It was confirmed a few years later by Michael Vaughan. 'The difference is that in county cricket you have to energize people,' he said. 'In international cricket you almost have to slow them down. With Test cricket you have to let it breathe a little. It is not all about energy.'

Goodness, Moores had been appointed less than a day after Duncan Fletcher resigned. The ECB had done this without advertisement or interview. They will point to the fact that Moores' appointment to the head of the National Academy job had come after a lengthy process of recruitment, during which for example the Australian Tom Moody, many people's favourite to succeed Fletcher, had been interviewed. Yes, it was a different role, but Moores had come out on top. 'He was very well regarded at the Academy,' says the then ECB chairman David Morgan. 'The chairman of Sussex, David Green, who was then a director of ECB, was very strong in recommending him. He was simply regarded as an outstanding candidate.'

Privately it may be a different story. One ECB official told me that had he interviewed Moores there was no way on earth he would have appointed him. While, when it came to appointing Andy Flower in 2009, a firm of head-hunters, Odgers Ray & Berndtson, were employed to recommend a shortlist of candidates. Mind you, the ECB got criticized for that too!

Things did not begin too badly for Moores. That first series against the West Indies was won 3–0. England lost the subsequent three-match series to India (home) and Sri Lanka (away) 1–0, but were never disgraced, and in one-day cricket, although they lost 2–1 to the West Indies, there were hugely encouraging series victories over India (4–3) and Sri Lanka (3–2).

It was in New Zealand in 2008 that cracks began to appear. That was actually my first overseas tour as a journalist, having just been appointed to replace Mike Atherton as the *Sunday Telegraph*'s cricket columnist. He was still in that position on that trip, however, and I went as correspondent in place of Scyld Berry who was otherwise engaged with editing *Wisden*.

England had lost the one-day series 3–1, but it was the tied match in Napier, where New Zealand managed to equal England's score of 340, that had begun to cause problems for Moores' regime. Remarkably after such a gruelling match, England's players were asked to go out and train. It didn't go down well, especially with the senior players.

It is, of course, the sort of story that is easily embellished, and it does seem that it was not a wholly compulsory session. One player told me that Moores had said 'Let's get out there and show them we're harder than them!' But team analyst Mark Garaway is not so sure those words were uttered. 'It was the sort of language Pete might have used,' he says, 'but it wasn't the full squad that went out by any stretch of the imagination. I remember it as being the group that didn't play in that match and a couple of lads who played but didn't do much.'

Graeme Swann, in his autobiography *The Breaks Are Off*, claims that everyone was ordered to do the running. 'He [Moores] announced that the whole squad was to return to the field of play,' he wrote. '"Those New Zealand boys will see us running on the square, and they will shit their pants, because they'll know that we mean business," he claimed. Shit their pants? More like piss their pants.

'The Kiwi lads thought it was absolutely hilarious as we trooped out into the middle with our fitness trainer. Our opponents sat there watching us from their dressing-room balcony, beers in hand, laughing their heads off.

'They couldn't believe what they were seeing, and I have to say it's the most humiliating and degrading session I have ever been involved in. For half an hour as we shuttled back and forth we had to ignore their mocking laughter.'

It is the gist of the story, but see what I was saying about embellishment?

Moores agreed to be interviewed for this book, which I wasn't expecting. Whether owing to the legal niceties of his departure from the ECB or not, he has rarely talked about his time as England coach since. And I was hardly his greatest supporter in the media.

He seemed to know the Napier issue would be asked about, and there does seem to be some regret on his part now. 'There are certain things I'd do differently,' he admits. 'There was an incident when we trained after one of the one-dayers [Napier]. It was sort of optional. What we were trying to do was to try and get ourselves fitter and stronger. If I'm being honest, when we first started we weren't in the right shape to be really competitive as an international unit, so the idea was that if we tagged in a quick twenty minutes then we wouldn't have to train for two days. I think the players saw it differently, especially the senior ones. That for me was a frustration.'

There was clearly a lot of frustration on that tour. It did not really become public at the time. There were murmurings, of course, but nothing explicit. Little did we know at the time that captain Vaughan was on the brink of resignation. He had texted ECB chairman Giles Clarke during the tour asking to talk. Had they done so Vaughan might have resigned there and then. Instead, before the flight home Vaughan spoke to Hugh Morris, who was also out in New Zealand, and voiced some concerns about Moores. Vaughan has since admitted that he flew home determined to resign, even though

England won the third Test in Napier to take the series 2–1.

That Test has become well known for the saving of Andrew Strauss's Test career. He made a duck in the first innings, and then 177 in the second innings. He was then batting at number three as a reluctant Vaughan opened with Cook at Moores' insistence on a right-hand/left-hand partnership. 'It was schoolboy logic,' said one player. Strauss had been dropped for the previous tour of Sri Lanka and it has since been said many times that it was good for him. I have never believed that. Listening to such an argument you'd think he came good immediately in New Zealand. He didn't. Had he got a second-innings duck, he might never have played Test cricket again. Yes, our double-Ashes-winning skipper might have been on the international scrapheap, a victim of a clash between two regimes.

As it was, Strauss managed to resurrect himself in an environment where Moores was unwisely attempting to break up the band of senior players that had been so loyal to, and generally so productive for, Fletcher.

Given what we know now I think it might have been better had Vaughan resigned after that tour. It was just not working with Moores. The next summer was simply a water-treading exercise. Just take what Vaughan wrote in a personal report, as revealed in his autobiography *Time to Declare*, before departing New Zealand: 'I feel that Peter [Moores] has been a little bit disrespectful to the old regime. He believes the Schofield report and has listened to it too much. He wants to change everything including personnel.'

Of course, following Fletcher was never going to be easy. But I have heard it said among the current England management that it was Fletcher's greatest fault that he did not create an environment where his successor could easily take over. I'm not sure about that. As mentioned earlier, Fletcher would have quite liked a hand-over period.

Moores handled the situation poorly. One comment he made

in our interview has stayed with me: 'How Duncan did the job I don't really know,' he said. He went on to say: 'It's a difficult thing to comment on coaching sometimes unless you're a player in there.' But surely it was Moores' job to find out what Fletcher did. There were clearly things that worked very well for Fletcher. It might have been an idea to incorporate some of them into his own methods.

Instead Moores, as Vaughan said, believed everything in the Schofield Report and blasted in with his methods. 'I knew how I could coach,' he says, 'and if I was not authentic to myself: one, the players would know; two, it wouldn't be me. I knew how I was going to coach and was prepared to see where it took us. I was just looking to be my own man.'

I was not in Moores' dressing room, but I was in the Glamorgan dressing room when Fletcher left in 1999 and a good-hearted but clumsy Australian called Jeff Hammond took over. It seems to me that both Hammond and Moores made the same mistakes. They railed against the Fletcher regime. I am certain Hammond felt inadequate in his shadow and I guess deep down Moores felt the same way.

Hilariously, Hammond made his first speech to us and promised a period of considered observation. Within a few minutes of the subsequent net practice he was vehemently advising our left-arm spinner that he couldn't possibly take first-class wickets with such an action and being rather rude about the stance of one of our young batsmen. Carrot and arse were mentioned in the same sentence.

Moores wasn't as tactless, of course. But he immediately tried to do things significantly differently. He was definitely not going to play Fletcher's consultant role. 'They certainly had different styles of coaching,' says Ashley Giles, who played under Fletcher and was a selector under Moores. 'Fletch's style was more sit back and watch and far more technical; Moores' style was more direct, and more directive. "This is what is going to happen now and this is what is going to happen then".'

It obviously did not sit well with his England captains. Vaughan resigned, Paul Collingwood resigned as one-day captain, and then there was the Kevin Pietersen farrago. It is actually forgotten that Strauss was Moores' first captain. For that Test mentioned at the very top of this chapter, Strauss was captain because Vaughan was injured.

The charge against Moores is that he wanted to be in charge too much. I put this to him. 'You play the role that the side needs at the time,' he said. 'It depends on the maturity of the team and where you're at. As a coach you are actively part of that team. You are in that team. I don't think coaches want the credit of the successes of their teams. Coaches don't want that. But managing anything is leading. You can't help that. Fletch was a leader. He can tell you what he wants. He was a leader. You arrive in the morning and have an influence.'

Fletcher was indeed a leader, and he does not think any coach can be worth his salt unless he is a strong leader, but it is the way you lead that is the key. In cricket the captain must still be the man in charge. It is difficult for a leadership model to work any other way. It is not like football or rugby where the manager or coach is always the leading voice and direction. It is why England's three-captains decision in 2011 was, as Andy Flower admitted at the time, 'a gamble'. It was lucky that none of the three appointed skippers – Strauss for Tests, Cook for one-day internationals and Stuart Broad for Twenty20s, which became five (Eoin Morgan and Graeme Swann also captained an ODI and two T20s respectively in the summer of 2011) – was like Nasser Hussain in character and outlook. It would have stood no chance then.

Vaughan made another point about Moores in that personal report quoted above: 'I get the feeling he would like a young captain that he can control and brainwash.' I suspect that may have been right. I think he quite fancied Ian Bell as captain.

Vaughan bears no animosity towards Moores. 'I had a decent relationship with Pete,' he says, and Vaughan phoned him before the release of his autobiography to warn him that he had been critical. 'I just think he got that job at the wrong time. It can be quite difficult for an Englishman to take it, because you almost know too much and can be too cosy with the counties, wanting to be best mates with all the coaches etc.'

None of this is to say that Moores is a poor coach. He is an exceptional coach. Talk to people at Sussex and Lancashire and they swear by him. He brought Sussex their first county championship pennant in 2003, and, in 2011, Lancashire their first title outright since 1934. He changed the culture at Sussex. They worked their socks off, especially at the disciplines like fielding and running between the wickets that are so easily improved by sheer graft. Sussex truly became a team, even if their critics will say that their success was mainly down to Mushtaq Ahmed. There is some truth in that, but truer still is that Moores took an almighty punt on Mushtaq, initially placing him on a small retainer contract with larger incentives for wickets and wins. Most observers considered him 'gone' as a cricketer when Moores signed him for the 2003 season after a few games for Surrey in late 2002.

Under Moores, Sussex did things differently. They were the trendsetters, using video analysis, a baseball coach for throwing, a vision coach, and tennis balls for fielding practice (improving reflexes and 'give' in the catch) before other counties. Once in pre-season the Sussex players arrived at the ground to find pots of paint waiting for them. The ground as a whole needed a lick and the players duly provided it without complaint. A team motto was introduced: 'United we believe, together we achieve'.

At Lancashire Moores did something similar. Nobody gave them a prayer in 2011. One esteemed former player said at the start of the season that it was the worst Lancashire side he had ever seen. They were certainly a young side, and indeed a small squad, without any stars, and it helped that they played all their home games that season away from Old Trafford (mostly at Liverpool) while it was being redeveloped, but Moores worked them hard and created a good spirit. To win the championship was a remarkable achievement given some of the great Lancashire names who had failed to win the title outright (they shared it in 1950): from the locals Brian Statham, Roy Tattersall, Jack Bond, David Hughes, David Lloyd, Mike Atherton, Neil Fairbrother, John Crawley and Andrew Flintoff to the overseas players such as Ken Grieves, Farokh Engineer, Clive Lloyd, Wasim Akram, Michael Holding, Colin Croft, Patrick Patterson and Muttiah Muralitharan. No matter that it was a poor championship year in terms of quality (if not in excitement, as it went to the final afternoon), it was still a mighty success and a romantic story.

Speak to Flower and the admiration for Moores is both huge and sincere. Indeed Flower cites no greater influence as a coach. 'I could never do what he does,' Flower once told me. 'His energy is unbelievable. He really knows how to run a cricket team.' And I don't think it's just because Moores appointed him as his assistant with England. Indeed I'm told Flower has run his England team in very much the same way Moores did his. One player told me 'Mooresy was all about getting fitness levels to a standard where we could train harder and for longer', which in essence has worked fantastically well, but the important difference is that with Flower the 'message is not so overpowering'.

Moores also made some other good appointments: Richard Halsall as fielding coach (as he had done at Sussex in 2003 too) and Mushtaq as spin-bowling coach, even if that was a controversial move because Mushtaq had been implicated in Pakistan's Qayyum Report into match-fixing in 2000. But Mushtaq has remained under Flower as an important part of the coaching team, doing a hundred days a year with the team. When the spot-fixing allegations against Pakistan arose in 2010 he quite naturally came under the spotlight again, but Flower countered with this: 'He's a cricket coach – that's what he is – and we're very comfortable working with Mushy. He's a lovely man, and a good man for our system. I'm quite happy with that.'

While his technical spin coaching may not have always worked – Adil Rashid has been a conspicuous failure, though that may not necessarily be Mushtaq's fault – he is used as much for his Test-match strategic thinking. He has a fertile cricketing brain. And he is definitely popular, ever-smiling. He calls Flower 'Mr Andy' and Swann 'Mr Swanny'; in return Swann calls him 'Mr Mushy'. On his much-talked-about Ashes 2010/11 video diaries one of Swann's best lines was to suggest that Mushtaq's long beard, with streaks of white in it, was sponsored by Adidas (after their famous three white stripes).

Moores introduced or reintroduced a number of players to international cricket. 'Swann, Prior, [Ryan] Sidebottom, Trott [picked for two T20s against the West Indies in 2007] and [James] Tredwell – a lot have carried on and had international careers,' Moores emphasizes. 'So I look at that and see it as a real positive. I don't look at that to steal anyone's thunder. I just look at it as a positive. We didn't have a lot of senior players, if I'm honest. As a coach you are trying to look for today but also looking for tomorrow. The players are only playing for today. I look back at other things and, knowing that you're going through transition and change, then there are not many supporters of it at the time. Nobody likes change. But sometimes it's a necessity. You just want things to evolve. I think they have evolved. I loved my time with England. I've got no regrets about it.' Indeed Moores has acted all along with great dignity. He has never criticized anyone or appeared bitter.

It's just a shame then that Moores could not build a relationship with any of his England captains, especially as he had had such a strong rapport with Chris Adams at Sussex. That took time, though, according to Moores. 'It became a very strong relationship,' he says, 'but at the start it wasn't like that. We had masses of disagreements. You are finding your space together and trying to make it work, like a marriage really. Relationships take time. A frustration for me was that I never got that time to build a relationship with Vaughany.'

Well, he did actually. Despite all his injury problems, Vaughan captained eighteen Tests under Moores, but by the third home Test against South Africa in 2008 he'd had enough. The Test had started on a Wednesday, so by Saturday South Africa had been set 281 to win. Nobody really expected the match to finish that day. I certainly didn't as the *Sunday Telegraph* columnist, and so set about doing a second piece for my column on Vaughan; on how, despite twin failures with the bat again, he should continue as captain.

But Graeme Smith played better than anyone could have expected, making a magisterial 154 not out, and the game was won late that Saturday evening. So late that neither I nor my colleague Berry could make the press conference on the other side of the ground at Edgbaston. While we were writing up our pieces, however, the man from the Press Association, Richard Gibson, returned from that press conference to announce, 'Something's up.' He thought some of Vaughan's responses were indicative of a man about to resign. It certainly caused some consternation in the press box. I made a couple of calls but could raise no one. As Berry later said, we should really have gone to the England team hotel that night. Instead we drove back to Bristol together where Berry dropped me off at the Parkway railway station. As I waited for my train all I could think was 'I hope he hasn't resigned'.

The following morning the dreaded text message arrived. Something along the lines of 'The ECB will hold a press conference at Loughborough at blah, blah, blah . . .' I didn't need to read the rest. It meant only one thing: Vaughan had resigned.

And the readers of the *Sunday Telegraph* were probably shaking their heads in disbelief at their cricket columnist's lack of acuity. 'Calls for his head are ridiculously premature,' I'd written. Oh no. He'd already topped himself.

Consolation came in the fact that I knew within an hour that Pietersen would be Vaughan's replacement, and indeed Collingwood's as one-day skipper, as he too had phoned Hugh Morris on that Saturday night to tender his resignation. That Collingwood went straight to Morris and did not even tell Moores speaks volumes about their relationship, or lack of it. It had stooped to its lowest level that summer when Moores forced Collingwood to apologize after a run-out incident involving New Zealand's Grant Elliott at the Oval. Elliott had collided with Ryan Sidebottom as the bowler went for the ball and the spirit of the game suggested that Collingwood should have withdrawn his appeal. But he didn't, and there was an almighty rumpus. Despite winning by one wicket, the New Zealand team slammed their dressing-room door in Collingwood's face as he left the field. Moores then told Collingwood he should apologize. He did, but he did not want to.

In the coming weeks I discovered that this had happened, and wrote as much in my column in a piece the week after Vaughan's resignation. It ran with the headline 'Discord seeps into Peter Moores' England dressing-room', because it was becoming ever clearer that that was the case. Collingwood and Moores were incensed that it had slipped out and apparently accused Flower of leaking it to me. I can say here and now to both of them that I had not got that information from Flower. But it was clearly correct.

As some consolation for my Vaughan shocker in 2008, the following year when Vaughan retired from all cricket I did at least manage to help break the story. I was sitting at home on Saturday, 27 June 2009 with no work planned for that day when a text arrived. 'Is Vaughan announcing his retirement in the Sun

Tel tomorrow?' it asked. Word was obviously being bandied around that that might be so. Vaughan was, and still is, a columnist for the Telegraph Media Group but I knew there was no planned column from him the following day. I made some calls, and, not knowing Vaughan that well, asked Berry to phone him. Vaughan confirmed that he was about to retire, but would not be quoted. Story!

My editor Peter Mitchell, the man to whom I owe everything in my journalistic career, at first thought it best for Berry to write Vaughan's 'obituary' so on such a pleasant summer's evening I decided to go for a cycle (my new fitness fix these days since those knee operations precluded running). I'd gone some distance, probably fifteen miles or so, when I came to the bottom of a steep hill near Bassaleg School outside Newport. I thought I could hear my phone ringing. Eventually retrieving it from the back of my cycling top, I discovered I'd missed sixteen calls! I was doing the Vaughan obit and I had just over an hour to complete it. I was still some way from home.

Don't panic.

I think it is fair to say that it was an interesting hour. It must have been well spent, though, because Berry later claimed it was one of my better pieces. Retirement as a sort of death for a professional sportsperson has always appealed to me as a writer, so off I went on that angle, relating along the way my favourite cricketing retirement story, that of Glamorgan's Emrys Davies, who told his skipper Wilf Wooller one July morning in 1954 after being bowled by Frank Tyson, 'I am finished. I can no longer see the ball.' The best part, though, is that Davies then went on to become a first-class umpire.

I ended the piece with this: 'Vaughan served England with distinction. He was a tough cookie, a great tactician, a very good batsman and, just as importantly, a very good bloke.' That's a pretty fair summation, I reckon.

So Kevin Pietersen was appointed. Atherton immediately

wrote with great prescience: 'I have a horrible feeling that this is going to end in tears.' It was such a contentious appointment that I understand the chairman of the ECB, Giles Clarke, seriously considered using his power of veto, as Ossie Wheatley did in 1989, in his capacity as chairman of the TCCB's cricket committee, as regards Mike Gatting, and as Morgan now wishes he might have done in relation to Andrew Flintoff in 2006/07 Down Under.

But the problem was the selectors wanted one man as captain, and with Vaughan and Collingwood gone, and Strauss not then in the one-day side, there were not too many candidates. I was told by one insider that Moores was 'adamant' he wanted Pietersen as captain. It is, I suppose, understandable, given what happened later, that Moores is rather reluctant to admit that, entering his very best cross-country mode before answering that question. 'At the time there was a strong move to unify the captaincy,' he says. 'KP got his chance, and nobody quite knew how he was going to take it. I wasn't adamant I wanted him, but we had lost a lot of seniority. One of the strengths of the Aussies over the years has been getting players to the last third of their career. Over recent times with England that has been difficult to do. It's a shame because Fletch had done so much good work and players like Tres [Marcus Trescothick] and Gilo [Ashley Giles] didn't get that last part of their international careers.'

Moores and Pietersen had to meet before Pietersen agreed to take over, and it was generally assumed that Pietersen had demanded the meeting. As he said afterwards of Moores, 'He likes to challenge us on a daily basis. We have lots of strong characters who can be very opinionated. The crux of the meeting was to decide where we can take the team together.' But I understand that it was Moores who phoned Pietersen and asked for the meeting, which eventually took place at the Hilton Hotel in Northampton.

The ECB had little time to work with – there was another Test starting at the Oval the following Thursday – but this was a rushed job. It was interesting that when England were seeking new captains for their one-day and Twenty20 teams in 2011, they conducted formal interviews with prospective candidates. That, as one ECB official has admitted to me, is what should have happened here. Despite their meeting, there were still too many grey areas between Pietersen and Moores. Pietersen thought he was in charge, and so did Moores.

Pietersen began with a bang, with a hundred and a Test win at the Oval, followed by a 4–0 series victory in the one-dayers afterwards. But trouble lay ahead, first in the form of an American chap named Stanford. I seem to recall that his first name was, and still is, Allen, although everyone at the ECB would rather forget everything about him, even if in 2011 they had to play two Twenty20 internationals against the West Indies at the end of the summer in order to fulfil contractual obligations with Sky that were a relic of the deal with the man. In the ECB's annual report for 2008 his name was not mentioned once in fifty-two pages.

But this was the man who on 11 June that year had landed his helicopter (or rather one we later discovered he had rented from nearby and to which he had had his company logo added) on the Nursery Ground at Lord's. The sight of ECB officials fawning over Stanford sickens me to this day. I know one or two of them who are mighty glad never to have been photographed with him. But there he was, arriving at the home of cricket as if on some state visit, using that old trick so favoured by American politicians of waving and pointing to make out he had some friends in the crowd. He had none.

Stanford had roped in some legends of the game to stand alongside him on stage: Sir Ian Botham, Sir Gary Sobers, Sir Everton Weekes, Sir Vivian Richards, Curtly Ambrose and Desmond Haynes. Sadly they were as gullible as the ECB's administrators, in particular chief executive David Collier, who, as others are very quick to point out now, was the driving force behind the whole Stanford deal. Money does indeed make a man blind.

Inside the Nursery Pavilion it was announced that England and a Stanford All-Stars XI would play five Twenty20 matches for $20 million each over five years. A perspex casket was brought out, supposedly with $20 million in it, and Nasser Hussain, who was presenting the ceremony, said, 'Gentlemen! If you've ever wondered what twenty million dollars looks like, here it is!' It was subsequently revealed that there may actually have been as little as $100,000 in there, and that the notes were probably fake.

Should the ECB have known that Stanford himself was a fake, as first alleged the following February when, ironically as England played a Test on the island of Antigua that had knighted him (since revoked), it emerged that he had been charged by the Securities and Exchange Commission with fraud 'of shocking magnitude'? There were certainly warning signs. South Africa, India and Australia had all spurned Stanford's offers. So had the ICC.

There had been a remarkable meeting between Stanford and ICC officials in Johannesburg on the morning of the World Twenty20 final in September 2007. He had previously met with president Percy Sonn and chief executive Malcolm Speed in the West Indies during the World Cup there earlier that year, outlining his proposals for a Twenty20 tournament involving his Stanford Super Stars. But negotiations had stumbled on the fact that Stanford wanted his team rather than the West Indies to play in this proposed competition. The ICC understandably said it could not sanction such a tournament as 'official' cricket. Stanford was not happy, but the ICC agreed to consider it further.

So another meeting was scheduled for the Sandton Sun Hotel in Johannesburg. Ray Mali (acting ICC president after Sonn had passed away in May of that year), Speed, Morgan (who was then ICC president-elect), Dave Richardson (ICC's general manager of cricket), Brian Murgatroyd and Campbell Jamieson (both senior ICC managers) were present as the ICC delegation. They were waiting for the Stanford group to arrive in the room they had hired when they were informed by a member of the hotel staff that Stanford and his cohorts were in another room. There were simply too many of them! In the other room were many great names of West Indian cricket like Richards, Weekes, Haynes, Wes Hall, Michael Holding, Lance Gibbs and Joel Garner. The president of the West Indies Cricket Board, Julian Hunte, was also present.

Mali made a polite introductory speech and then Speed got down to the business of the meeting to say that the ICC had considered carefully the offer Stanford had made. Before he could get any further, Stanford stood up, put his hand in the air and said, 'Forget all that. I now want to play the winners of today's match [the final was between India and Pakistan].'

The meeting degenerated from there. Speed tried to articulate the ICC's proposal (that the higher ranked of the two teams to tour the Caribbean each year would play the last match of their tour against the Stanford Super Stars, but it would be 'unofficial'), but Stanford lost his rag and stood up, knocking his chair over loudly in the process, and left the room. Haynes launched a rant at Speed, and Richards began banging both hands loudly on the table. 'It was the most amazing incident in which I was involved in eleven years of cricket administration,' wrote Speed. 'The walkout was childish.'

Thanks to the diplomacy of Morgan the meeting was rejoined, and Morgan calmly rebuked Haynes for his behaviour. It ended with Stanford saying that he would go to the ICC box at the final. He never did.

The ECB knew about this meeting. But as Morgan indicates, 'Had I still been chairman of the ECB I would certainly have explored Stanford. I would have been more wary after that meeting, but the ECB were still right to explore.'

As an unrepentant Collier has said since, 'Stanford had been recently knighted, Forbes referenced him as one of America's leading entrepreneurs and he had worked successfully in helping to promote West Indies cricket as well as many other sports.' And the ECB will point to the fact that they were helping the impoverished WICB as part of the deal, that it was intended to extend its own Chance To Shine scheme (promoting cricket in schools) in the Caribbean and that grassroots cricket in England and Wales, especially the funding of coaches, was to receive substantial benefits too.

There was pressure not just from the Indian Premier League but the unauthorized Indian Cricket League too. England's players were certainly miffed that they were missing out on untold riches at the IPL (none of the centrally contracted players appeared in the first instalment in 2008), typified by Chris Gayle's text messages to Pietersen at the time. First he asked why Pietersen was not playing in the IPL. Pietersen replied that he could not, so Gayle responded with a text consisting just of dollar signs. But, with England and India at each other's throats, this was about something more: about securing the West Indies' support in the fight against India's increasing dominance in cricket's politics.

My greatest gripe was with the nature of the match that was played in Antigua on 1 November 2008. Money should never be at the heart of one's desire to represent one's country. I went to the announcement of the England squad in September and felt genuinely sorry for Morris and Geoff Miller as they sat there, shuffling uncomfortably, trying to justify a match for which they should never have been asked to provide a team. That team that they did select should never have been termed 'England'. It was disrespectful to anyone who has represented England in 'official' cricket.

Miller described it as 'part of the process'. What process? 'The match has no cricketing value whatsoever,' I wrote afterwards.

'Indeed to call it cricket at all will be difficult. For Nov 1 will be the night cricket is turned into reality TV, where some grisly voyeuristic fare is served up for those of a short attention span. The ECB may come to regret this match.'

So they did. Even though one senior journalist told me it was the most attentively organized cricket trip he'd ever been on, the Stanford week was a shambles in so many other ways. England lost the match, which is probably just as well. But they were never in the right frame of mind to win it. The recession had arrived with the iciest of blasts and here were England's cricketers out in the heat of the Caribbean set to earn $1 million a man for winning a Twenty20 match. It was obscene. 'I respect what is happening in the world,' said the captain Pietersen ahead of departure for Antigua. 'I've got friends who are struggling and some who have lost their jobs and there's no way I will accept any of our players carrying on like clowns should we win this money.'

The only chap acting like a clown was Stanford, as his behaviour annoyed the England team intensely. He marched around with his own cameraman in tow, saying 'Howdy!' to everyone, trying to enter the England dressing room and then sitting Matt Prior's pregnant wife on his knee while Prior and his England colleagues were out on the field.

The ECB immediately announced it would undertake a review of its deal with Stanford, but by December the Texan had closed down his cricket office at his Coolidge ground and disbanded his Stanford board of legends, who were paid around $10,000 a month. But nobody foresaw the events of 17 February 2009. I certainly never thought I'd be standing, as I was on the morning of 18 February, in a queue outside Stanford's bank in Antigua seeking quotes from disgruntled customers as they waited to withdraw their life savings. When word came that day that he might actually be on the island, I did have wild visions of chasing him and unearthing his location on some remote part of the island. But then reality dawned. As a supporter at Newport's Rodney Parade rugby ground once advised me, 'Stick to the cricket, James!'

I called for Clarke's resignation as ECB chairman that weekend. 'Clarke should do the decent thing. But he won't,' I wrote. 'Decency departed English cricket's administration long ago: the day it prostituted itself to Stanford.' And he didn't resign. He was never going to. As I write, Clarke is still chairman of the ECB. He has recovered rather well. The ECB is in rude health, with Clarke poised for a third term in office. As for Stanford, in March 2012, he was found guilty of 13 out of 14 counts of fraud.

After that Stanford debacle in November 2008 England did at least have some 'proper' cricket: a tour to India no less. It was my first trip there. And it was going pretty much as expected by the time England were 5–0 down in the one-day series after defeat at Cuttack. The hotels in the up-country venues had been awful. 'You are staying in the second-best hotel in town,' the local agent would inform us religiously upon arrival at the airport. Translated roughly, it meant the players were in a decent establishment; we were in a shit-hole. I'd suffered Delhi-belly and England's bowlers had been smashed everywhere. Yes, the clichés were all in order.

Not even a Pietersen century had been enough to avoid defeat at Cuttack. So off we trudged from the ground to contemplate the rigours of a trip to Guwahati the next day. Then on the car journey from Cuttack to our hotel in Bhubaneswar news began filtering through of shocking events in Mumbai. Text messages from home along the lines of 'Where are you? Are you OK?' were worrying signs of something truly terrible happening.

The reasons for and the extent of that worry became apparent when we adjourned soberly to our hotel rooms and turned on the TVs. Indian TV clearly does not do picture censorship. The pictures being shown were horrifically graphic, with dead bodies being dragged across the road and blood everywhere in scenes of unfathomable butchery. Just as shocking was that the backdrop to these scenes was the Taj Mahal Palace Hotel in Mumbai, where we had stayed just two weeks earlier, indeed where the England team had left in storage their Test whites and other items of clothing for use later in the tour.

I was scared. We might have been nearly a thousand miles from Mumbai, but there was no knowing the extent of these atrocities. It was said Westerners were targets; the England cricket team and its entourage would seem easy targets in that case. I wanted to go home, and so did England's cricketers. It was the natural reaction. Of course, there were some brave comments from those sitting in the safety of their armchairs back in England. And there was the rigidity of those asserting that cricketers would never be targets. I never believed that for one minute, and appalling confirmation of as much duly came later that winter when the Sri Lankan team bus was attacked on the way to a Test match in Lahore.

But it took until 9.40 p.m. the following day in Bhubaneswar before it was finally announced that we were going home, with the two remaining one-day fixtures cancelled. It was fortunate that Morris was there in India. He played a blinder on that Thursday. Until then the question of what exactly Morris did was being asked frequently, just as it was with his counterpart at the Rugby Football Union, Rob Andrew. In rugby's case that was never fully answered, as Andrew was eventually demoted, shifted sideways and given all manner of other manoeuvrings seemingly in a bid to keep him in a job.

But Morris gave one of many compelling answers that day at the Mayfair Lagoon Hotel in Bhubaneswar in negotiations with the Board of Control for Cricket in India secretary N. Srinivasan, while keeping Clarke (on business in Colombia) and Collier (on holiday in Los Angeles) abreast of events. We the media were, of course, not staying at that hotel, but spent the whole day there lurking and listening. At one point Morris walked past and smiled. 'To think we only used to worry about scoring runs,' he said. It was indeed rather strange that the former Glamorgan opening partnership should end up in this position. But here was Morris proving that the best cricket administrators are usually those who play the game to the highest level first, then acquire the necessary management and business qualifications afterwards, as Morris did in gaining his executive MBA from Henley Management College.

Of course, everyone going home was not the end of it. There were still two Tests scheduled. Upon leaving I thought there was no way the players should return. Flintoff certainly agreed, as he told me in a rare conversation we had at the hotel bar later that night. I think the only reason he spoke to me was to tell me that the Lancashire dressing room were very unhappy with me, having been miffed at something I'd written the previous summer. 'You had a good career out of county cricket,' he said. 'Don't be so negative about it.'

We actually talked about the England A tour of Kenya and Sri Lanka in 1997/98, which we were both on and during which there was a similar situation after a huge bomb went off in Kandy where we were due to visit soon afterwards. Both Flintoff and I were keen to go home (my wife was pregnant), but it was somehow reported in the press that we had persuaded the others to stay ('an unlikely combination' we were called).

There was little doubt here who wanted to return to India, and Flintoff and his mate Steve Harmison were not among them. Pietersen did want to return, but then there were those who considered IPL riches in the next year his strongest motivation. I actually thought Pietersen led the team well in this episode. He said the right things and appeared to be in control. Apparently that wasn't the case. One player I later spoke to about him and his captaincy just giggled in response.

Confirmation of this came in Swann's autobiography. 'There

is no doubt that Kev is a good player, a really fine batsman,' he wrote, 'but he was never the right man to captain England in my opinion. Some people are better leaders of men and Kev, for all his abundant talent, is not one of those natural leaders.'

There was actually much confusion about what was happening because the atrocities were still continuing. Morris had told the players that they had to go home immediately, but they interpreted that as meaning the whole tour was off. That was never Morris's nor the ECB's intention. They always felt that, if safety and security could be guaranteed, the tour would continue at a later stage.

But it was not easy to do that. So first, after five days on every one of which each of the players had been telephoned to keep them informed of happenings, the players were flown to Abu Dhabi for a holding camp, and from there Morris and his name-sake, Sean, then the chief executive of the Professional Cricketers' Association, flew to Chennai where the first Test was scheduled to take place (the two original venues of Ahmedabad and Mumbai were replaced by Chennai and Mohali). There they met with Reg Dickason, the ECB's security adviser. Dickason, the moustachioed Australian whose ever-present smile conceals a steely character, was once easily derided as another of England's so-called unnecessary support staff, but here he proved his worth and much, much more.

Dickason demanded a 'ring of steel' of crack commando troops for the players should they return to India. And he was right to demand more security. On the day after the Mumbai atrocities a group of us journalists had accessed the England team hotel through the side entrance of an adjoining coffee shop. It hardly required the skills of Darcy Dugan to get in.

The ECB had to be sure that Dickason's security plan was going to be implemented to the letter, and Morris (Hugh that is) recalls standing before the Commissioner of Police in Chennai as Dickason went through his plans in great detail. The commissioner agreed on every point. 'Thank you very much,' said Morris. 'Now all I want is all that in writing with your signature on the bottom.' The commissioner's face dropped. It was getting late in the evening, and the two Morrises were leaving for Abu Dhabi early the following morning. They needed confirmation to present to some very nervous cricketers. Sure enough there was a knock at the door early the next morning. The signed document was there.

So the Morrises went to Abu Dhabi and addressed the players. There were two obvious dissenters in Flintoff and Harmison, with a number of other initial waverers that apparently included James Anderson, Bell, Prior, Cook and even Swann, who soon decided he rather wanted to play Test cricket. (He hadn't played at all then, remember.) But eventually all decided to go. It was a decision that was received with admiration and respect throughout the cricketing world, and beyond too. The Prime Minister, Gordon Brown, called the team 'brave and courageous'.

England lost the first Test in Chennai. It is tempting to recall the words of former England rugby skipper John Pullin, whose team went to Dublin in 1973 at the height of the political troubles there after Wales and Scotland had refused to do so the previous year. England lost 18–9, their eighth consecutive loss in the Five Nations championship, and at the post-match dinner Pullin declared, 'We may not be very good, but at least we turn up.' This England cricket team were better than that, with Strauss scoring twin centuries in the match, but India chased down 387 on the final day on a wearing pitch for victory.

However, it was not just the brilliance of Sachin Tendulkar (103 not out) that did for England there. There was trouble in the camp. Pietersen had already decided that he could no longer work with Moores. Tactically the captain had been exposed on that final day, but the die had been cast before the match when Pietersen had been to see ECB chairman Clarke and told him that Moores must go. Pietersen wanted the South African Graham Ford to take over, and told Clarke as much. England could easily have won that first Test, but Pietersen insisted even that would have changed nothing.

The ECB had naturally gone to India with much of its hierarchy. Clarke, Collier, Morris, Dennis Amiss (vice-chairman) and selector Giles were all there. But by raising the issue with Clarke (in Chennai, where the first Test was held) and bypassing Morris, Pietersen made a huge mistake. There was never going to be a simple and easy solution after that. Clarke is not a man to wear his authority lightly. This was clearly a big deal. He wanted it sorted.

Many a meeting took place in India, so that by the end of the second Test, which was drawn, Pietersen, seeing no resolution, threatened to resign. Morris had left for home by this stage, so Collier mollified Pietersen by asking him to email Morris with his plan to take England forward in 2009.

Off everyone went for Christmas, with all of us in the media still unaware of these alarming developments. Not even the announcement of the party to tour the West Indies in January, with Vaughan omitted against Pietersen's wishes, changed that. Pietersen was by now on a safari holiday in South Africa.

On Tuesday, 30 December I received a phone call from my *Telegraph* colleague Derek Pringle asking what I knew about a rift between Pietersen and Moores. At that stage all I had heard were murmurings that Pietersen was not enjoying the captaincy. I made some calls. Something was definitely bubbling. I told Pringle, who was working on the story with Nick Hoult, that they should do a speculation piece that day. You never know how long these things will last.

As they were still gathering information, they rightly waited until the next day. Unfortunately their excellent story for the New Year's Day edition was posted on the internet a little too early, at around tea-time on New Year's Eve. Both the *Daily*

Mail and the *Sun* seized on it and ran the story as 'exclusives' the following day. The cat was out of the bag.

Who let it out has been a matter of much debate ever since. 'Something was leaked, I don't know who by, I would love to find that person,' said Pietersen later. I think Pietersen thought it was Clarke. That's why he didn't speak to him for almost a year afterwards.

I'm not sure it matters who did leak the story. It certainly wasn't Pietersen, who on the day he was sacked (or resigned) issued a statement saying 'At no time have I released any unauthorized information to the media.'

The assumption has always been that the same conclusion would not have been reached had it not been leaked. From what I know now, I disagree. It is as wide of the mark as the commonly held belief that Vaughan's non-selection tipped Pietersen over the edge. As I said, once Clarke had been informed ahead of other management before the Chennai Test, there was no way that the conciliation Morris would by nature have been inclined to would suffice.

But what the leak did do was emphasize the powers of twenty-four-hour news. Quickly the story took on a life of its own. It ran more quickly than Usain Bolt ever has. Suddenly the politics of the England dressing room were being speculated upon, and Morris was canvassing some of the players to ascertain the exact details of any supposed rifts.

The truth is that many players did not even know there were such big problems. As Moores himself said to me, 'It wasn't like it was a raging feud.' But there were problems. I wrote at the time: 'For some time this England side have been unravelling like a ball of wool pawed by a frisky kitten. Forget the Oval Test win over South Africa and the subsequent 4–0 one-day success. They were mere diversionary morsels. Come the Stanford series and India the kitten was playing again. And the suspicion remains that the little beggar's name was Fred.'

Flintoff was indeed a problem. He and Pietersen never got on in the team environment, a clashing of egos as they jostled for the position of Top Cat. And Flintoff was more than happy to position himself in Moores' camp. He liked the coach from the start, especially when Moores offered to go with him to a specialist's appointment when injured. It was a level of care he never felt he'd received from Fletcher. But was Moores just being cute? Flintoff was a powerful dressing-room presence. I've heard that Moores used that relationship in his defence.

By a twist of fate Pietersen sent his email outlining his proposals on the very day the story broke in the *Daily Telegraph*. 'I really wanted to get this right for English cricket . . . In my email I said that I can't lead this team forward and take it to the West Indies if Peter Moores is coach,' he later said.

I asked Moores what the problem was. 'The whole issue revolved around respect,' he replied. 'It was about whether he felt he respected my view and whether together we could have moved it forward.' Well, there clearly was no respect. But as Moores emphasized, 'A lot of things have been said but nobody would have known that not everything was normal.'

Unsurprisingly they have not spoken since, or they hadn't when I spoke to Moores in the summer of 2011. 'Not deliberately, though, on my part,' says Moores. 'You have a county circuit and an international circuit. Occasionally they cross but generally they are different worlds.'

Pietersen was expecting to meet with ECB officials on 8 January 2009, the day he was due to return from holiday. But he never did have that meeting. Instead he was informed over the phone that his resignation had been accepted, followed by an email to that effect. Of course, he hadn't officially offered to resign, not since the end of the Mohali Test anyway, but these were mere semantics. Maybe his email had been taken as an offer of resignation, but in truth he had been sacked. And he had been warned this might happen before an ECB meeting on the evening of Tuesday, 6 January. So too had Moores, and so they were both sacked at that board meeting. A press conference at the Oval the following day confirmed as much. It would have been at Lord's but the banqueting manager was on holiday. It rather summed up the mess. Poor Morris did not take any questions. Given the dangers of employment law he would have been eaten alive.

He had been faced with the trickiest of situations. As I said earlier, he would have preferred to try to make the pair work together. There were two other options that didn't look particularly workable: firstly that Moores went and Pietersen stayed as captain, but that would have set highly dangerous precedents in terms of player power; secondly that Moores stayed as coach and Pietersen was stripped of the captaincy – but just imagine the dressing-room tension then. No, quite simply, the only option was that both men were sacked.

Of course, Pietersen came off worst. 'DeTested' screamed the *Sun*'s headline, before describing him as 'cricket's most hated man'. Much was made of those soundings Morris had taken with some players and the conclusion was reached that Pietersen had been shafted by his colleagues. I do not know what was said, but, yes, some probably did denigrate his captaincy. As I mentioned earlier it was not exactly rated inside the dressing room, but this was not the reason he was sacked. He probably should have returned from his holiday earlier, but again it is doubtful that would have made too much difference. As it was, he flew into Heathrow airport amid a welter of media scrutiny. He even had to ask for police protection via the ECB.

This imbroglio was, and still is, considered the result of his unstoppable ego. But the truth is that it was not just Pietersen. Others were just as unconvinced with Moores, as the coach himself admits. 'I've had lads turn round to me and say they loved it,' he says, 'and others who haven't.' There is little doubt that the whole affair was for the better. As I wrote at the time:

'England play cricket again in a fortnight. It might just be that they have a better captain and coach than the last time they did so.'

As Pietersen himself said, albeit with typical gaucheness, after England had retained the Ashes in Melbourne in January 2011, 'We would not be here today if I had not done what I did. I got rid of the captaincy for the good of English cricket. There is no way in this world that we would have succeeded under that regime and won the Ashes again in Australia after twenty-four years.'

Not that he had been a happy man in the intervening period. 'His conduct ever since has been terribly disappointing,' an ECB insider told me. 'He has allowed his showbiz friends to consistently convince him that he has been so badly wronged.'

Pietersen is easily disliked. I was still playing county cricket when he first came to England, and he soon acquired a poor reputation on the circuit. I actually broke his leg once in a match against Nottinghamshire at Colwyn Bay. Well, OK, he fell awkwardly when stopping one of my chinks to mid-wicket, and it was later discovered that he had broken a small bone in his leg. But the crucial point is that there didn't seem to be too much sympathy for him.

I admit that I took this attitude into my journalistic career. Early on I rarely passed up an opportunity to be critical. 'The man of the match might easily have lost England the match' I wrote at Edgbaston in 2006 when Pietersen's dismissal (for 142!) two balls after his stunning switch hit for six off Muttiah Muralitharan precipitated an England collapse.

I've come to like him, however. When on tour around the hotels and at grounds anywhere he is as polite and courteous as any England player. I think I quite like him because he is everything I wasn't as a cricketer. Deep down we'd all probably like to carry off that sort of cockiness and naked ambition. But it is just not an English sort of thing to do. Little wonder he was so disliked in the shires.

Pietersen is different. He craves and needs the spotlight as a child does milk. So in terms of management, he is high-maintenance. There is always something to deal with. He often engages mouth before brain. He sometimes makes poor decisions. Take what happened after his early return from the World Cup in 2011 with a hernia injury. With the Ashes and its tagged-on one-day internationals afterwards, it had been a long, long winter. Like the other England players, Pietersen was missing his family. So where does he find himself just a couple of days after returning home? In a Soho nightclub with his agent!

Add to all of this the fact that he is not English and it is easy to see why Pietersen attracts so much opprobrium. And he is not English, despite the tattoos and the early over-the-top attempts to prove as much. He's South African. I bet he still supports South Africa at rugby. Nay, I know. But we need to get over that. He came to England to play cricket. He fulfilled the qualification criteria and now scores lots of runs for England. If we feel so strongly about it, the qualification rules must be changed. Go back to seven years of residency if necessary. But the world is a smaller place now. People emigrate. People move easily. And, unfortunately for him, people are removed easily too.

The Saturday evening following the double sacking was the only occasion I have fallen out with Hugh Morris since I became a journalist. Pietersen was writing a column for the *News of the World* then and was about to pronounce his feelings about the farrago that Sunday, so all of the other Sunday journalists were under pressure to produce some sort of slant of their own on the story. 'Kevin Pietersen: I was betrayed by ECB as England captain' screamed the headline to my piece. Then on the front of the main paper: 'Betrayed!'

I had been told by a reliable source that Pietersen felt betrayed by three high-ranking ECB officials, whom I did not specifically name, but whom Pietersen felt had assured him before he went on his safari holiday that Moores would be removed as coach.

They were clearly Clarke, Collier and Morris, although I was unsure how the selector Giles fitted into the picture. Morris and I had a heated debate late on the Saturday night, when my piece appeared on the internet. He'd been copping flak all week, and I suppose a late little dagger from an old friend was not exactly what he wanted. I think we've made up now anyway. And I don't think there ever were any guarantees to Pietersen.

At his Oval press conference Morris had also said something else: 'Andrew Strauss has agreed to lead the team to the Caribbean.' Now there really was only one option, even if Strauss did mention to Morris that it might have been better to consider someone younger like Cook. The ECB cannot beat themselves up about a lack of an interview process here.

It was not headline news, of course. It was low-in-the-piece stuff compared to Pietersen and Moores. And at that moment it only referred to the Test matches in the West Indies. By the Friday it had been extended to the one Twenty20 international and the subsequent one-day internationals at the end of the tour. It had also been extended to being in charge of the tour, because Strauss left for the Caribbean very much as an old-style captain. Flower would remain as assistant coach, with no head coach appointed.

'I will be taking over a lot – the lead coach's responsibilities – but my job title is staying as assistant coach,' Flower explained at the time. 'I think it's better that way. I'm not sure if I want to apply for the job yet. I want to play it by ear and see how things go. Pete [Moores] brought me into the Academy set-up. We were good mates, and still are. I had a good think about it before I decided that I wanted to do this role. I would say it's unlikely that I would be offered the job full-time.'

Ah, the modesty of that last sentence. Just like Duncan Fletcher, albeit in very different circumstances, Flower wasn't sure whether he wanted to be coach of England. But it was the truth too. I spoke to Flower quite a lot during that period and those quotes reflect his feelings faithfully. He felt horribly awkward about immediately taking the dead man's clothes, about jumping so quickly into his mate Moores' shoes. He deliberated long and hard before accepting the role, talking at length with Morris about its parameters before doing so.

Was it awkward? I ask Moores. 'Not at all,' he responds. 'I've spoken to Andy all the way through. He is a mate. The opportunity came for him and he took it. He is a loyal bloke. We went into it as a team, and he knew it was a tough job. We went through some good times and some tough times. We had to make some really tough decisions. I mean leaving out Hoggy [Matthew Hoggard was dropped for the second Test in Wellington in New Zealand in 2008 and never played again] was a really tough decision. We thought it was right to play Jimmy [James Anderson] at the time and Stuart Broad also came in for Harmy [Steve Harmison]. They were big decisions.'

There was another complication: Pietersen had called for Flower's removal too. Flower had noticed a change in his attitude as the India tour wore on. He had become colder and more distant. And he wasn't the only one. During Moores' reign I had heard other players question Flower's ability to perform his assistant coach's role. Indeed one evening over a couple of beers one player told me in great detail how he much preferred Matthew Maynard as a batting coach. Flower himself will admit that he made mistakes early on as a coach. He was too critical, especially of some of the batsmen's techniques. But as he said then, 'When you are assistant coach you are always supportive of the coach and your most heated debates are behind closed doors, which is a healthy thing. Then you come out and speak with one voice.'

The Flower had been in its bud all that time. It was nothing new. It had been the same when he played for Essex for five seasons. There, domineering characters like skipper Ronnie Irani and Darren Gough rarely allowed him his say. 'I don't think his knowledge of the game was utilized enough in our dressing room,' admits coach Paul Grayson now. 'We had Ronnie as captain and Goughy, who both had very strong opinions in the dressing room. Maybe those two overpowered him a bit too much but whenever he did speak up it was always sensible and you always knew that when Andy was speaking everyone was listening.'

What a waste. I'd like to think that would not have been the case had Flower joined Glamorgan, which could easily have happened in 2001 when I became captain. Flower was keen (not to keep wicket, though, so as not to scupper the opportunities of our homegrown keepers, as he didn't do with James Foster at Essex), but his Zimbabwe Cricket Union contract would not permit.

But if you think Glamorgan fans might be miffed at missing out on Flower . . .

9

The Growing of a Flower

Cricketing folk of New Zealand, read this and weep. Andy Flower could so easily have been one of yours. And his brother Grant. That's because in 1978 the whole Flower family – father Bill, mother Jean and their five children Stephen, Gary, Andrew, Grant and Megan – were about to leave their home in Johannesburg in South Africa and emigrate to The Land of the Long White Cloud. The passage had been booked by liner from Durban, and all their possessions had been packed and crated. They were off to settle in Wellington where Bill had secured a job as an accountant. Melbourne in Australia had also been seriously considered, but windy Wellington it was going to be.

But there suddenly arose a problem. When Bill had made his application for a work visa, he and Jean had only four children. But in 1976 Megan had been born. At the very last minute the New Zealand authorities declined Flower senior's application, because he now had one dependant too many. Little Megan saved the day for Zimbabwe cricket. And, maybe, further down the line, England cricket too.

Mind you, the family could have stayed in South Africa, a decision that would have pleased the ten-year-old Andy. He was rather enjoying himself at Boskop primary school in Randburg (in the northern suburbs of Johannesburg). 'I didn't want to leave because we lived this idyllic outdoor life,' he said recently. 'Most white Rhodesians were making the opposite journey – leaving for South Africa [ahead of independence in 1980]. But my dad decided it was time for us to go back to Rhodesia.'

Bill accepted a transfer offer to be company secretary in Salisbury with the same international organization that had employed him for the previous ten years. Looking back, it does seem a curious decision. Whites were leaving Rhodesia in their droves, but the family had faith that things would ultimately work out for the better.

Bill, born in Johannesburg in 1937, and Jean, born in Umtali in eastern Rhodesia in 1939, had met at school in Bulawayo in 1952. Both had been brought up in Rhodesia, and eventually married in 1962. Bill swept Jean off to northern Rhodesia (now Zambia) where he was employed in the copper mines. They established a home there and produced their first two sons, Stephen and Gary. Andy was subsequently born in Cape Town, Grant in Salisbury and then Megan back in Johannesburg.

Bill was not an outstanding cricketer ('purely a league cricketer who bowled leg-spin and batted at number three or four', he says). He possessed and still does possess the most remarkable passion and energy for the game. But in 1982 he had a heart attack, and in 1984 underwent a triple bypass operation. He decided it was time to give up accountancy. 'I decided that if I stayed behind a desk I'd find an early grave,' he says, 'so I retired and applied for a job as bursar at Peterhouse [a school in Marondera, east of Harare]. I got involved in coaching sport there.' He was to become one of Zimbabwe's finest schoolboy cricket coaches.

'Wild Bill' is what Andy and Grant call him even now. But it is said in jest, in gratitude even. They know the early games they played with their father and brothers made them the cricketers they became. 'At every opportunity we'd be out in the garden kicking, hitting or chasing a ball of some description,' says Bill. 'Those family sessions set the boys off with their ball skills. I can't accentuate their importance too much. Stephen loved his cricket but never took his sport seriously and Gary, well, he never professed to be a sportsman of any description. But when it came to those family games he was up there with the rest of the family.'

No one can recall why Andy batted left-handed and bowled right-arm (some filthy medium-pace to which, to my lifelong embarrassment, I once succumbed in a club match in Zimbabwe), while Grant batted right-handed and bowled left-arm. 'Andy can play squash right- and left-handed,' says Bill, 'and he plays golf right-handed – although he can play it left-handed – and writes right-handed. Grant writes left-handed and plays tennis right-handed.'

Andy was certainly not instructed to bat left-handed, as the Flowers' great friend Alistair Campbell was by his late father 'Pol', the sagacious headmaster of the well-regarded Lilfordia School. Campbell was right-handed at everything, but his father recognized the benefits of a strong top hand in batting and so encouraged the southpaw stance. The result was one of the most graceful batting talents I've ever come across. Sadly there was not quite the temperament to match, even if there was a shrewd cricketing brain lurking within.

In their Johannesburg days the Flower family did not even have a lawn at first. Bill created one. In Salisbury they did have a lawn, but this was no typically affluent property of the white Zimbabwean. 'It was not the usual "easy street" with two house-maids,' says Bill. 'We struggled financially, so the family knew the value of money. They had to take their turns in cleaning the pool and mowing the lawn. It was good for them.'

Indeed Bill acknowledges that he was a strict father, and admits to having dished out a few deserved hidings along the way. He told me he was particularly severe if the children had misbehaved for their mother while he was away at work.

Andy went to Vainona High School in northern Harare, as did his brothers Stephen and Gary. Grant, meanwhile, went to St George's College. 'Education was beginning to turn,' says Bill. 'We foresaw problems and Grant needed to be pushed.' It was not a popular decision. 'My parents only wanted the best for me but I hated it,' says Grant. 'I wanted to go where Andrew was.' But the Jesuits did at least get Grant through his A levels.

Andy and Grant played international cricket together, at times forming an important opening partnership in one-day cricket with their rapid running and judgement between the wickets. They are so very different in character, but remain close friends, and enjoy some playful banter, which can sometimes be a little unsettling to those who don't know them.

Andy calls Grant by his nickname 'Gobs', which is short for 'Gobshite', and which in Africa is not as derogatory a word as it is in Ireland. It was given to him when he was the youngest member of the Zimbabwe side. By contrast when Andy made his first-class debut, appearing for a Zimbabwe Cricket Union President's XI against a West Indies B side as an eighteen-year-old in 1986, his older team-mates called him 'Petals'. Many of his team-mates at the Old Georgians (OGs) club where he made his debut at fifteen called him 'Maggots'. Nobody seems to know why. The Glamorgan players used to call him 'Self-raising', which always made me chuckle. Andy calls me 'Big Nose', so I call him 'Flat Nose'. Neither of us could sue. Such is the banter between sportspeople.

I met Grant for the purposes of this book in early April 2011. He'd been at the World Cup as Zimbabwe's batting coach and had just arrived back at his Chelmsford home to find a huge tax bill waiting for him. He was in a flap. He was late for our meeting. The first person he'd phoned? His brother Andrew. 'He's generally had a bit more confidence than me,' admits Grant. 'I've always hovered in the background a bit. I've got him to do things for me and I still ask him for advice, whether about cricket or life skills.'

Mind you, I did once ask Andy who he would turn to first when he was a player and was struggling with his game. The reply was instant: 'Grant.' Having witnessed the hours they spent together in the nets, it was little surprise really. 'We used to talk about cricket all the time,' says Grant. 'We knew each other's games really well.' Bill confirms this: 'They were always both very deep thinkers on the game. Grant knew Andrew's game backwards. He didn't need camcorders or any of that stuff. He could just pick up a fault by looking in the nets.'

Andy wasn't too shabby at spotting technical minutiae either. I remember sitting with him watching Worcestershire's first match of a pre-season tour against Mashonaland Country Districts at the once lovely Harare South ground, now tragically defunct as a cricket ground after being overrun by the war veterans at the height of Zimbabwe's problems. Graeme Hick, fresh from a winter with Queensland in Australia, came out to bat, and immediately Flower became quite animated. 'Look at his pick-up,' he said. 'He's flattened it out [meaning the face of the bat was not open]. They do that in Australia to counter the bounce.'

As a player, Flower was always analysing opposition batsmen's techniques, especially from his unique vantage point behind the stumps as a wicketkeeper. He noticed, for instance, that Sachin Tendulkar would gently rock back on his heels in his stance in order to maintain his balance. And early on in his Test career he marvelled at the New Zealander Martin Crowe's balance at the crease, unusual for such a big man and especially as he was hampered by knee problems late in his international career, allowing him to play peerlessly through the leg-side.

Crowe made 140 in Zimbabwe's and the Flowers' third Test in Harare in 1992 and it made a lasting impression on Andy, even if his admiration for Crowe went against the grain. Crowe was not popular among the Zimbabwean cricketing public or indeed with many of the Zimbabwean players whom he belittled in that first series between the teams. At the start of that Test, after Zimbabwe had drawn their first two Tests, a sign had been put up above one of the tents at the Harare Sports Club proclaiming Zimbabwe as 'The only unbeaten Test nation in the world!' At the match's conclusion – a New Zealand win by 177 runs – Crowe went over and pulled it down. His arrogance was not well received. But there was something Flower liked in him, a great batsman playing in a poor side. It was exactly what Flower was to become. Crowe was an inspiration.

There was also a time when Grant and Campbell called Andy 'Arrogance'. It was tongue-in-cheek from two cheeky mates, but they considered that there was some justification to it. 'He could be aloof,' says Campbell, who is not exactly short of confidence himself. 'He was one of those blokes who knew what he wanted to do and he wasn't tolerant of fools who mucked around while he was trying to achieve that.' And as Grant says, 'He did have that sort of aura about him. But most good sportspeople have a certain amount of arrogance about them.'

If only Grant had had that. It is a common assumption that Andy was the more talented cricketer of the brothers. I am not so sure about that. Talent-wise they were fairly similar, but that is not to say that the good Lord lavished too many of his cricketing gifts upon them. As I mentioned in the introduction to this book, Andy's batsmanship was not immediately eye-catching.

It is just that Andy had more confidence. And even that is, I reckon, a self-taught confidence. He is not an extrovert. He is naturally modest. Praise him and he just guffaws. Just this once, by way of illustration, I do not think he will mind my revealing a text he once sent me. When he and Andrew Strauss received OBEs in the 2011 Queen's Birthday Honours List (in which Alastair Cook also received an MBE), he replied to my congratulations with this: 'Just strange to go from OGs to OBEs!' He truly was humbled.

I have certainly never found him arrogant. In fact I've never heard anyone really say a bad word about him. But then I've never really had an in-depth conversation with Kevin Pietersen about him. There are always players who will slate a coach, at any level.

He is a loyal friend. All his friends confirm that even at the busiest times of being England coach he will always return calls and messages from his mates, however long it might take. Tickets are always sorted for those who want them – within reason, of course. And while there has obviously had to be a slight change in our relationship with me as a journalist and him as England coach, it hasn't altered dramatically. He has a gentle side. Once he came to my house in Cardiff and played golf on the Wii with my young daughter Bethan, who every time I go to cricket now says, 'Say hello to Andy for me please!'

Very early on as a cricketer Flower decided that he had to be tougher than others if he were to succeed in the game. 'I never actually had a high regard for whatever talent I had,' he once said. 'Seeing the ball, hitting it, there were plenty of other cricketers who did that far better than I did. But I thought one area where I could be better than them was to be more determined, more hungry and not give anything away.' The result was a cricketer who could not be messed with. As Campbell says, 'When he's got his "game-face" on, he's a very serious bloke.' There may have been an expletive in that quote too. A well-placed expletive, as it happens, because it does emphasize how serious Flower can be when the time comes for sporting action. Campbell is spot on. Flower's 'game-face', as a cricketer and as a coach, truly is the stuff of legend.

While Grant trained maniacally in the gym, Andy trained hard but also set about developing his mental toughness. He enlisted the help of a chap called Eugene Moody, a black belt in karate, to train differently; to train smarter.

Now I'm a bit of a fitness fanatic myself, but I can honestly say that I've never seen anyone train as hard as Grant. If I tell you that I have seen him do weights for four hours in the morning, go to net practice at lunchtime, go for a long run in late afternoon and then go for more nets in the evening, then I would not be lying. He might even fit in a game of squash some-where too. At one stage during his time at Essex the fitness staff told him his body fat levels were 'dangerously low'. I'm not surprised. 'I overtrained,' he confesses. 'Andy trained smarter and I burnt myself out because I thought the harder you trained the better it would be, and that I just had to give myself the best possible chance. I didn't spend enough time on the mental side of things.'

Andy was always reading books on sports psychology and listening to tapes on the subject. 'He was a pioneer of self-help,' says Campbell. 'I would read the books and listen to the tapes also,' says Grant, 'but I didn't take it in as much. Andrew wanted to understand it better. I found the physical side a lot easier – to deal with and learn from.'

None of this is to say that Andy was an obviously natural leader back then. 'He goes against that perception that great leaders are born,' says Campbell. 'If you'd seen some of the things he got up to as a youngster, you'd have said "no chance". If you speak to guys who went to school with him, he was a bit of a rebel.'

Flower will admit that his youth was a little wild. I have heard of him giving talks to young aspiring England cricketers and saying as much, although he does then emphasize how he came to realize how important fitness is. I'll never forget him turning up to training at Harare Sports Club once (we visiting English pros were often allowed to train with the Zimbabwe squad) and taking his shirt off to begin a physical warm-up. He glanced down at his midriff and pinched the smallest amount of flab. 'I'm supposed to be a professional sportsman,' he said angrily to himself, and there may have been an expletive in there then too. He trained like Grant that day.

Alcohol and sport mix as easily in Zimbabwe as any other country. For me, spending winters playing there was just an extension of the five years I spent at university. There was ample time to train, play and party. The Flowers and Campbell seemed to like playing student drinking games, especially that old favourite 'Bunnies'. So with two former Combined Universities colleagues Adrian Dale and James Boiling (who now teaches at my alma mater Monmouth School) joining me in Zimbabwe for two consecutive years there were some raucous times. 'We could never get Andy drunk in those games though,' recalls Boiling. 'He was too smart. He always had his wits about him.' Flower does, though, suffer from hangovers that are as bad as the ones I have to endure. 'Alcohol poisons him,' I remember his wife Becky saying with a shake of the head one morning in Zimbabwe.

In general, however, Flower is little different from most other Zimbabweans. They have a certain streak of madness in them. As I've mentioned, Duncan Fletcher had that too. I put this to Grant, and he knew what was coming. He knew I was going to talk about a trip we took to Lake Kariba over the festive season of 1991/92. 'They weren't big crocodiles!' he said unprompted, with a laugh. He was talking about the rather inebriated habit some Zimbabweans have of catching small crocodiles at night by shining a light across the water and pouncing on the red dots the crocodiles' eyes produce. The closer together, the smaller the crocodile. 'You never know though!' Grant admits with a nervous chuckle.

On that same trip one day Andy thought it was a good idea

to cool off after a warm day's fishing and drinking by lying in the shallow waters. I'd like to think that my impassioned screams of 'Get out of the water, you mad bastard!' may have helped England become the number one ranked cricket side in the world. But the truth is that he wasn't listening.

Flower still seeks adventure as England coach. On the South Africa tour of 2009/10 he was seen climbing the floodlights at Buffalo Park in East London with wicketkeeping coach Bruce French, who is a keen climber, Huw Bevan, Richard Halsall and a player who'd probably better remain nameless (the last three only went to the top of the pole so could not be seen like Flower and French, who popped out and had their photographs taken). On tour he will often spend a day off riding huge Harley Davidson bikes with Bevan. And when in Australia for the 2010/11 Ashes he, Bevan and French went tombstone diving in Fremantle, Western Australia, as well as climbing in the Adelaide Hills.

What is it with these Zimbos? 'I just think it's the culture we were brought up in,' says Grant. 'We had an outdoor lifestyle and went on holidays to places like Kariba and Victoria Falls. People take chances. You've had a civil war to deal with and a lot of people have had trouble on their farms. If you're weak, then generally you get singled out and you don't survive and don't come through the system. It is a bit mad, yes, but people who are brought up in London are more savvy to the world. We come to England and have to do things like go on the Tube and it is a big shock to the system.'

It was actually a trip to England in 1986 that began Andy's cricketing odyssey. In his last year at Vainona he was selected for the Stragglers club tour on which they played sixteen games in three weeks. 'They blooded him on that tour,' says Bill.

It was also in England on that tour that Andy's view of the world, especially in terms of race, was challenged. 'I was billeted with a lovely family in Esher,' he said in an interview with

THE GROWING OF A FLOWER

The Times in 2011. 'They had a son of my age and I remember having a discussion with him about interracial relationships. I was truly astonished when he said that he would contemplate having a non-white girlfriend. We argued for hours one night about it. I began to realize something was deeply wrong with my beliefs.

'It is amazing how easily racist ideology is absorbed by young people. It is a form of indoctrination because you just don't realize how your own ideas and assumptions have been coloured by what you are told and the norms of the culture you are living in. It was only when I got to my late teens and early twenties that I first started to ask the question: "What the hell am I thinking here?" My views were very backward, which is deeply embarrassing to admit today.'

Flower clearly learnt much, on and off the field, on that Stragglers tour, but returned home to work for the Anglo American Corporation as a trainee accountant. He was there for eighteen months, but the problem for him was that leave specifically for cricket would not be granted; he always had to take personal leave in order to play. Soon he decided he had had enough and went back to England to play in the Birmingham League for Barnt Green. It was a felicitous move. He was given accommodation at the club chairman's home, and Andy soon discovered that the Hampson family had a delightful daughter called Rebecca. She is now his wife and mother to three children, Jamie, Sam and Dani.

The following year (1989) Flower played in the Lancashire League for Heywood as an amateur, returning in 1992 and 1993 as a professional. In between times he spent two years in Holland, playing for Voorburg in The Hague. There followed stints with West Bromwich Dartmouth and Eastbourne (where he played alongside England fielding coach Halsall), as well as coaching posts at Epsom College and Oxford University.

This was no easy road into professional cricket. Grant was just as nomadic, taking in spells in Somerset at Winscombe, Cheltenham, Wallasey in Merseyside, Widnes and Harrogate. He also followed Andy to Voorburg and Epsom College.

But the crucial thing was that Andy was coaching, employed by the ZCU and gaining qualifications on courses run by Les Lenham, the former Sussex batsman. He coached the Zimbabwe age-group sides, visited the better schools in Harare on a rota basis, as well as youngsters in the underprivileged areas. All the while he was taking it a little more seriously than the two rapscallions Flower G. and Campbell, who were also working under the coaching director Dave Houghton. 'To be honest I didn't think about coaching then because I was playing,' admits Grant. 'It was a means to an end. I think Andrew might have thought about it a bit deeper than that. I was pretty naive and immature in those days, and Alistair [Campbell] and I were messing around. Andrew has always been a bit different.'

I'd agree with that. There was always a little bit more mystery to Andy than the others. He was certainly harder to get to know than his brother and Campbell. No harder than Fletcher, mind. 'Andrew doesn't let people in easily,' says Campbell. 'To gain his trust takes a process.'

But even Andy admits coaching was not necessarily always on his mind back then. 'I found it quite hard coaching five days a week,' he says, 'because all I really wanted to do was play. But it's interesting that when I applied for the England job I spoke about being involved in the study of coaching and maximizing my own and other people's potential for twenty years.'

In 1991 Andy was appointed to take over from Houghton as director of coaching at the ZCU. Campbell reckons this was a turning point for Flower, a time to recognize his responsibilities. 'There were no pros then so that was the highest position for a player,' says Campbell. 'My abiding memory of him is always walking around with a black Filofax under his arm. He was very structured even then. He wanted reports on where everyone was and what they were doing. He was never afraid of calling someone in and hauling them over the coals.'

I think that may mean that Campbell received the odd bollocking. And doubtless it was justified. He is an extremely humorous and gregarious fellow, but he was a lazy bugger then. His nickname is 'Kamba', which means tortoise in Shona, and it is very apt.

And none of this is to say that Flower and Campbell don't get on. They do. Famously. In 2006 they were on holiday in Mauritius with their respective families when Campbell told him he'd soon be coach of England. It was a big call given he was still playing at Essex, while doing some coaching with the National Academy. 'I told him, "You'll be England coach!"' says Campbell. 'I just thought it was a natural progression, knowing the personality and how he'd be able to distance himself from all the egos and the high life that is abundant there in the England cricket team. I knew he could bring a sense of normality.'

It was some remarkable prescience from Campbell. But as he says, he knows the character. He knows what Flower went through to become the number one ranked batsman in the world. He was his captain between 1996 and 1999, between Flower's two tenures as Zimbabwe captain.

Thinking about it, Flower must have been an awful captain. He was the only one of many I encountered in a 245-match first-class career who allowed me to bowl. Just the two balls, mind. Don Shepherd, the Glamorgan great so cruelly deprived of an England cap, took 2,218 first-class wickets at an average of just 21, so he is rather well qualified to comment on the quality of my bowling. 'The worst I have ever seen,' he once said. And he meant anywhere, not just in first-class cricket. Yes, I was rubbish – a huge disappointment given that my father had been a wicket-taker par excellence, in the Shepherd off-cutting mode as it happened, for Lydney and Gloucestershire second eleven. But

Flower allowed me to bowl, against his brother Grant of all people, at the end of a Mashonaland versus Mashonaland Under 24s match in Harare in 1994. They needed three to win. It was a surprise it took Grant two balls.

More seriously, there is something else I recall from that Logan Cup match, in which the Flowers were opposing captains. Andy won the toss and inserted the opposition on a dampish pitch at Harare Sports Club. They crawled to 284 in 152 overs. At the end of their innings as we walked from the field on the second day, I said to Andy, 'I reckon we should just get up to their score as quickly as we can, then declare.' The comment was based on two things. Firstly, a chronic lack of faith in my ability at the time. I could not score a run and was looking to take pressure from myself as the fear of failure took grip. And secondly, much less importantly in my mind, it seemed the only way for us to breathe life into a game that was dying. There just didn't seem time for much else.

So as I prepared to open with Paul Bourdillon, a Zimbabwean with whom I'd played some university cricket in England and indeed on a Combined Universities tour to Barbados captained by Mike Atherton, with Flower at number three and Trevor Penney at four in a strong side, Flower relayed this message to the team.

It went well. We were all out for 75. There was plenty of time left in the game all right. We lost by ten wickets. It has been said many times since that Flower is a good listener, but listening to a doubting, pusillanimous English pro that day was not one of his better moves.

Flower had been captain of Old Georgians at just twenty-one. He was already learning how to shape a cricket team. 'There are no mysteries,' he says. 'You need to have mutual respect for your team-mates, enjoy working together and enjoy sharing hard work.' Captaining older players is never easy, but it certainly shaped his attitude towards younger players. 'He ruled by fear a bit,' says Grant. 'Some players even left OGs because of it [I bet they weren't very good]. He didn't tolerate fools. He obviously had good knowledge, but his man management let him down sometimes.'

Flower himself will admit this. 'One of my weaknesses as captain was dealing with people,' he said recently. 'I look back and cringe at some of the things I did. I judged people too harshly, too quickly. I did not have empathy with people.'

One of the occasions he might be recalling is a Zimbabwe Under 24s match against Natal Under 24s in Durban during which he sent one of his players, Hitesh Hira, off the field. I'll let Campbell take up the story: 'Andrew felt Hitesh didn't go for a catch, so he threw his keeping gloves down, walked over to him and said: "This has been happening for too long. I'm sick and tired of you not trying. So get the fuck off the field!" Hitesh just walked off. Dave Houghton [who was coach] was in the changing room and hadn't seen what had happened. So Hitesh walks in and Houghton says, "What's wrong? Have you got a hammie [a hamstring injury]?" And Hitesh said, "Andrew has just sent me off for not trying!"'

Interestingly Fletcher also sent one of his players back to the dressing room, when he was captain of the Alexandra club side in Harare. He was a chap called Cecil Grimmer, who had been in an argument with one of his team-mates. Fletcher told him to leave the field, but Grimmer would not go. 'Get this man off the field,' said Fletcher to the umpires. Tough men, Flower and Fletcher.

Flower actually led Zimbabwe to their first Test win, in 1995, when they hammered Pakistan by an innings and 64 runs in Harare. Had I not been there I wouldn't have believed it, but I was there, with leg in plaster after partially severing my patella tendon on a glass door. It was not alcohol-related. Honest.

It was Henry Olonga's Test debut – a wake-up call, too. Not just because he was called for throwing, as he had been in the tourists' previous match against the ZCU President's XI at Harare South. He did throw at that stage of his career too, before undergoing remedial work with Dennis Lillee. I know that for certain because I had been coach of the Zimbabwe B side for the couple of years previous to that, and Olonga had played for us against Northern Transvaal B (coached by Surrey's Keith Medlycott) earlier in the month before his Test debut. It was obvious he was throwing, but I had no idea what to do. It was best I stuck to journalism, I think.

'Andy was a hard task master,' Olonga recalls of that first Test. 'He was a no-nonsense guy. He always demanded the best from his players and didn't tolerate weak excuses. I was eighteen years old and it was a case of "welcome to the world of men". Test cricket was harder than I imagined. I was a little kid and Andy didn't suffer fools gladly. You drop a catch or miss a run out and you will know about it.'

There were some weird happenings in that Test, which I thought nothing of at the time. It began at the toss. Flower tossed the coin and the Pakistan captain Salim Malik mumbled something inaudible. The match referee Jackie Hendriks immediately stepped in and put his hand over the coin, with Malik claiming he had called 'Bird' in relation to the Zimbabwe Bird, the national emblem that was on one side of the dollar coin then. A re-toss was made, which Flower won, and he and Grant put on 269 together for the fourth wicket, Grant making 201 not out and Andy 156. Both played quite superbly, but there were some curious bowling changes and tactics. Given subsequent events, it does make you think.

I was also there when Zimbabwe played their inaugural Test, against India in Harare in October 1992. For some reason, and with no idea what I was doing, I was Zimbabwe's press liaison officer. My main job was to ensure that the press box phone bills were not too expensive. I failed horribly apparently.

I was shocked that Test status had suddenly come to a group

of blokes who basically played club cricket on Sundays. It was good club cricket, I grant you, played over sixty overs, but I was genuinely worried that it was going to be too big a step up for most of them. But a flat pitch helped allay fears and Grant made 82, Andy 59, and Houghton, making his Test debut at the age of thirty-five, hit 121.

The decision to grant Zimbabwe Test cricket was, of course, politically motivated. India used it as a means of garnering another vote at the ICC's table, and duly arrived as Zimbabwe's first opponents. It shouldn't have happened, but you do wonder what might have happened had it not. What would have become of the career of Andy Flower? Would he have played for South Africa? Mark Boucher might be glad that this decision was made.

It was made, and suddenly Test and one-day international cricket was on Bill and Jean Flower's doorstep, with two of their sons as the prime actors on the stage. 'Flower Power' became a rather overused cliché. But it was always apposite. You could find no prouder and happier parents in world cricket than Bill and Jean, sitting transfixed at Harare Sports Club.

Then in 1996 tragedy struck the Flower family. At the age of just thirty-three, the eldest son Stephen was killed in an accident on his farm in Zambia. 'He was the farmer in the family,' says Bill. 'He was running a large rose operation from York Farm just outside Lusaka. And he was building a refrigeration unit on the back of his farm truck to use when he came to Harare regularly to visit family. It was a freak accident, by electrocution.'

I spoke to Bill in late March 2011. He and Jean had just moved from Lincolnshire to Surrey, to be nearer daughter Megan and her family. And Bill had just had another heart attack, on New Year's Day, in fact, while Andy was out in Australia preparing for the final Ashes Test. Andy very nearly came home. 'He asked his mother whether he should come home,' says Bill, 'and she said no, which was the correct decision.'

When I spoke to Bill he was still recovering. He was easily emotional. And recalling the tragic story of Stephen quite naturally affected him. He remembered it as if it were yesterday: 'It was a Saturday afternoon, I was being interviewed at the ZBC [Zimbabwe Broadcasting Corporation] studios about the cricket development work I was doing at the time. I was summoned to the phone. Jean had received the news. I just went to pieces . . .'

Andy and Grant are not naturally emotional people, especially Grant. Andy can be more emotional, and I have heard that occasionally he becomes so when speaking to the England team, as he did at the end of the South Africa tour in 2009/10 when talking to the team about the tour as a whole, and again in Perth on the Ashes tour. It was the fourth morning of play, with England facing defeat at 81-5. There had been an incident the previous evening when Paul Collingwood was out when he shouldn't really have been facing had nightwatchman James Anderson done his job properly and taken the single so obviously on offer. Flower apparently said, 'Jimmy messed up yesterday evening, that's OK. We all do that, but let's appreciate everything he does for us.' As Strauss related in his Ashes diary, 'He actually got quite emotional, which Andy doesn't often do. He was talking about the way Jimmy bowls, and the fact that he actually embraces the nightwatchman's role. His voice was breaking a little. It highlighted to us just how much he cares and how passionate he is about us, not only as a side but also a group of individuals.'

There was another occasion, at the Oval at the end of the 4–0 Test series win over India in 2011. As Graeme Swann was later to reveal, 'An hour or two after the Fourth Test finished on Monday, we wandered on to the outfield, supped a couple of beers and had a final reflective chat about the Test summer.

Andy Flower was quite emotional as he spoke of the pride he felt in the team. It's great that a coach can be so happy that he chokes up like that.'

When Stephen died, Andy was in England coaching at Epsom College, and Grant was playing at Wallasey. Naturally they both returned home immediately. 'They both gave the outward impression that they had everything under control,' says Bill, 'which I don't think is a good thing. You carry that grief for too long. I tried to get them to agree to counselling before they went back to the UK. But I think that by the time they came back to Zimbabwe they had had their own private grief release.'

Bill does, though, think that it played a part in shaping Andy's future management skills. 'It helps make you what you are,' he says. 'You have to learn to suffer losses like that. That's life. That's why he is so good with his man management. Players can talk to him.'

Grant, too, thinks it had an effect. 'It might have made us a bit tougher,' he says. 'It puts things into perspective. When you think things are the end of the world, well . . . We've never been the most overly emotional people, Andrew and I, and the rest of the family expected us to show our grief more. But we didn't because we tried to be strong around them. That was our method.'

Andy gave up the Zimbabwe captaincy at the beginning of that 1996/97 Zimbabwean season. It was nothing to do with Stephen's death, rather that the job had been getting too much for him as a whole. I have often been asked why Flower was not always captain of Zimbabwe, if he is such a good leader. The answer is obvious. Captaining Zimbabwe is not like captaining any other Test country. It's like captaining, say, Cambridge University in first-class cricket. You just keep losing. And that must get you down.

Flower returned to the captaincy in 1999. He intended to be in it for the long haul, but was sacked in 2000 after a pay dispute with the Zimbabwe board during the tour to England. ZCU chairman Peter Chingoka held Flower personally responsible, and, unbeknown to Flower, just before that triangular final asked Heath Streak to take over the captaincy in the upcoming season. Flower did not discover this until he returned to Zimbabwe some time afterwards following a holiday in France. To say he wasn't happy would be the grossest of understatements.

But rejection can focus the mind. Flower decided that it was all going to be about him from then on. He'd spent all that time trying to carry an under-strength side on his shoulders. So he set himself a personal goal. He wanted to become the number one ranked batsman in the world. At the time he was ninth, with Alec Stewart, Justin Langer, Inzamam-ul-Haq, Ricky Ponting, Saeed Anwar, Brian Lara, Steve Waugh and Sachin Tendulkar above him.

He began by taking a piece of paper and in the centre of it marking a huge number one. Around the number he made notes of various things he felt he needed to do in order to reach that goal, whether they were mental improvements, technical adjustments or even changes to his social habits. That piece of paper was always with him, whether he was at home or in his hotel room on tour, with only his closest friends having any knowledge of it. He kept adding notes as time moved on.

By December of that year he was up to second in the rankings, with only Tendulkar ahead of him. That was due in no small part to a couple of remarkable Tests in India, where Flower scored 183 not out and 70 in Delhi, and then 55 and 232 not out in Nagpur. It confirmed him as a quite exceptional player of spin. Anil Kumble and Harbhajan Singh may not have been playing in those Tests (at Delhi the spinners were Sunil Doshi and Murali Kartik, and at Nagpur they were Doshi and Sarandeep Singh), but Kumble, Maninder Singh and Rajesh Chauhan had been playing in 1993 in Delhi when Flower made

115 and 62 not out. And both Kumble and Harbhajan were playing when Flower made 92 at Delhi in 2002. In five Tests in India overall Flower averaged 117. It is a stunning statistic. But then few could sweep or reverse-sweep like him. In Nagpur especially he reverse-swept the Indians to distraction.

In June 2001 Zimbabwe beat India in Harare, with Flower hitting the winning runs. But unusually he was batting at number eight, having broken his thumb while keeping. Until then he had played in every one of Zimbabwe's 52 Tests and 172 one-day internationals. He missed four ODIs and two Tests before returning against South Africa in September. In the first Test in Harare he made 142 and 199 not out. Still Zimbabwe lost, but the rankings could no longer deny Flower. Since being sacked as captain in 2000, he had made 1,407 Test runs at an average of 108. He was the number one batsman in the world, and remained so until December.

That piece of paper had worked. Sound familiar? Throughout his tenure as England coach he has been seen studiously taking notes on the sidelines. Whereas before he had been plotting his own path to the top of the world, now it was England's.

10
Changing of the Guard

The West Indies is the hardest tour for a cricket newspaper journalist. Of course, it's not the hardest in terms of the lifestyle and hospitality, but it is the hardest in terms of filing to ever-shifting deadlines. In Australia you know that by the time your stuff appears in the newspaper it is dated, so you write accordingly. You write carefully! But in the Caribbean, with the time difference being about five hours behind, you are constantly filing live copy. And things can change very swiftly.

So there I was in 2009, acting as the *Sunday Telegraph*'s correspondent again, with Scyld Berry doing his *Wisden* editorship. The first Test was in Jamaica, and Saturday was the fourth day. My first edition copy had to be in by just before lunchtime. The pitch had been slow, and therefore so had the match, with most interest centring upon events far away in India where the Indian Premier League auction had taken place on the third day, with Kevin Pietersen and Andrew Flintoff both fetching a record $1.55 million each. After Pietersen had been dismissed for 97, aiming to reach his century with a six, he was memorably dubbed 'Dumbslog Millionaire', after the Oscar-winning film *Slumdog Millionaire*. Two other England players, Paul Collingwood and Owais Shah, were also bought at the auction, as was Ravi Bopara, not then on the England tour but later called up.

On that fourth morning the West Indies had only just completed their first innings, crawling to a lead of 74. The match had 'draw' written all over it so I wrote a piece suggesting as much. Just as I was finishing it, Alastair Cook was out for a duck. I was not particularly worried. Openers get ducks. Neither Cook nor Strauss had reached double figures in the first innings. The home side's opener Devon Smith had failed similarly, even if his partner Chris Gayle had made a century on his home turf.

Then for a few overs before lunch the left-arm spin of the tall Sulieman Benn was introduced. At the fourth ball of the last over before the break, Ian Bell attempted a limp cut to a wide one and was caught behind for 4. England were suddenly 11-2 at lunch, trailing by 63, and already my sports editor Peter Mitchell was on the phone advising that I tickle my 'intro' so as to reflect the possibility of some impending doom.

But nobody could have foreseen the depth and the rapidity of that doom. By 2.34 p.m. that afternoon the match was over. England had been bowled out for just 51. Only Flintoff, with 24, reached double figures. England had lost by an innings and 23 runs. Jerome Taylor recorded figures of 9-4-11-5. With the third ball after lunch he bowled Pietersen for 1 with a wicked, late away-swinging yorker. 'London Bridge is falling down' blared the music from Chester's Bar. At 26-7 soon afterwards it had collapsed.

My second edition 'intro' was rather different. 'This was an utter disgrace,' I wrote. 'Another shameful chapter of English cricketing history was written here, as England's batting collapsed inexplicably and spinelessly to 51 all out, their third-lowest score ever. Only the 45 against Australia in Sydney in

1887 and the infamous 46 in Trinidad in 1994 stand below this effort in the record books . . .'

Get stuck in, son.

After the quotes had been gathered from a despondent England press conference, Mitchell then decided, quite rightly of course, that this required a further comment piece. Another eight hundred words.

'How long have I got?' I asked.

'Twenty minutes,' came the response.

Jesus.

'Whither England now?' I wrote. 'How do you recover from such a shambles? Skipper Andrew Strauss described his dressing room as being a "pretty disconsolate place". You can bet it was a lot worse than that. It will have been a place of devastation and embarrassment . . .' I recounted a tale of my own, of how Middlesex had bowled out Glamorgan for just 31, in 1997 of all the years, the year we won the county championship, with Duncan Fletcher as our coach. I went home after that debacle and lay on my sofa for the rest of the day with my face turned inwards. I couldn't even face my wife.

Imagine how Andy Flower felt. What a first Test for the care-taker coach. Well, we discovered how he felt the very next morning in a press conference at the team's Hilton Hotel in Kingston. Let us just say that he had obviously dealt with it a lot better than I did in 1997.

The conference had been scheduled for right beside the pool, but was moved to beneath a nearby palm tree. Not even there was there any shade for Flower from what one writer described as 'the microphones and cameras that were jabbed, almost pugilistically' into his face.

As Flower had walked to his chair, he had glanced at me and smiled. I genuinely felt sorry for him. At that stage I did not think he wanted the job, and I did not think he would get it. As I wrote later that day, 'Baby-sitting should really have no place in international sport. He [Flower] is the best-paid nanny in the country, waiting until the real boss comes home.'

But I was underestimating his resilience. He was quite brilliant at that press conference. As one gnarled old hack observed, 'It's almost disarming to hear straight questions being returned with straight answers.' Yes, Peter Moores had never been particularly good at that.

Flower ducked nothing. 'As a team we've underperformed,' he said, 'and it's all our jobs to do something about that. And if we don't do it, we'll be out of jobs. What you've got to do in inter-national cricket is handle the pressure and we didn't do that yesterday. I'm in charge – the buck stops with me.'

The last comment was impressive. It would have been so easy for him to blame others. He was, after all, only the 'assistant coach' in title. He had had no say in selection, because the squad had been chosen before the double departure of Moores and Pietersen.

It should really have occurred to me then that Flower wanted to make a fist of this. He wanted to be coach of England. Or 'team director', as the grand title now is. What's more he was clearly up to that task. Hugh Morris and Geoff Miller were standing at the back of the press conference, and they clearly thought the same. 'He was very close to getting the job that day,' admits Morris. 'He was hugely impressive in a really difficult situation. He was incredibly honest and straightforward.'

He was relaxed. There was no sense of panic. There were certainly no 'naughty-boy nets' for the players, as quite a few of them went off to play golf. 'I think after a day like yesterday it's best to stay calm,' he said, 'and reflect on what's happened and not to have knee-jerk reactions on selection. There is a time when we need to reflect on what has happened and also for the learning of the players and the coaching staff. We will have our team meeting tomorrow.'

The following day, having flown to Antigua, they did have

their team meeting. It was a meeting that was still being talked about years later. In his newspaper column in 2011, just before the third Test against India at Edgbaston, with England on the verge of becoming number one in the world, James Anderson wrote – or his ghost did anyway – of the ten steps that had brought England to that position. First on the list was the 51 all out scenario. 'After we were rolled over, assistant coach Andy Flower and Strauss led a team meeting which went something like: "You're grown men, it's time to take a bit of responsibility for yourselves, your practice, your preparation." They did not just want the captain to be the leader. Their formula was based on having a team of leaders. A key moment.'

The meeting took place at the Grand Royal Antiguan Hotel in Deep Bay, St John's. Mark Garaway was then the England team analyst, and had been since 2006. It was actually his last tour, because when Flower took over the reins permanently one of his first moves was to remove Garaway from his position. The reasons were twofold. Firstly, Garaway was very close to Pietersen, indeed they were habitual running partners in the West Indies, and it was perceived that he was heavily involved in the Moores saga. Secondly, under Fletcher, Garaway had been encouraged to coach, as well as work as the analyst. That was Fletcher's way. He liked his support staff to help out in a coaching capacity. And Garaway had been coach of Somerset, remember. But Flower didn't want that. He wanted an analyst pure and simple, even if Garaway's successor, in a job-share arrangement with Gemma Broad (Stuart's sister), was Nathan Leamon, a Cambridge maths graduate and former maths teacher at Tonbridge and director of coaching at Eton who is a qualified cricket coach. 'Numbers' the players call him, and that's what he deals in. He doesn't try to coach.

You might think Garaway is bitter. He is not. He quickly moved on to become the high performance director for Ireland Cricket (he left in 2011 to set up his own business). 'It wasn't a shock to me,' he says of his removal from the England camp. 'I'd been tipped off that was the way he [Flower] was going to go. I made no secret: I wanted to coach and I wanted to lead more importantly.'

Garaway remembers that Antigua meeting as the moment Flower stood up as a leader. 'We didn't really find out a lot about Andy in the first twenty-two months,' he says. 'During that time it was always Mooresy's message, and Andy is a loyal Zimbabwean. He never said or did anything to undermine Mooresy. But this was where we really saw what the bloke was about. I walked out of the meeting thinking, "This bloke is definitely going to get the job, and if he does get it, he is only going to get better and better."'

Strauss wrote in his Ashes diary that Flower was 'brilliant' in that meeting. 'It was the moment that we all realized that he had something special. He was very honest about his own view and some of the things that he hadn't said before, and then he encouraged other people to talk, but did it in a way that was very constructive and sympathetic to their point of view. So it wasn't "You're saying something I don't agree with, so you're talking rubbish". It was "OK, that's interesting. I don't necessarily agree with it, but I can see why you're saying that." A lot came up about the players not having bought into the team side of things. There were some pretty hard conversations going on.'

Garaway agrees it was a 'punchy' meeting. 'We all know that in cricket dressing rooms people come out with clichés,' he says, 'but here Andy and Straussy really set their stall out. A lot of the bullshit chat that had gone on before was not going to be allowed. People just wouldn't be allowed to get away with talking in vague language.'

Garaway says that everyone in the room, including the support staff, was challenged about his role. And he recalls, in particular, that Pietersen was confronted strongly. 'I remember one conversation where they were challenging KP,' he says, 'and somebody challenged him about his lifestyle, about being in the papers all the time and living in Chelsea. KP quite rightly went at them, saying, "I train as hard, if not harder, than anybody else, and I believe my results speak for themselves. I can back it up."'

Garaway then revealed that 'two or three of the senior players who didn't always see eye-to-eye with KP actually backed him up'. He was undoubtedly talking about Andrew Flintoff and Steve Harmison. 'Yes, Fred particularly,' he admitted. 'It was a very unusual thing to happen, but it was just the environment that the two Andys had decided to put in place at the time. Before that there wouldn't have been the strength of environment for them to back him up.'

As Strauss says, 'In the space of one meeting we'd gone from a team that never said anything honest to one in which people could say almost anything to each other.'

The most obvious upshot of the meeting was that Bell was dropped. Patience had run out. He was told in no uncertain terms that he needed to shape up, and toughen up. He'd played forty-six Tests by this stage of his career, with eight centuries, but with that killer statistic still hanging over his head: all of those centuries had come after a colleague had also made a century in the same innings. The accusation, which became a cliché, was that he was a piggy-backer, a soft follower rather than a tough leader. The Australian Stuart Law had once called him 'that timid little creature', and during the 2006/07 Ashes Shane Warne had nicknamed him the 'Sherminator' after the ginger-haired geek in the *American Pie* films. Mike Atherton described him as 'the man-boy'. Mentally, Bell was certainly not Flower's type of batsman at that stage.

Bell was not fit enough, or tough enough. I remember being outside the Hilton Hotel in Barbados later in the tour, talking to Flower as he prepared to leave for practice. Out of the hotel came Bell, all alone and dressed in running gear. He had a quick word with Flower, and off he ran.

'Good effort,' I said to Flower.

'Yes, he's got a lot of work to do,' was the response.

Indeed he had. For the rest of the tour barely a trip to the ground or back after play went by without a sighting of Bell running. Sometimes others were with him. Goodness, I even saw Harmison running back from the ground in Barbados once! Bell would rise early and do boxing sessions with the team security man, Reg Dickason. Bell knew the score. 'It wasn't technically that I was struggling,' he later told me. 'It was about how to make myself tougher and physically better. Reg put me in a tough place.'

It got tougher. When Bell returned from the West Indies, his Warwickshire colleague Darren Maddy put him in touch with Darren Grewcock, a rugby fitness guru with experience with the Leicester Tigers. Grewcock in turn introduced him to a cage-fighter called Barrington Patterson. By the time Bell returned to the Test team for the third Ashes Test later that year, he was a different person.

Just like Bell, the England team as a whole resolved to be different. They too resolved to be tougher. Their first step was to make themselves harder to beat. They could not win any of the three remaining Tests (four if you include the ten-ball abandoned debacle at the Sir Vivian Richards Stadium in Antigua, where the sandy outfield was soon deemed unplayable), but they did not lose any either, playing all the cricket in truth. In the hastily rearranged Test at the St John's Recreation Ground in Antigua, England had ten overs at the West Indies' last pair but, agonizingly, could not force the last wicket, and then in Trinidad the hosts were hanging on grimly with eight wickets down.

There was, inevitably, criticism of England's conservatism, with declarations seen to be too tardy, but both Flower and

Strauss were laying down markers. Test cricket is no playground. It is not like the old days of three-day county cricket, when enticing declarations were made and the result was forgotten as soon as the next match started, which was usually the next day. Test-match declarations matter. Those that lead to defeat are remembered. Everybody recalls Gary Sobers' generous declaration in Trinidad in 1968 that handed England victory, so too David Gower's at Lord's in 1984 that gave the West Indies an easy win.

At least England won the subsequent one-day series 3–2. It was the first time England had ever won a one-day series in the Caribbean, and this at the seventh attempt. In the series Strauss was the leading run-scorer (204 runs at 51, with a strike rate of 86.80) – not bad for a chap who hadn't played an ODI for nearly two years, who was ignored as soon as Moores took over after the World Cup of 2007. Between now and the 2011 World Cup, after which he retired from ODIs, he would rejuvenate his one-day batting, averaging nearly 41 in forty-nine matches with four hundreds at a strike rate of 87.68. Overall in his ODI career he averaged 35.63 with six hundreds and a strike rate of 80.94. So the improvements were obvious. He knew that he had to expand his game at the top of the order, and he did, even if I still think he was better suited to the middle order, where he batted around 2004.

Fletcher always insisted that in order to flourish as an ODI opener you need to be able to hit high and hard down the ground. So around that period in 2004 Fletcher used Strauss at number four. A game that readily springs to mind is the Champions Trophy semi-final against Australia at Edgbaston, where England chased down 260 with 3.5 overs remaining. Strauss made 52 not out from forty-two balls at number four.

Fletcher always saw his number four in one-day cricket as the lynchpin. He wanted his top three to be aggressive against the new ball in the Powerplay overs, with the realization that the number four could stabilize things if early wickets were lost. The number four also had to realize that, if the start was good, he might have to drop down the order. A lot of this applied to me at Glamorgan. A natural opener, it was Fletcher who eventually persuaded me to bat in the middle order – after much debate and argument, it does have to be said.

It always irked Fletcher that he could not improve England's one-day cricket more. And, in truth, under Flower there have been many of the same old problems, as evidenced by Fletcher's India's 5–0 win over England in the autumn of 2011. Under both coaches there have been encouraging times. But there have also been dispiriting times. Fletcher is a good one-day coach. His main worry when taking the England job was whether he could coach Test cricket. But the problem in England is that one-day cricket is the poor relation. To the counties and the ECB it is simply a money-making venture; any consideration for the standard of cricket being played often falls by the wayside. There is the difficult problem of English (and Welsh) pitches being so very different from most others around the world, and the accompanying hazards of power hitting in the Powerplay overs on seaming pitches. But that does not excuse some of the ludicrous scheduling. One-day internationals should be played as curtain-raisers to Test series, just like they were so successfully before the 2005 Ashes, not as closing credits that are so easily switched off.

The one-day series victory in the Caribbean at least gave Flower a small achievement with which to enter the interview process for England team director. The ECB had had thirty applicants for the job, but, with the help of the hot-shot recruitment agency Odgers Ray & Berndtson, who were heavily involved in the early parts of the process (presumably approaching potential candidates still under contract elsewhere and so avoiding embarrassment for the ECB), had whittled that down to a shortlist of four. The names of those four are still closely guarded today because of the jobs they were in at the time, but the New Zealander John Wright was certainly among them (he was interviewed on the phone apparently), and the then South Africa coach Mickey Arthur probably was.

The interview panel consisted of Morris, Gordon Lord (the ECB's elite coach development manager), Dennis Amiss (the ECB deputy chairman), Angus Fraser (recently appointed managing director of Middlesex after leaving the *Independent* as cricket correspondent) and Floyd Woodrow (a former head of recruitment at the SAS used by the ECB to train many of its younger cricketers. It was quite rightly felt that Woodrow knew a bit about leadership.) The candidates were interviewed for two hours, and then re-interviewed later in the day. If Flower did not already have the job, he soon did. He was informed later that evening that he was now England's new team director.

The appointment was not greeted with universal acclaim. The 'robust and transparent process', as described by the ECB, was derided. At the press conference to trumpet Flower's elevation, Morris mentioned on more than one occasion Flower's 'potential to be a world-class coach'. Not too many people believed him.

I did. That is not arrogance or my proclaiming any brilliant prescience. I believed then that potential was enough, and Flower had that. I also believed that none of the other proposed candidates were that good anyway. For the *Wisden Cricketer* I wrote, 'Those promoting a raft of better coaches out there, available or not, are spouting nonsense. Tom Moody? Ask his former Worcestershire charges in private; the Guard is changed less often than captains were there. Mickey Arthur? He does what he's told; Graeme Smith is a strong man. Graham Ford? Reliant on Kolpaks and Kent got relegated. Gary Kirsten? He was less experienced than Flower when he took the India job. John Dyson? No coach had previously lost a match single-handedly before his recent Duckworth/Lewis blunder. Andy

Moles? Twice troubled by player power in other posts before becoming New Zealand coach. And so on.'

England were ranked sixth in the world in Test cricket when Flower took over properly. They'd dropped from fifth after the 1–0 loss in the Caribbean. It had long been the ECB's stated aim to be number one in the world. First they'd said by 2007, then by 2009. But this was the first time the England team had spoken about it as a motivational tool. Flower told them that the only way they could become number one was by becoming number five first. So that was their aim for 2009. They achieved it by beating the cold and uninterested West Indians 2–0, and not even winning the Ashes at home later that year altered that position. Fifth they remained, behind India, South Africa, Australia and Sri Lanka, as 2010 dawned.

It is interesting to look back at the team Flower and Strauss picked for their first two Tests in that first home series of 2009, against the West Indies. Flintoff was unavailable, having had knee surgery for an injury sustained playing for the Chennai Super Kings in the IPL, and having missed the final two Tests of the West Indies tour with a hip injury. That quite naturally raised the old chestnut of whether to play four or five specialist bowlers. In Barbados in the first of those two away Tests, England had played six batsmen, with Ravi Bopara scoring a century from number six. He was promptly dropped for Trinidad where England preferred two spinners.

This was now a very different West Indies side away from home. In truth they were poor. They had managed to defend their 1–0 lead at home on the flattest of pitches, but now skipper Gayle set the tone, as had New Zealand's Dan Vettori the previous year, by missing the early part of the tour while staying at the IPL.

Flintoff's injury at the IPL caused much anger. He missed the ICC World Twenty20 as well as the West Indies Tests, and critical comment was only increased when it emerged that Pietersen, who like Flintoff was given a three-week window to play in part of the IPL, had an Achilles tendon problem that had been troubling him on the tour of the West Indies, where he had been clearly ridding himself of frustrations over the Moores scenario by doing a lot of long-distance running. He would not last beyond the second Ashes Test at Lord's before undergoing surgery.

The IPL is a problem, but I do not think it is now a huge problem for English cricket. Of course, dripping opulence turns heads initially, as the Stanford fiasco amply demonstrated. And because of the IPL the finer details of central contracts became hugely complicated, and for a couple of years their signing by the England players was completed about as punctually as the arrival of a train on the British rail network. But one only has to consider the deleterious effects it had on India's Test side in 2011, in particular its meaning that India's best players do not get an off-season, to realize that England's strict command that players can only go for short periods is working. For instance, before that Test series here in 2011 Virender Sehwag played eleven IPL games with an injury that required surgery, and the delay meant he missed the first two Tests. In the third he bagged a 'king pair'. Cricket does have a natural justice system after all.

Anyway, in that first home Test in 2009 England opted for five bowlers, with both Graham Onions and Tim Bresnan making their debuts in the first Test at Lord's. I think the selection was a classic case of the captain getting the side he wanted. Strauss wanted five bowlers; Flower was keener on four. It was why later in the summer, when Flintoff was deemed unfit for the fourth Ashes Test at Headingley, England again went for five. They got hammered, and presumably Strauss told Flower, 'OK, we won't be doing that again!'

Guessing that first Test squad was mighty difficult. This was my attempt in my *Sunday Telegraph* column at the third seamer because I was convinced they would select six batsmen, with Vaughan at number three and Bopara at number six:

> So to the choice of third seamer. Inked in are the excellent James Anderson and Stuart Broad, with Graeme Swann (now thankfully minus 29 loose bodies found in his troublesome elbow) as the principal spinner. But then? Panic. Firstly the injury list is lengthy. Flintoff, naturally, heads it. Ryan Sidebottom has bowled some overs after surgery, but not in Nottinghamshire's championship side. Amjad Khan and Robbie Joseph are busying Kent's physiotherapist. Ditto Simon Jones and Kabir Ali at Worcestershire, Mark Davies at Durham and Steven Finn at Middlesex. Even good old Darren Pattinson is now crocked. Charlie Shreck too.
>
> So who? Steve Harmison, one suspects, is still fighting selectorial purdah. The burly Tim Bresnan has his advocates, as has Warwickshire's thoughtful young swing bowler Chris Woakes. Matthew Hoggard, Graham Onions and Chris Tremlett are less well promoted. Justin Langer suggests Liam Plunkett. But for me Sajid Mahmood's extra pace shades it.

I was wrong. Bresnan and Onions it was, alongside Anderson and Broad, while Bopara, fresh from his IPL stint at King's XI Punjab, was selected to bat at number three, ahead of Bell and Vaughan, who was still keen to return at that stage. Bopara duly made centuries in both Tests, making it three in succession after a hundred in Barbados that winter, as England won by ten wickets and then by an innings and 83 runs.

Bresnan was, and still is to me, a fascinating selection. I'll admit that he has shocked me. And I know of many others around the county circuit who share the same feeling. On first sighting he looked ordinary, and unfit. Time in the England set-up has certainly resolved the latter problem. As for the former, Flower never saw it that way. After those first two West Indies

Tests he asked me what I thought of Bresnan, who had done decently. 'A competent fourth seamer,' I replied. Flower was aghast. 'He's the best fourth seamer in the world, if that's the case,' he responded. You have to say that he has been proved right.

Flower did get something horribly wrong in 2009, though: his selection for the World Twenty20 opener against the Netherlands at Lord's. Collingwood was by now Twenty20 captain, having been persuaded back into the job by Flower. There really wasn't much choice. Strauss had captained the sole Twenty20 international in the Caribbean but had batted at number six, and had been omitted from the thirty-man provisional squad in April. The announcements said that Strauss had stepped down voluntarily, but Flower, already showing that sentiment would play no part in his decisions, knew that he was no Twenty20 batsman. Strauss was never going to be in that squad. So, with some gentle persuasion, Collingwood returned to a leadership role.

For the first match Adil Rashid was selected ahead of Swann. England were looking forward, experimenting even. It backfired. They lost. It was a humiliation. 'England got their just deserts on Friday night,' I screeched in my Sunday column. 'Cricket has a shark's nose for those daring to treat it with complacency, and so England were easy targets. For, make no mistake, England were complacent.'

Flower learnt an important lesson, as he admitted before the next tournament in the West Indies in 2010. 'We won't mess around with selection like we did against Holland when we didn't pick Graeme Swann,' he confessed to me in an interview. Had he been cocky? I asked. 'Yes, I suppose so,' he replied with a smile. His honesty was refreshing.

In 2009 England did actually beat Pakistan, the eventual winners, in their next match, but failed to make the semi-finals. In a worrying nod to the shambles of the 1999 World Cup there was a curtailed opening ceremony because of rain, but, in fairness, the tournament as a whole was a huge success for the ECB, and much credit for that went to tournament director Steve Elworthy, the former South Africa fast bowler who is now the ECB's director of marketing and communications.

Elworthy had also organized the inaugural tournament in his homeland in 2007, where England had performed predictably miserably. It became the tournament that awoke India, the surprise winners and previous sceptics, to the wonders of Twenty20, with Yuvraj Singh striking Broad for six sixes in an over and thoughts of an IPL first emerging. But England were hapless, with a poorly selected squad relying too heavily on Twenty20 journeymen. Flintoff, incapacitated by an ankle injury, hobbled through his overs when in reality he should not have been anywhere near a cricket field. 'Give him six months off,' advised Australia's captain Ricky Ponting.

England truly were in a muddle. Wicketkeeper Matt Prior broke a thumb while receiving throw-downs from coach Moores, and even Flower was in the wars, badly damaging an Achilles tendon while playing touch rugby before a match at Newlands in Cape Town. But most embarrassing of all, captain Collingwood had been found to have been in a lap dancing club after his team lost to Australia and back in England newly elected ECB chairman Giles Clarke had to face more questions about that than other matters in his first press conference in the role.

Disciplinary matters were still sadly affecting England's preparations when it came to the 2009 Ashes at home. On a trip to Flanders Field in Belgium Bopara forgot his passport and Flintoff missed the team bus after a late night spent drinking. Bopara can be dozy (when recalled to the Test side in 2011 he said he had invested in an iPad to help sort his life out, but then in the same sentence admitted, 'But I've forgotten to charge it up and at the moment it's lying dead in my car').

Flintoff's misdemeanour was more galling. From day one of their regime Strauss and Flower had preached the need for personal responsibility. They had gone to see a conflict-resolution specialist in London immediately after the Pietersen/Moores split, and he had suggested that the team themselves draw up a charter of values. One particular mantra that arose was that 'the team is not a lease car'. In other words it was not to be treated as if it did not matter what sort of condition it was in when you left it. And whether it was intended or not, Flintoff's behaviour went against that, suggesting the sort of cynicism towards the trip that the management had been hoping to avoid, even if this sort of trip was something new to English cricket.

The Australians had first done something similar in 2001, when Steve Waugh's squad went to Gallipoli to visit Australian war graves before the Ashes, and four years later they went to Normandy. Now this was not necessarily Flower's idea – Morris had previously talked with Moores about going to Flanders – but it was certainly something Flower embraced instantly and enthusiastically. As he said afterwards, 'This visit was part of ongoing efforts designed to broaden horizons and learn more about the role of leadership and team ethics.'

It has not always been all about cricket for Flower. I interviewed him once and asked him about the greatest influences on his cricket. He talked about the coaches Zimbabwe had had during his playing days. He especially liked the plain-speaking attitude of John Hampshire, the former Yorkshire and England player. He may have been a little old-school but Flower liked his simple fondness of the basics of the game. So too before him Barry Dudleston, the former Leicestershire and Gloucestershire batsman who, like Hampshire, became an umpire. Flower admired Dave Houghton's tactical and technical expertise, and learnt much from the Australians Carl Rackemann and Geoff Marsh. Unsurprisingly he didn't mention Don Topley, the former Essex seamer, bizarrely chosen as Zimbabwe's coach for the 1992 World Cup, where at Albury Zimbabwe famously beat England, captained by Topley's Essex captain, Graham Gooch. 'I'm going to remind you about this every day next season,' said a joyous Topley afterwards, to which Gooch gave one of the classic cricketing put-downs: 'I'm not sure I'm going to be at too many second-team games this year, Toppers!'

But Flower did reel off a list of other names from Zimbabwe cricket: John Traicos, Andy Pycroft, Kevin Arnott, Malcolm Jarvis and Andy Waller – three lawyers, a gym owner and a farmer. It was not just their cricket that impressed. It was their life balance. They managed to be professional at work and in sport, as well as find time for their families and have some fun too. It would take the farmer Waller two hours to get to practice, and another two to get home afterwards, but he was always there. Jarvis had fought in the war for independence. These were not cosseted cricketers. 'I thought the balance they found was amazing,' Flower said. 'They taught me about the disciplines you need to succeed in sport and life.'

So Flanders was the beginning of that sort of process for England's cricketers, of making them more rounded characters. Broad laid a specially made stone cricket ball at the graveside of former Kent and England left-arm spinner Colin Blythe, who died at the Battle of Passchendaele in 1917, and the players attended the daily service held at the Menin Gate where wreaths were laid by Strauss, Bopara and Alastair Cook before 'The Last Post' was played and singer Sean Ruane delivered a rendition of 'Jerusalem'.

'It brought us closer as a group. It was going to be harder for the Aussies to break us down,' said Strauss afterwards. Was it mere coincidence that in the first Ashes Test in 2009 a new spirit was instantly revealed? Probably not. The Cardiff Test, as the last pair of Anderson and Monty Panesar survived sixty-nine balls and forty minutes to salvage a draw, was the first one of three 'Great Escapes' from England in a year.

It was also the first ever Test at Cardiff. This was obviously surrounded in controversy. The decision in 2006 to award this match to Cardiff rather than Old Trafford or Durham had certainly been a shock. The ECB had introduced a new 'blind bidding' system and Glamorgan had played it cleverly to surprise their rivals, bidding some £3.2 million thanks to £1.2 million from the Welsh Assembly. Lancashire bid some £1.5 million and thought they were home and hosed. They'd been pipped on the inside.

So there was outrage when the result became known. The most withering criticism came from Hampshire chairman Rod Bransgrove, even though his county had pulled out of the bidding (they would host their first Test in 2011, against Sri Lanka). 'Quite clearly the "W" in the ECB is silent, but very powerful,' he said.

I'll admit that I did not agree with Glamorgan's pursuit of Test cricket. I was still captain of the club when it was first mooted. Part of my argument against it was that they would only get Tests against Zimbabwe and Bangladesh. I was proved wrong on that one obviously! But the other part was a worry about too many Test grounds. If every one of the eighteen counties wanted Test matches, then what?

There are now nine Test grounds – Lord's, the Oval, Trent Bridge, Headingley, Old Trafford, Edgbaston, Cardiff, Durham and Southampton – as well as Bristol, which hosts one-day internationals and T20 internationals. It is probably too many. If the blind bidding system did have an upside, apart from providing easy money for the ECB, it did give grounds like Old Trafford a jolt. That ground was in serious need of re-development, which it is now receiving. And at least the bidding system has now been revised so that counties bid for packages of matches with predetermined prices.

Cardiff was the first Test in 2009 because the England management had not wanted to play at Lord's first.

England had not beaten Australia there since 1934, after all. And that was the only occasion in the twenty-seven Tests going back to 1899. That is one woeful record.

So having just avoided defeat in Cardiff – and Collingwood's gutsy 74 was as important as Anderson and Panesar's last stand – and with that sort of history looming over them, England probably did not want any extra distractions. Enter Flintoff with a huge piece of news: he was retiring from Test cricket at the end of the summer. It had emerged that he was still struggling with his knee injury, so the remaining Tests were going to be part of some grand tour of the country, with standing ovations at every turn. Roll up, roll up everyone for the last tour of Freddie's travelling circus.

The decision did not go down well. And not just with me. I've always liked the line given by former Australia fast bowler Carl Rackemann: 'You don't make a statement to let everyone know you're debuting, so why should you have to declare your intention to finish?' Especially these days when cricketers don't really retire; they just go to the IPL, or some such other Twenty20 extravaganza in the sky.

The England management weren't happy either. Plagued by injury, Flintoff had become something of an outsider to the team, rather like Meursault in Albert Camus's *The Stranger*. His closest friends had long departed. He seemed to have little understanding of the strong team ethos being developed under Strauss and Flower. He simply did his own thing.

Above that was the worry that such a decision had a history of backfiring. Both Alec Stewart and Steve Waugh had announced well in advance that they were retiring from inter-national cricket, and it affected them and their teams, even if, of course, they departed to fervid farewells on their home grounds.

In fairness, Flintoff immediately dispelled such concerns with a performance of rare brilliance at Lord's. On the final morning England required five Australian wickets for victory, and bowling ten unchanged overs from the Pavilion End, Flintoff took three of them to end with a five-wicket haul. It was a stunning victory, courtesy of a remarkable spell of bowling, unrelenting in its accuracy and hostility. The people's champion had delivered. Fredmania swept the country as quickly as swine flu did at the time.

How Flintoff revelled in the moment. He had become a highly commercial cricketer, always with an eye for a photo opportunity, always keen to endorse some product or other. For instance he had irked the England management earlier in the summer by turning up at Lord's for the West Indies Test wearing a hooded top bearing the name of his personal sponsor rather than that of the England team, and then sitting on the balcony one along from the England dressing room.

So now for his three wickets we had three wholly photogenic poses, culminating in the bended-knee, arms-spread-wide stance that followed the wicket of Peter Siddle – a picture that has become as famous as Flintoff's consoling of Brett Lee after the 2005 Edgbaston Test.

Unsurprisingly, Flintoff was named man of the match. 'Flintoff's match' some had already christened it by the next morning. Poppycock. Strauss should have been man of the match. The beginning of the match was much more important than the ending. Of course, it was wonderful bowling from Flintoff, but his wickets on that final morning were Brad Haddin, Nathan Hauritz and Siddle. Strauss made 161 on the first day when England desperately needed to make a strong statement after Cardiff.

For some strange reason Strauss is easily maligned and over-looked as England captain. At the end of the 2012 Pakistan series he had still won exactly half of his forty-two Tests. Only Michael Vaughan has won more Tests as captain (twenty-six in fifty-one Tests), and only Vaughan (50.98), Percy Chapman (nine from 17 Tests at a winning percentage of 52.94), Mike

Brearley (eighteen from thirty-one at 58.06), W.G. Grace (eight from thirteen at 61.53) and Douglas Jardine (nine from fifteen at 60.00) of those to have captained ten Tests have a higher winning percentage.

In the West Indies it had been declarations for which he was chastised. Here it was for not enforcing the follow-on. Brearley called it 'pusillanimous'. Attitudes have altered markedly on this over the years. My instinct was always to enforce it. But maybe that was because we never had that many opportunities to do so at Glamorgan. Or maybe it was because my often overriding fear of failure preferred to postpone the moment of judgement (in other words batting) and this was always a good opportunity to do so.

Then there was, of course, the famous Test in Kolkata in 2001 when India, following on 274 behind, sensationally beat Australia by 171 runs thanks to V. V. S. Laxman's 281 and 180 from Rahul Dravid. That deterred a few from doing that again, especially after it seemed that Australia had determined never to enforce again after Mark Taylor had done so against Pakistan in Rawalpindi in 1994 and suffered as Salim Malik made 237.

Sometimes, because of time lost, you have little choice, like at the Oval in 2011 against India, which worked out fine as England won. But generally the welfare of your bowlers must be of primary concern. When Vaughan asked Australia to follow on at Trent Bridge in 2005 Simon Jones had broken down instantly. When Vaughan did the same to South Africa at Lord's in 2008, and the visitors ended up batting for three successive days, Ryan Sidebottom had got injured. When Flintoff was skipper against Sri Lanka at the same venue in 2006, he too had asked his opponents to follow on and had bowled himself into the ground (fifty-one overs in the second innings).

So you could understand Strauss's reluctance here, what with Flintoff's knee and with Anderson suffering an ankle problem. When Australia resumed on the third morning on 156-8, Strauss was of a mind to enforce the follow-on. But the weather was bright and the pitch suddenly looked very flat, as Australia added fifty-nine runs in fourteen overs for those last two wickets. Strauss nipped off the field for an over to speak to Flower, and they agreed to bat. England won the Test. No more needs to be said.

Strauss has grown into an astonishingly good leader. There was a time when he was younger that he was rather too dopey. Among his nicknames were 'Mareman' and 'Muppet'. His occasional absent-mindedness concerned Fletcher a little, I know. But not his batting. Fletcher was waiting around for an ECB meeting one day at Lord's in 2003 when he spotted Strauss batting in the middle. He recognized a Test batsman immediately, with his back-foot technique revealing strong pull and cut shots.

It was something Ed Smith, a schoolboy adversary when Strauss was at Radley and Smith at Tonbridge, had noticed years before and articulated so well in *The Times* after the Ashes triumph of 2010/11. 'When I first met him, at an England Schools trial,' wrote Smith of Strauss, 'he was not the kid in the county tracksuit earmarked for professional greatness. He just clipped the ball deftly off the back foot, a rare skill for a schoolboy, and let others big-note about county contracts and bat deals. But when we played against each other at school, I was clear about one thing: he batted better against better bowlers. My school team-mates even mocked me for suggesting that he was the best player we played against. In time, he left the flat-track bullies behind.'

So Strauss has gradually left his captaincy critics behind. He just keeps making good decisions. Some view many of them as conservative, but he is not showy as a person, cricketer or captain (giving Swann the new ball in grey, swinging conditions at Lord's against the West Indies in 2009 is the only example I can recall of him trying to be a little too clever).

'The thing about Strauss is that he is so calm and always says the right thing,' said Swann of his captain after the 2011 India Test series. And he is so right. Strauss is a highly impressive statesman, as well as the England cricket captain. He showed it so obviously during the difficult summer of 2010 when the allegations of corruption among the Pakistan team emerged, most especially when the Pakistan Cricket Board chairman Ijaz Butt then claimed in a ridiculous act of retaliation that England had deliberately lost the third one-day international at the Oval.

England very nearly did not play the fourth ODI in protest. The night before the match they were locked in talks until the early hours at London's Landmark Hotel. Strauss, quite rightly, was extremely angry. Initially, like most of his team, he did not want to play the next day. But eventually he realized that the show simply had to go on. Rather than speak to the media – there was no time really – he insisted on a carefully worded statement. It was classic Strauss:

> We would like to express our surprise, dismay and outrage at the comments made by Mr Butt yesterday. We are deeply concerned and disappointed that our integrity as cricketers has been brought into question. We refute these allegations completely and will be working closely with the ECB to explore all legal options open to us. Under the circumstances, we have strong misgivings about continuing to play the last two games of the current series and urge the Pakistani team and management to distance themselves from Mr Butt's allegations. We do, however, recognize our responsibilities to the game of cricket – and in particular to the cricket-loving public in this country – and will therefore endeavour to fulfil these fixtures to the best of our ability.

Strauss was no less impressive on the eve of the third Test against India in 2011 when riots were sweeping the land. 'I think this is an opportunity for cricket to put a feel-good factor into the newspapers and show that not everything's bad at the moment,' he said. 'Clearly it's not our proudest moment as a country. When you watch those things on the TV it's horrific. All of us agree on that and it's very disappointing to see these things happen. But they haven't affected our preparations for this Test match.'

Strauss can be flustered, though. He does not enjoy being rushed. The fourth Test at Headingley in 2009 was an example of that. The third Test at Edgbaston had been ruined by rain, and was only notable for the absence of Pietersen, whose troublesome Achilles tendon required an operation after Lord's. In the early hours of the first morning of the next Test at Headingley – at 4.45 a.m. to be precise – a fire alarm had gone off at the England team hotel, the Radisson. Then during warm-ups Prior had suffered a back spasm, and it was uncertain whether he would play. Collingwood was suddenly busily brushing up on his wicketkeeping skills when team masseur Mark Saxby was hit flush on the forehead by a stray cricket ball and carried off. It was chaos.

Australia graciously agreed that the toss be put back by ten minutes, by which time England had decided to take a gamble on Prior. It was a toss Strauss did not really want to win. It was drizzling when the players had had their early morning call, but the pitch was dry with the sun beginning to show its head. But, as happens on such occasions, he did win it. He decided to bat, and then had to conduct the various media interviews (too many in my opinion) before going off to strap on his pads.

He should have been out first ball, lbw to Ben Hilfenhaus, but was reprieved. Clearly his mental state was scrambled, and he survived only sixteen further balls before edging Siddle to slip. His team were soon all out for 102 as the ball darted around, and defeat (eventually by an innings and 80 runs) was inevitable once that had happened. It was Strauss's worst morning as England captain.

The repercussions were not as calamitous, but Strauss was similarly distracted on the opening morning of the 2010/11 Ashes Down Under. There he had won the toss and elected to bat, but had been thrown by the national anthems taking place between that and the start of play. That had happened at Cardiff in 2009 (with the Welsh national anthem played as well as 'God Save the Queen' and 'Advance Australia Fair', as well as both teams being presented to Rhodri Morgan, the first minister of Wales), and England had not batted too well. But in Brisbane it had a greater effect. Strauss admitted to being too emotional, and was out third ball.

It is easy to overlook the difficulties faced by the skipper in such circumstances. The toss usually takes place half an hour before the start of play. Captains who open the batting have to be able to compartmentalize swiftly and easily. Often as a county captain, say, you have to tell a player that he has been omitted from the final eleven. He can, of course, be disgruntled. He may even want to argue with you over it. I remember on a couple of occasions as Glamorgan skipper telling the coach, John Derrick, 'John, please go and tell so-and-so he's not playing. He's going to be mightily pissed off, but just tell him that I'll speak to him later.' But still out of the corner of my eye I'd be spying on that conversation and watching for the reaction. And then I'd try to think about batting. Not easy.

Strauss had his own selection problems at Headingley even before Prior's late injury scare. The day before, he and Flower had decided to omit Flintoff on fitness grounds. He was clearly struggling at nets the day before the game. It was decided to rest him and try to get him fit for the final Test at the Oval. Flintoff did not argue.

But then Andrew 'Chubby' Chandler, his agent, caused a fuss in an interview with *The Times*' Atherton. 'I've seen a few disappointed sportsmen over the last couple of months,' said Chandler, a former European Tour golfer, who set up International Sports Management Limited in 1989 to look after golfers mainly, 'but I've never seen anybody as low as Flintoff on Thursday night [the night before the Test] when he was told he would not be selected. He told them he was fit enough to get through, that he felt no different to how he felt at Edgbaston [where the previous Test was played] and that he could get through and do his bit. They didn't want him. He was prepared to do whatever it takes, was prepared to put whatever needed to be put into his knee. What they didn't take into account during Thursday's practice was that there was no adrenalin. That was why he looked as though he was struggling so much. His presence would certainly have lifted the crowd and the team, because without him they don't have much inspiration.'

Agents, eh? Even Flintoff admitted later, 'The article didn't do me any favours.' Too right it didn't. Flower was very quickly on the phone to Flintoff, demanding to know what on earth was going on. Likewise Strauss phoned Chandler. The England captain felt that quite a lot of Chandler's comments were inaccurate. 'We had more important things to worry about, but I felt it was important I said something to him rather than just let it lie,' said Strauss.

It is true that Chandler and his employee, the former Lancashire and England batsman Neil Fairbrother, did help Flintoff in his early years by sitting him down and spelling out some home truths about the sacrifices required to become and remain an international cricketer. And in general agents have helped international cricketers earn the sort of money they deserve (I'm not sure that is the case in county cricket, where, in my opinion, wages have spiralled out of line with what a domestic cricketer actually merits, but that is another matter). But it should also be remembered that Chandler is from a golfing background. Golf is an individual sport. Cricket is an individual sport played in a team environment. They are two very different things.

Later in 2009 the announcement came on Flintoff's own website that he had turned down the ECB's offer of an incremental central contract so that he could supposedly travel the world playing in Twenty20 tournaments, and, if he felt like it, play for England in one-day internationals and T20s sometimes. He was going 'freelance', so it was said. Much was made of it, but in truth it was a non-story given unnecessary legs by what I called his 'concomitant cacophony'. Not least because Flintoff's knee never allowed him to play again after the final Test at the Oval that summer.

There is always sadness when a player's career is cut short like that, and Flintoff's case should be no different. He was an outstanding cricketer who provided some great moments and put in some great performances. He was also at times a great bloke, but celebrity changed him, as it might many of us. The England team that was to become number one in the world in 2011 was not sad to see him go. It made their absolute insistence on the team ethic so much easier. It made their insistence on supreme levels of fitness easier. With Flintoff still there, I doubt they would have been able to ignore Samit Patel purely on the grounds of sloth.

No one is irreplaceable. But it might have seemed so when England were being thrashed at Headingley without Flintoff. The lesson learnt, however, apart from ensuring Strauss is not rushed before batting, was that six batsmen must always play, despite the continuing claims of some of the game's romantics. England, with Broad at number seven, were exposed. And Flower and Strauss were spooked by the experience. Flintoff played at the Oval but thereafter until they became the world's number one team they played six specialist batsmen, a wicket-keeper and four bowlers in all of their twenty-four Tests bar one, the second Test against Bangladesh in Dhaka in March 2010, where they played two spinners. And Strauss was not actually captain then: Cook was deputizing while Strauss rested. That is a different matter anyway, having to fit in two spinners on turning pitches.

The Sunday of that Headingley Test was the last day, as England were hammered after some frolicsome, if vain, batting from Swann and Broad. It was also an interesting day in my journalistic career. 'Leaked dossier shows what the Australian team really think of England team' screamed the headline in the *Sunday Telegraph*. I suppose it could be said I had a 'scoop', even if it didn't feel like it. Indeed when I first saw the dossier that had been handed to me, I didn't think much of it. 'I'm not sure there's much in there,' I told Peter Mitchell, my sports editor. I was being very naive. In general I'd like to think I have a decent nose (yes, a big nose even) for a news story, certainly more so than some of my cricketer-turned-journalist colleagues, who often consider it stooping a little too low to become involved in such matters. But what I was forgetting here was the thrill for members of the public of being on the inside, however fleetingly; of suddenly being privy to thoughts and observations that are usually out of their reach. Every fan craves to be inside the dressing room.

I'll admit that when I first received a phone call about the dossier (that's what it was called by me and my paper, but in truth it was little more than some random thoughts) written by Justin Langer, then still at Somerset and now Australia's batting coach, I wrestled hard with my conscience. Yes, journalism is regarded as a low art, and in the wake of the phone hacking scandals its reputation has only fallen further, but it is not all about exposure. Most of us have a barrelful of stories we would never dream of publishing. Sources and contacts need to be kept, as well as protected.

I'd interviewed Langer down at Taunton earlier in the season.

He'd been engaging and interesting. But, after Mitchell had come back to me in a state of great excitement upon seeing the evidence, it seemed too good an opportunity to miss. After all, how the Australians had rejoiced and mocked when England's bowling plans had been leaked in Melbourne during the 2006/07 series.

What the hell . . .

Langer had emailed his thoughts to Australia coach Tim Nielsen, and Nielsen had printed the following off and given a copy to every member of his squad before the first Test in Cardiff. This was reproduced in full in the *Sunday Telegraph*:

Boys

Here a few thoughts from Justin Langer who captains Somerset and I have been in contact with in regard to the English squad and conditions. Have a read and use as you will

- the dukes ball usually takes a few overs to swing so don't get impatient with it. Sometimes you have to wait until the lacquer wears off before it starts to swing. England players work very hard on shining the ball after the lacquer is gone. They use Murray mints religiously to get it to shine up. Be aware of this from an opposition point of view but also from your point know the ball will shine up nicely if you work hard on it.

- English cricketers are great front runners. Because of the way they are programmed they will be up when things are going well but they will taper off very quickly if you wear them down in all apartments. Because they play so much cricket, as soon as it gets a bit hard you just have to watch their body language and see how flat and lazy they get. You can show this up by running hard between the wickets and pressurizing them in the field. They are the best in world of tapering off very quickly when things go a bit flat for them. This is also a time when most of them make all sorts of excuses and start looking around to point the finger at everyone else – it is a classic English trait from my experience.

- English players rarely believe in themselves. Many of them will stare a lot and chat a lot but this is very shallow and again will last as long as the pressure is back on them. They will retreat very quickly. Aggressive batting, running and body language will soon have them staring at their bootlaces rather in the eyes of their opponent – it is just how they are built. They like being friendly and 'matey' because it makes them feel comfortable. In essence this is maybe the key to the whole English psyche – they love being comfortable. Take them out of their comfort zone and they don't like it for a second. This can be done by aggressive bowling, confident body language and putting them back under the pump but not being too friendly with them – a good lesson learned from 2005 to 2007 series.

- Andrew Strauss is a very solid character and excellent bloke. His weakness is possibly his conservative approach. He will tend to take the safer options in most cases. He is batting well. He has played quite aggressively recently but can be cramped up just outside the off stump. He plays well through the offside, particularly off the back foot.

- Alistair Cook doesn't move his right leg towards the ball. Get him cover driving and he won't score and will also look vulnerable in the slips and gully position. He has a good all round game and very good temperament but good patient bowling full outside the off stump should bring him unstuck.

- Ravi Bopara is a good player. I have seen him caught at third man a couple of times. This might be tough at Cardiff but third man and high bouncers could be an attacking position. He will have a go at the cut and pull shots so third man and two men back behind square leg could bring him undone. He is a bit of a street fighter who is sure to wind the boys up by his strutting around but he is a respectful young guy who thrives on the chat and talk. I would leave him alone and just bowl at him rather than letting our egos take away our focus. I think you know what I mean here.

- Anderson is hugely improved and has gained a yard and is bowling well. He is swing the ball well but again can be a bit of a pussy if he is worn down. He is a classic as in my second point. Things have been going well for him so he is happy and confident but I am convinced he can be worn down and his body language could be detrimental to them if we get on top of him early.

- Swann is another one who is sure to wind us up with his ego and body language. I am not sure he likes short pitched bowling. He goes hard with the bat but will give lots of chances as he hits the ball in the air a lot. His bowling is on a par with N. Hauritz and he takes a lot of his wickets with the balls that don't spin much especially to the left handers coming back in and getting bowled or lbws

- Another point to be aware of especially for the younger guys is that the Cardiff crowd is feral and they will be brutal on you guys. They are very aggressive and it is something the boys should be aware of before the event. Awareness is the key. But they are a tough crowd. Also it might be worth the batsmen getting a good feel for the place leading up to the game because the changing rooms are a long way from the ground so it feels like you are miles away from the action. A small consideration but I know you will have plenty of time to adapt to this.

- Matt Prior – We played him a few weeks ago and I would definitely bowl wide to him. He loves to score and will go hard. A deeper point can be a catching position as can two deeper gully position. He scores a lot of runs to thirds man. He gets very very low in his stance. The key is he wants to score runs quickly and look good. He can be dangerous because he is a talented stroke player. Stop him scoring boundaries, even employing a point or deep cover boundary fielder, like Michael Vaughan did so well against us in 2005, and he will definitely give you plenty of chances. I would chip away at him about his wicket keeping and the pressure he is under to perform with the gloves on. I am not sure he actually likes keeping that much and from all accounts he has a massive ego so I would be reminding him about how his keeping could see him out of the team. I would definitely work his ego.

- Flintoff – for the batsmen who haven't faced him it takes time to get used to his pace and bounce. He has to be worn down and as we both know is the key to their attack with James Anderson.

I've not seen or spoken to Langer since. He was 'shattered' apparently. In his BBC online column he wrote this:

> Having spoken to Tim on Sunday night, he was upset and sadly apologetic that our written conversation had been exposed. Because of this, I am naturally disappointed that some of my personal and private thoughts to a close friend of mine in Tim Nielsen have reached the public domain. He had copied my thoughts down and given them out to a few of the less experienced members of the team before the Cardiff Test. Obviously one of the team left these lying around and, as they say, the rest is history. What interests me is why it has taken so long for them to come out? Sure there is journalistic liberty, but if my private opinion was so relevant, why wait until England had lost a Test match? Maybe that says something about the ruthless nature of the press in this country.
>
> From Taunton,
> JL

Well, the truth, JL, is that I did not receive the 'dossier' until the Wednesday before the Headingley Test. It was published at the first available opportunity in the *Sunday Telegraph*. That it came out on the morning when England were facing a heavy defeat was a complete coincidence.

For England it must have seemed like a kick to a beaten body, although Flower never complained to me about it. He just did what he does so well: he planned how to get England out of the hole into which they'd fallen. The series stood at 1–1 with just the Oval Test to come. He did not want the players to dwell too much on their defeat, so instead of allowing them to go home immediately he called a team meeting at the hotel that evening. As ever it was frank. It was pretty obvious what had happened, aside from selection and the chaos before the toss: the players had got ahead of themselves. They had been thinking about winning the Ashes rather than how they might go about winning the Ashes. It was the classic cliché beloved of the sports psychologist: they had been focusing on the outcome, not the process. Truths were told, and they moved on to the Oval.

Flintoff duly returned to the side, but Bopara was dropped. He had endured a difficult summer at number three. As well as those three consecutive centuries, he'd also scored three ducks in succession earlier in his career. The management considered him 'mentally shot', and, after a lengthy selection meeting at Trent Bridge where Warwickshire were playing Nottinghamshire in a county championship match (with the visitors' director of cricket and England selector Ashley Giles therefore in situ) on the Friday before the Test, selected Jonathan Trott instead.

These days there is usually more secrecy surrounding England selection than an SAS mission, but this was an exception. The following morning most of the newspapers confidently named the squad ahead of Sunday's announcement. There had been a leak. Or rather someone's bins had been rummaged. At Trent Bridge a small group of journalists had decided to visit the room used for selection long after the selectors had gone. What did they find in the waste paper bin? The squad on a piece of scrunched-up paper! It was careless.

With Trott's promotion, another South African was in the England cricket team. It naturally caused considerable comment, even if Trott had already played (in Twenty20s) in 2007. It prompted that superb writer Peter Roebuck, the former Somerset captain who had become very much an Australian before tragically taking his own life in South Africa in November 2011, to dub the England side 'Durham and the Dominions'. Yes, appearing from Durham in this series were Collingwood, Onions and Harmison.

But the South African point can be stretched. Strauss

was born there, but left at the age of six, spending eighteen months in Melbourne before settling in England. He went to Caldicott Preparatory School, Radley College and Durham University. That is a very English upbringing. Little wonder that another of his nicknames to add to those I mentioned earlier is 'Lord Brocket' (after the accent of the cocky aristo-crat who came into the public consciousness around 2004 in the TV programme *I'm a Celebrity . . . Get Me Out of Here!* rather than his personality). Prior's family came from Johannesburg to England when he was eleven. He went to Brighton College.

Trott and Pietersen spent a good deal of time in county cricket before appearing for England. Trott had played for Warwickshire's seconds as long before as 2002, making 245 against Somerset on debut, as it happened. Pietersen too had played one match for Warwickshire's seconds in 2000 (scoring 92), while he was playing that season for Cannock in the Birmingham League, but Warwickshire were primarily after an off-spinner to replace Neil Smith, and so did not sign him. Mistake! Nottinghamshire instead signed him and he played four seasons for them before moving to Hampshire in the winter of 2004/05 (although he was going to join Somerset and indeed drove around for some of that winter in one of their sponsored cars). Controversy stalked his every move, mind. At the end of the 2003 season Notts' captain Jason Gallian had thrown Pietersen's kit off the Trent Bridge balcony after it became apparent Pietersen wanted to leave. And in 2010 Pietersen left Hampshire, and struggled to find a county before Surrey took him, initially on loan before eventually signing him permanently.

The Australians were still at it in 2011 when they commissioned a report, based squarely on the Schofield Report of four years earlier, into the failures of their team. When making public its recommendations, Don Argus, like Schofield a non-cricketing man placed in charge of it, joked, 'I was thinking of putting in a recommendation that we put in a Zimbabwean coach and get four South Africans into the side.' He actually forgot that England had an Irishman, Eoin Morgan, too – he might have been able to make an even better rib-tickler.

One's place of birth can, of course, be misleading. If a man is born in a stable it doesn't make him a horse, and all that. Just look at some of these England captains and their birthplaces: Gubby Allen (Australia), Freddie Brown (Peru), Donald Carr (Germany), Colin Cowdrey (India), Ted Dexter (Italy), Tony Greig and Allan Lamb (South Africa), Nasser Hussain (India). Or how about the England side that played in New Zealand in 1992 containing seven players born outside the United Kingdom: Graeme Hick (Rhodesia), Robin Smith and Lamb (both South Africa), Derek Pringle (Kenya), Chris Lewis (Guyana), Dermot Reeve (Hong Kong) and Phil DeFreitas (Dominica)?

When selected Trott was, just like Pietersen, not a popular figure on the county circuit. He was perceived to be stroppy and selfish. And, of course, South African. Very much South African according to Michael Vaughan, who wrote in his auto-biography, 'It was a sad day for English cricket when on my last day against South Africa [at Edgbaston in 2008] I saw Jonathan Trott celebrating with South Africa, when the week before he had been our 12th man at Headingley. I was going into the press conference and I saw him patting them on the back. It hit home what English cricket has become like.'

It was all a misunderstanding, though, according to Trott. 'We were standing between the changing rooms when both teams were on the field at the end,' he said. 'I've known Paul Harris [South Africa's spinner in that game] since I was sixteen and we played together at Warwickshire. I just said something like "Cheers, well done on your victory".'

I can believe it was a misunderstanding. Trott is easily

misunderstood, both as a person and as a cricketer. At the beginning of his international career I fired some arrows in his direction, just as I had with Pietersen. But Trott won me over too. It seemed at first that his whole mien was based around irritation, from his time-consuming and obsessive pre-delivery rituals to his one-paced one-day batting. But the truth is much simpler. Yes, through marriage (to Abi, Warwickshire's press officer and the granddaughter of Tom Dollery, the county's first professional captain) and fatherhood he has mellowed as a character, and therefore improved as a cricketer.

Essentially, though, Trott just loves batting. And he bats extraordinarily well. He is easily maligned because he is old-fashioned, even down to his boots and his pads. As I once wrote, 'The former look heavy and outdated, the latter rather wide and as if they should be fastened by buckles rather than Velcro.' In an age fixated with Twenty20's pyrotechnics, he is a blocker. He still plays one-day innings that divide opinion sharply. Indeed in February 2010 he played a Twenty20 innings (39 from fifty-one balls) against Pakistan in Dubai that cost him his place in that format of the game, receiving a flea in the ear from Flower for his sins. But he scores runs. He keeps scoring runs.

The fuss over Pietersen and Trott was only exacerbated early in 2011 when Craig Kieswetter, who like Trott had played for South Africa Under 19s, was selected for England's shorter-form squads almost as soon as he had finished the requisite qualification period. Even National Selector Geoff Miller was moved to say on the issue of too many South Africans, 'Yes, we have to be careful.' Others, like Jade Dernbach and Stuart Meaker, have followed.

But it is no new issue. In any sport. In 1936, for instance, Great Britain won ice hockey gold in the Winter Olympics in Germany; of their squad of thirteen, nine had grown up in

Canada. Only one was born in Canada, but eleven had previously played there. Imagine that happening now.

In cricket the South African influence began as a very different issue with the late Basil D'Oliveira, who was considered a 'coloured' under the apartheid regime and therefore barred from first-class cricket, making his England debut in 1966. He was followed by Tony Greig (and it is easily forgotten that his brother Ian, also born in Queenstown in Cape Province, played two Tests for England), the Smith brothers Robin and Chris, and Allan Lamb, all of whom made their official Test debuts for England while South Africa was excluded from international cricket.

Now, with that argument redundant since South Africa's readmission to international cricket in 1991, the reasons for moving are very different. Pietersen made it very clear that he came to England because of the quotas imposed upon provincial cricket. Trott just felt he might not make it in South Africa. Indeed when he made his debut, South Africa coach Mickey Arthur made it very clear that he would not make South Africa's team, but did voice some frustration at Trott's defection, conceding he might be 'there or there-abouts' in national selection. Arthur was rather more interested in Kieswetter, phoning the Somerset wicket-keeper during the Champions League in India in 2009. As Kieswetter once told me, 'He [Arthur] wanted to know what my plans were. He said he could get me into one of the franchise teams, as they were looking at a replacement for [Mark] Boucher. I just told him I wanted to play for England. I didn't want to be rude. I just had to say no thank you.'

Kieswetter has a Scottish mother and a British passport. His family used to visit the United Kingdom for a couple of months each year. After passing his 'matric' at the Diocesan College (Bishops), Cape Town, Kieswetter decided he wanted to come to England. He spent a term and a half at Millfield

School, trialling at Kent before Somerset signed him. In 2011 I asked him about his 'Englishness' (it should have been 'Scottishness' really). 'For five years I've answered those questions and I think there comes a time when I'd rather people write about my cricket,' he retorted sharply. He had a point.

Do we, in these days of globalization, mass immigration and widespread multiculturalism, get a little too vexed about this matter? Consider the comments of John Woodcock, the cricket correspondent of *The Times* from 1954 to 1988, on Tony Greig: 'What has to be remembered is that Greig is English not by birth or upbringing, but only adoption, which is not the same as being English through and through.' And Vaughan, later in his autobiography, discussing Trott's century at the Oval, wrote, 'I suppose you could wish he was a bit more English.'

For the associated problems you need look no further than the example of when England wanted a team song in 2005. One of the management asked a friend to come up with some lyrics reflecting what it meant to play for England. This is what he initially provided:

> Our Army's been assembled,
> From Durham down to Kent.
> A joining of all counties,
> To Lord's we have been sent.
> To play for these three Lions,
> The rose on our shoulder too,
> To play for the glory
> Of the mighty 'Navy Blue'.

> No matter where we travel,
> From London round to Perth,
> We take great pride in playing

> For the country of our birth.
> Our aim is for her triumph,
> To glorify her name,
> To show all those who face us
> That cricket's England's game!

Somewhat hastily the first half of the second verse had to be changed to:

> With the Union Jack before us,
> Around the world we roam,
> Taking pride in playing
> For the country we call home.

I think the song was changed a bit more too, and there is now a very different song whose identity is closely guarded by the current squad. But this does rather stress the modern-day difficulties of nationality.

It is a complicated business, as I know myself, having once seriously considered playing for Zimbabwe. And I might have played all my years of professional cricket in Wales for Glamorgan, and indeed still live there, but I am fiercely proud of being English. So when I was asked to captain Wales against England in 2002 (a match we won by eight wickets, as it happened) I only did so when it was confirmed that it was an unofficial fixture. The presence of Jacques Kallis in the Wales side (he had played for Glamorgan in 1999) did rather give that game away, mind.

I also remember being a little bemused in 1997 when I went on an England training camp to Lanzarote and the one-day skipper at the time, Adam Hollioake, could not join us immediately because of visa problems concerning his Australian passport. I've recorded my thoughts already on Kolpaks, but, as I said then, rules are rules regarding international eligibility.

Cricket's are among the tightest. For instance the residency qualification to play cricket for England is four consecutive years, with at least 210 consecutive days in each of those years. By contrast for the England rugby union team it is just thirty-six consecutive months, and if you've got an England-born grandparent, you're straight in, which doesn't apply in cricket, even if a parent is England-born – presumably a reason why, when team manager Martin Johnson named his forty-five-man pre-World Cup squad in 2011, there were thirteen players born overseas in it.

As I write, the frenzy surrounding London 2012 is building. So too is the subject of what the *Daily Mail* has termed the 'Plastic Brits', athletes conveniently announcing themselves as 'British' just in time for the Olympics. Like Shana Cox, a 400m runner born and raised in the United States; or Shara Proctor, a long jumper from Anguilla; or the sprinter Tiffany Ofili-Porter, born and raised in the US to a British mother and Nigerian father. 'I've always felt I was British, American and Nigerian,' she said. 'I'm all three.'

Now that I do disagree with strongly. It is why it is good that rugby union, since the infamous 'Grannygate' scandal involving the Kiwis Shane Howarth and Brett Sinkinson, who played for Wales having falsely claimed they had Welsh grandparents, tightened its rules and deemed that you cannot play for two countries.

Technically you can still do that in cricket, but only fourteen players have ever done it in Test cricket, the first of them being Billy Midwinter, who appeared for both Australia and England, and with whom, by coincidence, I share the distinction of being the only international cricketers born in the Forest of Dean (Midwinter was born in St Briavels). Kepler Wessels was the last of those fourteen, playing for Australia and his homeland of South Africa once they were readmitted. Before him John Traicos (born in Egypt) had played for South Africa in 1970 and then Zimbabwe when they were admitted to Test cricket in 1992. In one-day internationals six players have represented two countries: Wessels, Clayton Lambert (West Indies and USA), Anderson Cummins (West Indies and Canada), Dougie Brown (England and Scotland), Ed Joyce (England and Ireland) and Eoin Morgan (Ireland and England). And in T20 internationals Dirk Nannes stands alone in this two-country representation, having represented the Netherlands and Australia.

I'll be surprised if we see another cricketer play for two countries in Tests. And I'll be even more surprised if this issue ever ceases. What fascinates me is where these players go once their playing days are finished. Lamb stayed in England, Robin Smith is now in Australia, and in 2011 Graeme Hick was planning to emigrate to Australia.

Wherever Trott goes, he will recall his debut fondly. It was a stunning entrance to Test cricket, in trying circumstances too: England's biggest Test match since four years previously when they'd reached the Oval 2–1 up with the Australians requiring a win to draw the series and retain the urn they'd had (metaphorically anyway) since 1989.

When the Australian observers weren't concerned about nationality, they were complaining about the Oval pitch. England had 'cooked the books', according to Roebuck. In other words they'd prepared a pitch to suit them. And so what? There is nothing wrong with home sides preparing pitches to suit. It was exactly what England did against India in 2011, and good on them. For too long England had been far too accommodating to its cricketing visitors. It used to irk Fletcher no end.

A draw was of no use to England. They had to win. So they requested a pitch resembling on day one the sort of wear associated with day three. They got what they wanted, with groundsman Bill Gordon receiving a standing ovation at the end-of-season dinner of the Cricket Writers' Club. It certainly began dry and spun like a top, so much so that England must have considered including a second spinner, Panesar, who was in their squad.

England were, though, grateful that they won the toss, and even more so that Australia made the unfathomable decision to omit their spinner Nathan Hauritz. Admittedly, Hauritz had not played in the victory at Headingley, but that was understandable. This was not. Swann took eight wickets in the match, including the final one of Mike Hussey, caught at short leg by Cook, on the fourth afternoon for England to win by 197 runs. For a long time afterwards the Australians were muttering darkly about what they called 'Spingate', and about the real reasons why Hauritz did not feature. It was even suggested that Hauritz, with his reticent body language, did not fancy playing.

One man who did fancy it was Stuart Broad. On the second afternoon he bowled the spell that turned the game on its head, announcing the arrival of a champion cricketer. It was supposed to be Flintoff's match, his fond farewell, but, in the general manner of these things, his was a muted exit, save for running out Ponting with a direct hit on the last day. Instead Broad took 5-37 in twelve overs of snorting hostility, combining swing and seam with a wonderfully naked spirit. It was an uplifting passage of play, forever etched into Ashes folklore. Once Australia were dismissed for just 160, and England held a first-innings lead of 172, there was no way back for the visitors. England had regained the Ashes.

It had been a curious series, though. Australia's batsmen scored eight centuries to England's two, and three Australians, Hilfenhaus, Siddle and Mitchell Johnson, stood at the top of the leading wicket-takers in the series. But England had won more of the big moments, as epitomized by Broad's spell at the Oval. You don't win the Ashes by luck. Five Tests is too many for a fluke.

But there was no open-top bus parade. And so there shouldn't have been. Strauss had been correct in saying earlier in the series that Australia had lost their 'aura'. They had. They might have begun the series ranked number one, but by the end they had slipped to number four. England began at number five, and finished there.

There was still work to be done.

11

Petals and the Weed

I should really have been thinking of the threat of spin in Asia, but instead the main question in my mind when England became the world's number one team in 2011: how would they fare against South Africa? Especially away from home if such a series had been scheduled. They'd been there in the winter of 2009/10 and drawn 1–1, with two more 'Great Escapes' beginning with 'C', at Centurion and Cape Town, to add to Cardiff in the 2009 Ashes.

At the time, though, this was actually an achievement. South Africa were number one at the start of the tour. Andrew Strauss reckoned the result to be every bit as impressive as the Ashes victory that preceded it.

Not that it showed so immediately in the grand plan. The plan to reach number one, that is. Before the tour at a meeting at Loughborough Nathan 'Numbers' Leamon, the team analyst, had gone through in great detail what was required to reach that summit. It must have been quite daunting for many of the players, not least because of the potential arduousness of Leamon's route.

As Andy Flower said at the time, 'One of the ECB's stated goals is for us to become number one and I wanted to get some idea of the task. So I asked our stats people to work out what it would take for us to get there. It was an interesting answer. Even if we win every single Test match over the next eighteen months we might still not be number one – and that's not just winning every series but every match. But I don't find that dispiriting in the least. We start by closing the gap on number four – that's our first task. We have huge scope to improve but we'd better remember exactly where we are – and that's number five in the world Test ratings. And the gap between us and number four [Australia] is huge. We're eleven points behind them.'

They were still eleven points behind Australia by the end of the series, but Australia had by then moved up to third and Sri Lanka in fourth were only seven points ahead of England. So some progress had been made.

But the ICC's rankings system is, by necessity, rather complicated. As we saw at the beginning of this book, it was once left to *Wisden* to rank the Test-playing countries, as initiated by then editor Matthew Engel in 1997. As he explained upon its introduction, 'The Wisden Championship has the advantages of simplicity, practicality – and a working model. The proposal is that each country should agree to play the other eight in at least one Test – home and away – every four years, the existing cycle for the traditional confrontations such as England v Australia. A handful of extra Tests would be needed on top of current schedules. Each series of whatever length – counting a one-off game as a series – would be worth the same: two points for winning the series, one for drawing and none for losing. The competition would be continuous, like the world ranking systems in golf and tennis, but every time a series was contested it would replace the corresponding one in the table.'

It was all admirable stuff, but it eventually encountered difficulties. In early 2003 South Africa went top of the rankings after beating Pakistan in a home series. But to everyone in world cricket it was clear that Australia were the best team by a distance, having beaten South Africa both home and away in their most recent encounters. The problem was that South Africa had played, and obviously beaten, Bangladesh and Zimbabwe in recent times, but Australia hadn't.

Change was required. So the ICC decided to adopt a system created by David Kendix, an English actuary, scorer and cricket statistician. It is a model based on the concept of a batting average, using results over the previous three or four years, with more relevance given to more recent results, but just as importantly it awards points on the strength of the opposition.

Even now it has its critics. I was one when I studied how India had reached number one status before being toppled by England in 2011. They had done most of their winning at home. And this was before England went top without winning in Asia. I contacted Kendix, and in fairness, his emailed response made sense:

There is no obvious reward that should be attached to an away win; some teams have broadly similar records home and away, others are starkly different. Also the contrast between home and away varies by fixture, so SL v India and NZ v Eng may have much less of a home advantage than say SL v Eng and NZ v India.

I don't see any problem in a team being Number 1 without beating anyone of note away from home. Being Number 1 means having a better recent record than everyone else. It doesn't necessarily mean having shown dominance in all conditions against all opponents. It just happens that during the prolonged periods of West Indian and then Australian leadership, they did indeed demonstrate that dominance, which is why they tended to lead the ratings by such large margins. Indeed, almost by definition, when the battle for Number 1 is interesting, with two or three teams closely bunched, you will not have one side who has shown a clear supremacy over the others. In a closely fought football league season, you may well have the champions who lost their away fixtures to the teams who finished 2nd, 3rd and 4th, but without it being suggested that their 1st place was in some way less worthy.

Of course, there is a similar rankings table for one-day internationals. Indeed the ICC had been using Kendix's model for ODIs since 2002. When that had begun England were sixth, and they were still sixth in September 2009 after a 6–1 drubbing at home from Australia. As of early 2012, they have never been higher than third, and have been as low as eighth. Flower had seen enough, though. It was time to make some serious alterations. England's batsmen had to be aggressive, their bowlers had to be more accurate, and their fielding had to be sharper.

Simple commands, really. But Flower wanted his batsmen to be really aggressive, his bowlers to be really accurate and his fielders really sharp. And as the start of a plan it worked pretty well. England reached the semi-final of the Champions Trophy in South Africa and then beat the hosts 2–1 in the subsequent one-day series. An important marker was put down in the dropping of Owais Shah after the Champions Trophy. He probably would have been dropped for that tournament, but ICC regulations stipulated the early announcement of squads. Shah did make 98 off eighty-nine balls when South Africa were beaten by 22 runs at Centurion, but minds had already been made up. After the Trophy semi-final against Australia he never played for England again.

I quite like Shah. He was a smiling, chirpy youngster on the England A tour I went on to Kenya and Sri Lanka in 1997/98, and it was obvious that he was a hugely talented batsman. But he is also a poor fielder (although he has competent hands at slip) and an even poorer athlete. He does tend to get run out rather often. He can be a moaner, often blaming somebody else, and not producing his best until he really needs to. Put simply, it seems to me that he is not the type of character Flower wanted in his set-up.

This period of one-day matches was also when it became clear that England possessed a seriously formidable bowling attack. They obeyed Flower's words, and more. Stuart Broad and Tim Bresnan were superb, but it was James Anderson who impressed most. This was the moment when it emerged that here was a truly world-class bowler. His 5-23 in a canter of a victory at Port Elizabeth were, and still are, his best ODI figures.

Anderson had been in the international game a long time by this stage (one-day debut in Australia in 2002, Test debut against Zimbabwe at Lord's in 2003), but, as can happen with genuine swing bowlers, his returns were infuriatingly inconsistent. It is a fiendishly difficult trade, which requires the most sensitive of treatments because the bowler's main weapon is at the mercy of a phenomenon that nobody wholly understands. Many and varied are the theories about swing bowling. The balls, the shine, the sweets used (illegally) to produce that shine, the overhead conditions, the new stands at certain grounds, a ground's water-table, its proximity to the sea when the tide is in, the bowler's action, the bowler's wrist position, and, of course, the position of the moon. OK, I might be exaggerating a little on the last point, but the others are all factors one day, and complete non-sequiturs the next. The truth is that some days the cricket ball swings, some days it doesn't.

Sometimes we writers pen a piece we later rue. And probably my worst column piece since taking over from Mike Atherton at the *Sunday Telegraph* concerned Anderson and his performance at Trent Bridge against New Zealand in 2008. But the worst thing is that I keep getting reminded of that particular piece. Just as a cricketer always insists he does not read the papers, so a journalist will always deny typing his name into an internet search engine to see what comes up. Don't believe it. Whenever

I type 'Steve James cricket' into my Google page, for some reason one of the first links to appear is a piece entitled 'Pressure and James Anderson do not mix'.

God, it was a crap piece. Anderson began the Saturday morning of that Test with all six New Zealand wickets. A fairy-tale ten-wicket haul beckoned. But Anderson was all over the place early on, and my conclusion? He'd bottled it! He did take one wicket that morning to finish with 7-43 in the first innings, as New Zealand were bundled out for 123. And he finished that series with nineteen wickets at 19. I can only apologize.

Not that Anderson was always undeserving of criticism, of course. Especially abroad, with the Kookaburra ball, he could be startlingly ineffective. He seemed to lack variation, and his body language suffered accordingly. Justin Langer's 'pussy' observation was harsh, but you could see what he was getting at.

Now in South Africa Anderson was transformed. That Kookaburra ball was not just talking; you couldn't shut the thing up. There were out-swingers, in-swingers, cutters, bouncers and slower balls. The crucial difference, in my opinion? The absence of Andrew Flintoff. Anderson was now the leader of the pack. Some bowlers shrink in the face of such responsibility. Anderson positively thrived upon it. Top dog status suited him. And one of the most important branches that helped England to the top of the tree first revealed itself here.

Anderson was not, though, England's star bowler in the drawn Test series. Surprisingly, given that the pitches at three of the four venues – Centurion, Cape Town and Johannesburg – had plenty of grass on them, that accolade fell to off-spinner Graeme Swann. At the Boxing Day Test in Durban, where England won by an innings and 98 runs, he took 9-164 in the match. After England had clung on in the first Test for a draw, nine wickets down at Centurion with Paul Collingwood reproducing his Cardiff blocking heroics with 26 not out from ninety-nine balls and Graham Onions surviving twelve agonizing deliveries, this was unexpected festive cheer from England.

I certainly needed it. Now, I am fully aware, and indeed eternally grateful for the fact, that I possess a dream job. I love cricket and rugby, and get paid to watch most of the top matches in both those sports. As a columnist rather than a correspondent, I don't even have to spend as much time away from home as many others in the profession. But there is always a downside to any job, and that Christmas of 2009 in South Africa was most certainly one. Spending Christmas Day away from your wife and two young children (Rhys was four then and Bethan eleven) is hard, and that Christmas Day, despite the efforts of the son of Denis Compton, Patrick, a South African journalist, to feed and water the travelling English press corps at his home, was one of the more depressing days of my life. That it rained was thoroughly apt.

But Boxing Day soon arrived, and with it a performance that skipper Strauss described at the time as 'not far off the best performance I've seen from an England side, certainly away from home'. That was no hyperbole. Strauss is not inclined to such stuff. There were centuries for Alastair Cook and Ian Bell, another match-turning spell from Broad on the fourth evening and, of course, Swann's continuing excellence, earning him a second successive man of the match award.

All were hugely significant performances in differing ways. Firstly, here was incontrovertible evidence, if there had not already been some during the Ashes earlier that year, that Swann was a world-class off-spinner. He'd passed fifty Test wickets in the first Test (thirty-three of those victims were left-handers), and, yes, I will admit that I was still shaking my head in disbelief. It was some transformation.

I played against Swann quite a lot in county cricket. He was different in many ways. As opposed to most other off-spinners in the English game, he bowled an attacking line outside off-stump, spinning the ball hard. He cracked a few meaty shots down the order – although the suspicion always was that, if the ball was short and fast, he was not so keen to crack anything – and he cracked more than a few jokes. Sometimes he irritated; sometimes he amused.

He was certainly chosen prematurely for England's tour of South Africa in 1999/2000. He was immature both as a cricketer and as a person. Much has been made of Duncan Fletcher's spurning of him thereafter, but it was hardly a difficult decision to do so. It was the correct decision, as Swann himself admits in his autobiography. He was what Fletcher might call a 'twit'. He was nowhere near ready as an international cricketer. 'The primary reason for me remaining on the sidelines was that at 20 I wasn't good enough,' Swann wrote, 'and my tendency to wind up the wrong people at the wrong time didn't help matters.'

Swann's move from Northamptonshire to Nottinghamshire was crucial. The pitches at Wantage Road were actually spinning too much for him. A spinner learns nothing then. Trent Bridge is where swing bowlers rule. So Swann had to learn the art of defence as well as attack. Not that it came easily. It required some stern words from Nottinghamshire's wicket-keeper Chris Read during the pre-season of 2007 for the penny to be removed from its jammed position in the slot machine. 'Stop looking for the dream ball every ball' was the main substance of the advice.

Bowling in the first innings had to become more of a holding operation. Patience became a new friend. And Swann had to learn new tricks. He needed to be able to beat the bat on both sides. So he developed the away drift from the right-hander that is such an important part of his armoury.

He has become absolutely vital to England's four-man attack, even if he has surprisingly admitted that it was a policy with which he disagreed at first. Without him England might have to consider five bowlers. But with him, because he is so adaptable as attacker and defender, and so can bowl so many overs on the first day even if the toss is lost on a flat pitch, there really is no need for a fifth specialist.

Not that Flower and Strauss recognized Swann's abilities immediately. For their very first Test in charge in Jamaica they did not pick him. Nor Anderson for that matter. Swann was not selected for the second Test either, the abandoned debacle at the beach that was the Sir Vivian Richards Stadium in Antigua. But then curiously he was included instead of Monty Panesar when the rescheduled Test at the Recreation Ground in St John's began two days later. What happened during the ten balls that were bowled at Sir Viv's stadium (not that the great man wanted to be associated with it after that) and the start of the rescheduled Test at the Rec?

Well, I'll tell you. England had a middle practice at the St John's Police Recreation Ground, and while Swann was bowling Flower called Strauss over. 'Look at how much he is troubling all the left-handers' was the gist of Flower's words to his captain. Strauss knew because he had just faced him, and struggled. As the West Indies had five left-handers in their top six, and six in their team altogether, it was a rather pertinent observation. Strauss agreed. Swann was in. He hasn't missed a Test since. Indeed he has mostly bowled like Jim Laker since.

As for Cook, the fact that he scored a hundred in Durban while undergoing a radical technical overhaul was testament to his remarkable resilience. At the end of the Ashes the previous summer he had decided, along with Flower and Graham Gooch (then just his Essex coach but soon to be appointed as England's batting coach), to make some significant changes to his technique, most notably his backlift. He tried to eradicate his natural double backlift by holding the bat aloft, as Gooch used to. But, worried that he was not holding it in the correct position, he kept glancing back at it, like some fleeing thief checking on his chasing victim. Allied to a change in his 'trigger' movements – he tried to make them earlier, avoiding his usual 'floating front foot' – he looked horrible, even uglier than normal at the crease. And that is saying something. As probably the ugliest batsman in county cricket in the nineties, I think I am well qualified to comment.

Strangely, Cook's changes appeared to bring instant success. He scored two centuries in three days for Essex in the NatWest Pro40 competition at the end of that 2009 season. It could not surely have been down to the changes so soon. It hardly fitted in with Malcolm Gladwell's theory in his excellent book *Outliers*, subtitled 'The Story of Success', that it requires ten thousand hours of practice to master a specific skill.

Indeed Cook scored two more Test centuries, away in Bangladesh, with this obviously unfamiliar method. But then came a period of sustained failure against Bangladesh and Pakistan in the home summer of 2010. The word 'drop' was even being mentioned. Not by the England team management I don't think, because I reckon they believed in him enough to have taken him to the Ashes Down Under that winter even if he had failed all that summer. But it was still a time of some crisis, as he nicely summed up later that summer in an interview I did with him. 'One day I walked into Tesco,' he said, 'and a little kid came up to me and said, "Are you Alastair Cook?" Yes, I said. "You're not playing very well are you?" he replied.' Ouch.

Before the third Test at the Oval in the summer of 2010, Cook had had enough. He went to Flower and said, 'That's it. I'm going back to how I was.' He did. He cleared his mind of all technical thoughts. He didn't glance back at his bat. His backlift was a double movement, as it always had been. He went back and across the crease, with his front foot 'floating'. He just watched the ball. And he made a century. Then he kept on making centuries, double-centuries even. Mark my words, he will score more Test runs than any England batsman (Gooch's

8,900 is the current best) and more centuries too (Geoff Boycott, Colin Cowdrey and Wally Hammond head the list with twenty-two). As I write, Cook is twenty-seven years old. He has 6,027 Test runs with nineteen centuries. With him on nineteen are Strauss and Kevin Pietersen. Bell has sixteen. And people wonder why England were so good in 2011.

One wonders whether Cook needed to go through that period of change. 'I feel pretty good that I can change my technique and still score Test runs,' he admitted to me, 'but it made me appreciate what I had before and also that you can't change things too much. You have to be true to what you are.'

'He needed to go through that,' said Flower to me later. And I could see why Cook did it. The grass is often greener for batsmen. I experimented with all manner of theories during my career. I didn't glue my top-hand glove to my bat handle, as New Zealand's John Wright once did, but I did just about everything else. It is a shame, but I cannot again watch one of Glamorgan's greatest triumphs, the claiming of the Sunday League title at Canterbury in 1993, complete with an emotional farewell from the aforementioned Mr Richards. I watched it once on tape and turned it off after watching myself face one ball. My technique was shambolic, with front foot splayed down the pitch, bat aloft, head moving, body crouching.

If there is a modern batsman I wish I could have imitated, it is Bell. He is elegance personified at the crease. That 2009/10 winter in South Africa was when he finally shed all the 'soft' tags. The century at Durban was important because he could easily have been dropped after another insipid performance at Centurion, making just 5 and 2 and being inexplicably bowled leaving the left-arm spinner Paul Harris in the first innings.

'I changed a few technical things at Centurion,' Bell said to me later in the tour. 'Sitting there watching, I was asking myself whether I needed to get my leg out of the way to Harris. But the best thing I did afterwards was to decide just to trust myself, to go back to what I normally do. I knew Durban might be my last chance – I needed a big score and something that helped the side win – but I didn't want to walk away having just feathered one negatively [as in the second innings at Centurion]. I just wanted to be positive.'

At Cape Town in the second innings of the third Test, Bell made 78. I thought his 72 in the first innings at the Oval in the Ashes decider had been a fine innings. But this was even better, as England somehow managed to save the game again, with Onions – 'Bunny' by nickname but not by nature on this trip – facing eleven of the seventeen balls that he and Swann had to survive as the last pair after Collingwood had produced another trademark low-backlift 'Brigadier Block' (as David Lloyd christened him) innings of 40 from 188 balls.

'That's it then. Argument over. Ian Bell cuts it. Anyone questioning his mental fortitude at the highest level henceforth should be dismissed with the sort of contempt reserved for irritating flies,' I wrote the next day. 'He showed the type and volume of grit England's roads could do with right now.' Yes, it was snowing back home, but in South Africa England's cricketers were working hard in the heat.

That England could not complete a series victory was a disappointment. But in Johannesburg, after all the guts they had shown previously of their own accord, they were suddenly eviscerated. The guts on show were a ghastly sight. Strauss won the toss and batted on a damp, green pitch – he was worried about later indentations – and was promptly out first ball. England were all out for 180.

Graeme Smith made a century, and that was that. Except it might not have been. Smith had made only 15 when he edged Ryan Sidebottom (a shock replacement for Onions in a decision based too much on statistics at the ground) behind, but was given not out. He did edge it. Given the loud noise, with bat well away from body as Smith attempted a cut, everybody knew he'd edged it, except umpire Tony Hill and then, on review, Daryl Harper, the TV umpire. Quite why Harper heard nothing became the subject of so many conspiracy theories that it was a surprise Dan Brown did not write a book about it. But it wasn't until six months later that the truth was confirmed: Harper had heard nothing because of a poor sound feed from the host broadcaster SABC. To compound matters, other broadcasters, especially Sky Sports, received a better sound feed so their commentators quite naturally slated Harper for what they perceived to be his mistake.

England were incensed at the time. They were firmly against the Decision Review System, and had voted against its intro-duction (it was a 9–1 vote in favour). I was never sure why, although one ICC official did mention to me that it might have been purely because Fletcher proposed the system in the first place.

Their first taste of it in the West Indies in 2009 had stirred controversy, not least because Harper was the TV umpire. Both he and the two teams failed to grasp the basic concept that the system was introduced to eradicate howlers. During the first Test in South Africa Flower had said he was 'not a fan' of the system, but here now the ECB chairman Giles Clarke dived into the debate with two feet, describing the system itself as 'damned dangerous' and its implementation here a 'shambles'.

They were unnecessary comments, not least because Clarke should leave the cricket to the experts. And it was forgetting that Collingwood's match-saving innings at Cape Town would not have lasted more than one ball without the DRS. He was given out caught at slip off Harris, but the review showed clearly the ball had hit his hip, not bat.

It was interesting how attitudes had changed by the summer of 2011 when India (with Fletcher now, of course, ironically their coach) would only accept a watered-down version of the system, while England, with Swann picking up so many of his lbws from it, were rather keener to use it. The system may still not be perfect, but it has been proven to increase the percentage of correct decisions. That has to be a good thing for the game.

It was also good, in my opinion anyway, that the day after the South Africa series concluded it was announced that Strauss was taking a break and missing the tour to Bangladesh. This was something new and different, and inevitably drew howls of disapproval from a legion of former England captains, including Mike Atherton, Nasser Hussain, Ian Botham, David Gower, Alec Stewart and Bob Willis. I thought I'd take them to task in my column. 'The old boys are talking tosh,' I began. I did, of course, give them the respect they deserve – 'Fine body of men' etc., etc. – but then 'But they are wrong. Just because they have, by various methods, been ushered to an early captaincy grave does not mean another, Strauss, has to follow them.'

The crux of this matter goes back to a point I made earlier in this book: English cricket simply does not understand the word 'rest'. Strauss was knackered. Absolutely knackered. The strain of dragging England from the mess of the Pietersen/Moores episode and trying to maintain the highest standards as an opening batsman during all that time had simply become too much.

I chanced upon him and his two young children in one of Sandton's shopping malls the day before the final Test in Johannesburg. His eldest Sam was bawling his eyes out, having hurt his arm. I wasn't sure whom to feel most sympathy for. Strauss looked shattered, not from child-minding, but just generally. I thought to myself, 'I bet he doesn't score many runs tomorrow.' As I mentioned above, he was out first ball, even if it was to a stunning catch at short leg.

Strauss is usually the most equanimous of cricketers. Neither barbs nor bouncers normally unsettle him, but in that Johannesburg Test when Morne Morkel hit him and followed it with some verbals, Strauss responded angrily. He needed a break. Yes, it was a departure from the policy adopted in 2001 by Fletcher that players could only choose formats and not tours. That was in response to Stewart and Darren Gough's desire to miss a tour of India and then travel to New Zealand later that winter. Fletcher told them they could retire from international one-day cricket if they wanted, but they couldn't pick and choose tours. It was an admirable policy, and in the end one that was well respected by the players.

But Strauss's decision was different. It was not just Strauss who made it. Flower, Hugh Morris and Geoff Miller all agreed with it. It was done with the Ashes in mind. And, let's be honest, it was done with the quality of opposition in mind. If you are going to miss a tour, if not to Bangladesh, then where? Some might scream about disrespect, but matches against lesser opposition can often be hardest for the more experienced, been-there-done-it-all players, as England showed when losing to both Bangladesh and Ireland in the 2011 World Cup. When England sent a virtual second team to play Ireland after the India Test series later that year, that was the correct call. And England won. If only narrowly in a rain-affected match.

So it was the right call to rest Strauss. It also allowed Cook some valuable leadership experience in Test matches and ODIs. When it came to choosing a new captain after that World Cup, the ECB knew their man. They quite rightly interviewed other players (including Eoin Morgan, who impressed so much that he was selected to captain in that aforementioned match in Ireland), but essentially their decision had been made. 'I think he has done brilliantly,' said Flower after Bangladesh. It was enough said.

Before that tour of Bangladesh, Flower had had reason to become excited about something else. In February 2010 England played two Twenty20 internationals against Pakistan in Dubai. They won one and lost one. I mentioned the latter match in passing earlier when talking of Jonathan Trott. He was not doing the exciting, though.

As I write, that was Trott's last T20 international, as his dawdling innings cost England the chance of victory. Flower simply does not abide selfishness, and this was never going to be swept quietly under the carpet. 'We've had some honest discussion about that, one-on-one and in front of the team,' Flower told me just before the ICC World Twenty20 three months later. 'He [Trott] got that innings wrong, no doubt about it, and that was a contributing factor to him not being in the side right now.'

Trott was then opening with Kent's Joe Denly, two players about whom I have been wrong in my predictions about their England careers. Even halfway through 2010 I was saying Trott wouldn't be in the team for the first Ashes Test that winter.

I honestly thought Denly could be the answer to England's problems at the top of their one-day order. He was aggressive, and liked to take on the short ball, and, importantly, he always seemed to score runs on television. I was at Loughborough one day in 2008 doing some interviews when Michael Vaughan walked past me as I was watching the TV as Denly took a century off Durham in the Friends Provident Trophy semi-final. 'He should be playing for England,' said Vaughan. He did play for England, but, sadly, he just couldn't cut it.

The excitement came two days before the first of those two T20s in Dubai when England had played England Lions in Abu Dhabi. The juniors had humbled the seniors, beating them by five wickets. But most importantly, Flower had suddenly seen his new T20 opening partnership. In chasing 158 to win Craig Kieswetter (a day after he had officially qualified for England) and Hampshire's Michael Lumb put on 86 for the first wicket in just eleven overs for the Lions.

Kieswetter was hastily added to England's squad for the one-day matches in Bangladesh, and when it came to the first match of the World Twenty20 in the Caribbean (against the hosts as it happened) he and Lumb became England's sixteenth T20 opening partnership in just twenty-six matches.

So much for the meticulous planning for which Flower has become famed. But as Flower said beforehand, 'We might get criticized for chopping and changing, but Twenty20s are so few and far between and there are such big chunks of time in between. We're on the search for the most effective opening combination, and that continues.'

It continued for some time afterwards actually. Since that tournament there have been a few more. Nottinghamshire's Alex Hales was the latest to be tried, in late August 2011. But Flower is right about international Twenty20. Its presence in the calendar outside of the global tournament that is now played every two years is rather arbitrary.

Indeed there are many observers who think that Twenty20 should not be played at international level at all. I tend to agree. But it's too late now, and it has become a little farcical that matches are played on their own at the start of one-day series, or in the case of England's tour to India in the autumn of 2011, at the end of it. The ICC is so worried about playing too much of it that they have set a limit on the number that can be played in a year: no more than six at home in a calendar year, and no more than three in a series.

Its introduction to the county game in 2003 was for a very specific purpose. Money. It was brought in (after a vote of 11–7 among the counties) as a means of helping ailing counties keep their finances in order. For some, like Essex, Somerset and Sussex, that has worked. But it was never about the cricket. Yes, it has extended the horizons in terms of one-day batting, but essentially it is the same game most of us played as youngsters in some local midweek league.

As Flower said before the 2010 tournament, 'There are all sorts of theories that abound about Twenty20 cricket, but I think, when you get down to the meat of the matter in the changing room, it's much more simple than people are making out.'

So England won their first global tournament by keeping things simple. It was the only way really, given that they left in late April with the county season in full swing, with some players having even played championship matches the week before. But they did possess five players – Pietersen, Collingwood, Morgan, Lumb and Bopara – who'd been appearing in the Indian Premier League beforehand. And if the captain Collingwood picked up one gem from that tournament it was that he had to have a left-arm seamer in his side. So Sidebottom played instead of Anderson. It was a surprise. But it worked. 'To me Sidebottom was non-negotiable,' Collingwood told me afterwards. 'In the IPLs so far the majority of the top bowlers have been left-armers. Right-handers struggle with their angle going across them.'

'Petals and the Weed, a strange combination to be sure,' I wrote before the final against Australia, in describing Flower and Collingwood (the England players, especially Pietersen, used to nickname Collingwood 'Weed' because of his perceived lack of hitting power) and the general surprise that England had done so well. For it was a surprise, with Collingwood having given up the one-day captaincy fewer than two years earlier when Flower was an assistant in a regime that was not universally popular. The odds on those two leading England to their first global trophy would have been long. 'Of the sort offered to the deluded father who thinks his three-year-old can play football for England,' I wrote. '"Don't be silly, but 10,000-1 anyway,"' the bookmaker might have said.

But win England did, and in some style. They benefited firstly from a settled side. They made only one change throughout the tournament, and that was because Pietersen returned home for the birth of his son Dylan, missing the match against New Zealand, with England already through to the semi-finals.

Pietersen, batting at number three after the quickfire if never lengthy opening partnerships of Kieswetter and Lumb, ended up as Man of the Tournament for his 248 runs at an average of 62 and a strike rate of just under 138.

The bowling followed a familiar but successful pattern. Sidebottom and Bresnan opened, with Broad as first change. Usually once the six Powerplay overs were over, the spin twins of Michael Yardy and Swann would operate in tandem. And the quintet had to adapt to two very different types of surface during the tournament, excluding the slow pitch in Providence, Guyana, where England played their two initial group games, and very nearly exited the competition after rain and Duckworth/Lewis tried to conspire against them, but where they only bowled 9.2 overs in total: the pace of the Kensington Oval, Barbados, which evoked memories of years gone by and the Ends named after Malcolm Marshall and Joel Garner, and something slower in St Lucia, but not as slow as Guyana. Only on two occasions did England deviate slightly from their plan: against Pakistan Collingwood bowled a single over, as did Luke Wright in the final.

It was also obvious that England were by far the fittest side on show. In the tight-fitting shirts worn these days they looked like athletes. And there was a reason for that: the work of fitness and conditioning coach Huw Bevan. If you'll pardon another brief hint of braggadocio, I'd like to take some credit for that. (But even as I write that is being taken away from me. I've asked my wife a question about Bevan and she's just replied, 'Don't try and take the credit about Bevs. That was my idea!')

To explain. In 2002 I was captain of Glamorgan, and we were looking for a part-time fitness trainer. It is crazy to think that counties did not employ full-time fitness trainers then. But they didn't. And they didn't until the ECB provided them each with £25,000 p.a. specifically for that purpose. Anyway, my wife Jane was then the physiotherapist at Cardiff RFC, and she said the best fitness trainer they'd had at Cardiff was Bevan. By then he was at Bridgend RFC before joining the Ospreys in 2003, when the Welsh game went regional. He'd been a no-nonsense hooker who'd played for Bridgend, Cardiff, Swansea and, very briefly, Llanelli. He'd also always been a keen Glamorgan CCC supporter and was living (and still lives) a stone's throw from Sophia Gardens. So one evening Jane and I were having a few drinks at the Cameo Club, a well-known watering-hole in Pontcanna near Sophia Gardens, and Bevan was there too. We got chatting and Jane just asked him if he would like to help out at Glamorgan. To say he was keen to do it would be an understatement.

So Glamorgan had a new fitness trainer. And, boy, was he good. I still talk to some of the players about the famous Friday afternoon sessions we used to endure at the David Lloyd Centre in Cardiff. They could be brutal, but they were always good fun. Jane had talked about how at Cardiff the squad would split up into forwards and backs to do 3km runs. Bevan would run with one group and finish near the front, then straight away go with the second lot and run most of them ragged too. At Glamorgan very few of us could stay with him. As for his favourite gym exercises, chins and dips, he was unbeatable.

Unfortunately in 2008 Bevan left the Ospreys. The New Zealander Andrew Hore, once the Wales team's fitness trainer, had come in as elite performance director and that was always going to spell the end for Bevan. They'd never really got on. For a while Bevan was without a job. He was beginning to fret. He had been a PE teacher at Heolddu Comprehensive in Bargoed for ten years but did not really fancy returning to the teaching profession. To fill time he did work with various Welsh tennis players and amateur boxers.

Then I mentioned to him that there was a job coming up with the ECB. He already knew. He applied, and asked me to be one of his referees. I doubt if I helped much, but in November 2008 Bevan was appointed as the National Cricket Performance Centre conditioning coach. Soon he was taking six young bowlers – Maurice Chambers (Essex), Jonathan Clare (Derbyshire), Jade Dernbach (Surrey), Chris Jordan (Surrey), Mark Turner (Somerset) and Chris Woakes (Warwickshire) – to Florida for training at the famous IMG multi-sport facility in Bradenton, where Nick Bollettieri's tennis academy is situated. That winter he also went to South Africa with the England Under 19s and to Malaysia with the Under 18s. By the time the World Twenty20 was being held in England the following year in 2009 he was being asked to work with the senior side. So impressive was his work that he has never been away from the main side again, with the man in situ, Sam Bradley, shifted back to the NCPC.

There has been no fitter England side than the one under Flower, Strauss and indeed Bevan. Not that Bevan will take any credit. He is simply not that type of bloke. Ask him and he will say it is a team effort, along with fielding coach Richard Halsall, physiotherapist Ben Langley (and before him Kirk Russell) and long-serving masseur Mark Saxby (there for many of the Fletcher years too). As he said to me during the 2010/11 Ashes, 'Under Straussy and Andy there is a very proactive culture where it is part of the players' responsibility to be in the best physical condition they can.'

But Bevan has transformed the thinking. Central to this has been the realization that cricket is actually a power sport. For a long time cricket fitness was a bit of a joke; if any was done at all, it was just some light-hearted long-distance running. When I first joined Glamorgan in the mid-eighties there was only one test conducted at pre-season training, and that was a three-mile run that had to be completed in twenty-one minutes. It was hilarious. Some of the older sweats wore their cricket whites and caps. One chap even sported his cricket spikes to wear them in on the concrete part of the course. And, of course, plenty knew a short cut, and used it too.

Cricket might be played over a long period of time, but the movements made by cricketers are actually very dynamic. They require speed and power. That is not to say endurance is not needed too, but plodding along for, say, an hour on a treadmill is a rather poor use of time unless you need to lose a considerable amount of weight. A 5km run is probably enough for those who are used to such activity, as you will often see Bevan doing with, say, Strauss on tour. You are more likely to see the bowlers performing a series of 40m sprints – say twenty-four in total, in sets of six repetitions in order to replicate bowling four overs, but with shorter rest periods.

Weight training also plays a crucial role. But here Bevan has had to endure some uninformed criticism. The easy conclusion among those who have never lifted weights seriously is that it automatically puts unnecessary muscle bulk on the participant. It doesn't. It is actually very hard to put weight on. Strength can be acquired without excess weight. Bevan does not want muscle-bound fast bowlers. He wants them lithe and powerful. It is not like rugby where bulk is obviously required.

In a remarkable new initiative during the 2010 season, Broad and Steven Finn were taken out of the game completely to work on their fitness and conditioning. That went down well among the old guard! But as Bevan explains, 'Because of all the cricket we play, it is difficult to make any gains in terms of strength, and any gains you make are difficult to maintain. Other sports will have an off-season which we don't necessarily have, so to make real improvements you need a block of time to train. We are trying to build up each of the players' training age. By that I mean if you do weights for twenty years then stop training, you won't lose strength rapidly. But if you only train for a short period of time, you will make gains quickly but also regress quickly.'

But still, whenever a bowler is injured, there is a temptation for some to criticize the training methods. So for instance when in Bangladesh Sidebottom, Broad and Onions were all lame, Flower had to defend his man, and did so very well. 'I think the game is played at a different intensity – if you look at old footage I think it is pretty obvious,' he said. 'The pace at which the game is played is such that there is a lot of stress put on bodies, especially if you play in all three forms of the game.

'I have heard some criticism of the amount of work the guys put in in their physical preparation but I think to play at the intensity required these days in both limited-overs and Test cricket people will continue to seek constant improvement in their physical shape.

'You don't want people to overtrain but you are always trying to get that balance right. Fast bowlers are going to get injured. It's a stressful job that they do. If we could morph a physical trainer and an ex-fast bowler into a package then that might be quite useful but I trust our medical staff and I certainly trust our trainer, Huw Bevan, who has been excellent and has done some really good stuff with our squad.'

These days the ECB set out what they call their 'Fitness for Selection Policy'. This is not just for the England team but, as they say, 'the minimum benchmark standards which would be expected of all professional cricketers'. It includes a minimum score of 12.5 on the dreaded Bleep Test (a continuous series of 20m shuttle runs with the pace increasing at every level); sprint scores of 1 second over 5m, 1.74 seconds over 10m and 3 seconds over 20m; and being able to bench press 80% of your body weight for five repetitions, squat 120% for five repetitions, and do five chin-ups with a 10% load added to your body weight.

The problem is that not all county cricketers are as fit as they should be. There have been a number in recent seasons who have made it into the England squad and then had to be brought up to speed (if you'll excuse the pun) by Bevan. Some counties are superb in their dedication to fitness, but some are still of the old-school view that practising cricketing skills alone is sufficient fitness.

There is also the problem of how to punish a cricketer for poor fitness levels. Nottinghamshire's Samit Patel is the classic example. England did not pick him for a long period – he should have been their second spinner at the 2011 World Cup but simply wasn't fit enough – and his county were well aware of, and indeed frustrated by, his apparent laziness. But to drop him or release him entirely would have been self-defeating because another county would instantly have signed him. He is a good cricketer after all. Indeed England were so keen to include him that they dropped the Bleep Test target to 12 for him, which he just about achieved in 2011 and so was picked for the T20s and one-day series against Sri Lanka and India.

As Bevan says, a lot of the work he does is not actually measurable. 'How do you measure athleticism?' he asks. 'There is no objective measure for the footwork and agility required for fielding.' But there is little doubt that he has formed a formidable partnership, and indeed friendship, with Halsall.

Rugby is a common talking point between those two. The Zimbabwe-born Halsall was once a promising back-row forward at Arnold School near Blackpool. He coached rugby at both Brighton College and Wellington College. Just after he began work as England's fielding coach before the 2008 season he had to take a day off to go to Twickenham to see his Wellington Under 15s beat Millfield to win the Daily Mail Under 15s Schools Cup for the second time.

Halsall was something of a surprise appointment by Peter Moores. He had become county cricket's first fielding coach when employed part-time by Moores at Sussex in 2003. And now Moores decided, quite rightly and in line with Recommendation No. 10 of the Schofield Report, that he needed someone similar with England. Another Zimbabwean, Trevor Penney, from the same Old Hararians club as Fletcher and having helped England in 2005, was approached but was unavailable as he was emigrating to Australia to be assistant to Tom Moody, with whom he'd been working for the Sri Lanka team, at Western Australia. (Ironically Penney was back in England in 2011 as Fletcher's newly appointed fielding coach for India.) Jonty Rhodes was sounded out by England too, and Gloucestershire's Mark Alleyne was interviewed, but Halsall was always going to get the job.

I'd met him a few times out in Zimbabwe in 1994 when he'd returned there for a couple of seasons. He'd left the country for England aged four, and was now there playing some representative cricket for Mashonaland Country Districts. I couldn't remember him being a particularly outstanding fielder, but as he says, 'coaching is far more than just showing'.

I interviewed him at Loughborough just after he'd got the job, and he gave me a lovely line about how he was going to put a patch over Monty Panesar's eye ('sensory deprivation stuff', he called it) in order to help his catching. How the paper loved that. But he did counter the inevitable comparisons with, say, a Rhodes by stating confidently, 'If it's about diving full length and stopping the ball then Jonty might be better. But if it was lasering the ball in from sixty metres then I'd be better than him. And as for having to write a fielding programme for a Level Three coaching module, then I'd back myself.'

Halsall has transformed England's fielding sessions into highly organized and highly scientific practices. It took some time, because I remember watching a few early on that were rather chaotic with players clueless as to what they were supposed to be doing. Now they are like military operations. Halsall uses a specially adapted bowling machine that fires balls from ground level, often on to orange ramps that deflect the balls in different directions. Sometimes they use heavier balls so that when the real ones are used they appear ridiculously light. The short leg and silly point fielders take balls off springy nets. Flower edges catches for the slip fielders left-handed, and team manager Phil Neale does it right-handed – just as Fletcher and Neale used to in a previous regime. Fletcher was, and still doubtless is for India, a quite brilliant 'nicker' for slip catches, being able to edge a ball so fine that it is a catch for a wicketkeeper standing up. Deliberately. You try to do that. It is nigh on impossible. Both Fletcher and Flower are very good at hitting catches for gully and backward point, which is also a very difficult skill to perfect.

I think Fletcher would have enjoyed working with Halsall. He was a decent cricketer. He studied sports sciences at Brighton and Cambridge, winning a Blue and also appearing for Sussex second eleven, as well as an England amateur eleven. And he is fit. When he lists one of his key tenets as 'physicality', he is well placed to comment. He spends long periods in the gym, with the players or maybe even just with Bevan. 'He doesn't like running, though,' jokes Bevan. Little wonder the players call him 'Stick', on account of his skinny legs.

Halsall's other two tenets are 'precision and sacrifice'. 'Sacrifice comes in many forms,' he says, 'but in terms of fielding it means all those extra yards that only your team-mates really appreciate. It's about diving full-length on rock-hard outfields that cut and scrape your body, chasing down what appear lost causes, sprinting forty yards to congratulate a mate, or simply backing up a throw just in case something happens. Sacrifice also means practising a skill a hundred times so you can execute it the one time in a hundred you need it.'

In that early interview Halsall talked about how England cricketers in general were poor at hitting the stumps. 'We seem obsessed with getting rid of the ball too quickly,' he said. 'You need to give yourself a photo moment as I call it – set yourself, get your base and then throw.' He has even got his players to practise archery in order to utilize the correct feet positions. He talked about how on DVD he had a perfect example of Marcus Trescothick doing so at Durham in 2005, running out Australia's Andrew Symonds from mid-off. 'It's beautiful,' he purred.

He's got a better example now, that of Trott running out Simon Katich without facing a ball on the first morning of the Adelaide Test in 2010. The fourth ball of the Test had hit Shane Watson on the pad and gone out towards square leg. As the Australian pair hesitated over a single, Trott moved around from mid-wicket, picked up the ball, took a step, stopped for that 'photo moment', took aim and hit the one stump that was visible. He ran around the ground like a striker who had just scored the winning goal in the FA Cup final.

Ricky Ponting was then out first ball to Anderson, and by the third over Australia were 2-3 (that's two runs for three wickets in the English way of telling the score, or 'three for two' as they say in Australia).

England's fielding in general during that Ashes was outstanding, their supremacy over Australia evident at every turn as England's ground fielders adopted a 'pack mentality', as Halsall likes to say, hounding the Australian batsmen, with everyone committed to saving every run possible and everyone also prepared to run huge distances to congratulate a colleague when he'd done so. Such showy slaps on the back can look a little too contrived, even a bit silly, but they can also produce a togetherness and an energy that exude purpose. That was certainly the impression given here. The statistics said that over the series England's fielders saved runs on 109 occasions compared to Australia's 68. That's a convincing victory.

England's catching was also superb. Of the ninety wickets they took in the series, sixty-six came from catches. That is a high proportion. England's wicketkeeper Matt Prior took twenty-three catches compared to Australia's stumper, Brad

Haddin, who took just eight. The best of England's catches was undoubtedly Collingwood's to dismiss Ponting at Perth, diving high to his right at third slip. His low left-handed grab off Swann to get rid of the same batsman in Adelaide wasn't bad either.

England effected four run outs to Australia's none in the series. Trott was responsible for two of them, his effort in Melbourne to run out Phillip Hughes (with a good take from Prior in front of the stumps, as Fletcher had preached to Geraint Jones all those years before) earning special praise because he had just batted for 486 minutes for 168 not out, and also because when on 46 he had dived full-length to avoid being run out. Hughes here did not dive. It told a story, as did the sight of Trott in hotel gyms early on Test-match mornings during the tour – evidence of a man who, as he later told me, had taken to heart Flower's mantra that 'fitness and fielding are non-negotiable'.

Flower was impressed. 'Trott has worked incredibly hard at his fitness and his fielding over the last year,' he said afterwards. 'He is lighter and quicker and actually hits the stumps quite often in training. The fact that he had just come off 168 not out and was still quick enough and fit enough and alert enough to effect that run out, I think is a great example of all the hard work he has put in, but also of the contributions that the back-room staff have made too. Huw Bevan has worked to get him fitter so that he can concentrate for a long time, while Richard Halsall will have done the same on his fielding. That's what makes me proud as a coach when you see something like that, rather than only his batting.'

At the World Twenty20 in 2010, England's throwing at the stumps had not appeared to be that good. In the final Australia might have been buried earlier had hits from Collingwood and Lumb (twice) been on target. But their catching and ground fielding was exceptional throughout. And as Halsall has said in convincing defence since, 'It is also useful to know how many times the people hit the stumps when it really matters. A percentage of one in four turns out to be very high – you're doing well if you can manage that.'

When he took the job, Halsall reckoned England were the fourth best fielding side in the world behind Australia, South Africa and New Zealand. By 2011 they were surely the best. And Halsall must take the credit. 'We may just have another Troy Cooley on our hands here,' I'd written at the start, 'an unknown gem of rounded knowledge and clever communication.'

Cooley had indeed been a superb bowling coach, especially in 2005. At the World Twenty20 England had a new bowling coach, David Saker. He had replaced Ottis Gibson, who had taken the job in the autumn of 2007 and had now been unable to resist the call from home, returning to the West Indies as head coach.

Gibson left with his reputation enhanced, which was a surprise to me. It might even have been a surprise to Flower, because I was never sure how highly he rated Gibson. I was never sure how well Gibson had made the transition from player to coach – unsurprising given that he had hopped between the two, coaching for the ECB for three years before returning to the professional playing game with Leicestershire in 2004.

Gibson had played for Glamorgan in 1994 and 1996, and while the raw talent was there for all to see, he was obviously no thinking cricketer. But he clearly learnt. By the time he finished his first-class career at Durham he was the canniest of fast bowlers. In that final season in 2007, at the age of thirty-eight, he took all ten Hampshire wickets in an innings at the Riverside, Chester-le-Street.

And so the ever-smiling Bajan learnt as a coach too. His early days with England were difficult, as he struggled to work with Steve Harmison and Matthew Hoggard. He would hardly have been against the decision to drop them both for the second Test at Wellington in 2008. By the time of the 2009 Ashes he was starting to earn public praise from the likes of Andrew Flintoff and Stuart Broad. Flintoff made a point of signalling to the dressing room at Lord's on the fourth morning when he dismissed Australia's Katich because a plan – bowling wider on the crease and so moving the ball across the left-hander from outside leg-stump – had been hatched that morning with Gibson. Then when England triumphed in Durban that winter, it was Gibson who was credited with outsmarting his opposite number, Vincent Barnes. England had achieved reverse swing; South Africa hadn't.

With Gibson gone, England first wanted the Australian Mike Kasprowicz. Flower phoned him and asked about his avail-ability, but Kasprowicz eventually decided he could not justify the time away from his family. This was kept quiet at the time. The only reason I am mentioning it here is because I know Saker knows about it. Indeed he was taking the mickey out of Flower about it just before the Perth Test in 2010.

But they can laugh about it now because Saker has proved an outstanding appointment. And Saker does enjoy a laugh, especially at himself. His humorous personality is infectious. He was on a shortlist of five that also included Craig McDermott, former Warwickshire all-rounder Dougie Brown, former Gloucestershire bowler Stuart Barnes and Allan Donald, who had been England's bowling coach in the summer of 2007. So keen was Saker to land the job that he paid for his own flight from Melbourne to attend the interview.

Saker made an instant impression. 'One of the things I quite liked about him,' says Flower, 'was that he has always had a leaning towards coaching and helping other people learn, even when he was playing [in seventy-two matches for Victoria and Tasmania]. We did a lot of research on him and all the inform-ation coming back was very positive.'

Saker had coached the Delhi Daredevils IPL side of which Collingwood had been a part. Collingwood had liked what he saw. And so did England very quickly. By the start of the 2010/11 Ashes tour managing director Morris was already negotiating a new contract with Saker, and by the Test series' end he had signed for a further three years. There was to be no repeat of the Cooley impasse. Ironically, Cooley was moving on from Australia's job to their centre of excellence and there was talk Saker might apply for that. No chance. He'd already made up his mind.

Saker's great strength is that he keeps things simple. He is not a biomechanist. The art of bowling interests him more; he is more of a strategist and planner really. But he is also a fine 'people person', so important with bowlers, who can be an irascible, moody group of individuals!

Flower likes simplicity. It is why he also appointed Gooch as batting coach. That move surprised, even worried, me. I'd worked with Gooch on my only England A tour in 1997/98. I loved his work ethic, as does Bevan, who says of their now regular training sessions 'He just doesn't know when to give in!', but I was unsure what he could offer technically. Maybe he thought I'd reached a ceiling technically, and it was best not to confuse me.

Or maybe not. 'I coach run-making, not batting. Anyone can bat, but can you make runs? They are two different things,' Gooch says of his philosophy. 'We do a lot of overs practice so that the lads bat for a certain number of overs while we switch the bowling from over the wicket to around. It creates a similar environment to the middle. We also get them running between the overs, carrying bricks, or doing physical exercises. That's really to test their mind and their concentration – it's nothing to do with fitness. We call it distraction.

'Sometimes we put coloured discs down on a length when we are throwing to the batsmen. If you hit that coloured disc, the ball deviates a bit and misbehaves. But the main lesson for the players is that they've got to concentrate on the ball, not on what might be sitting on the surface of the pitch.'

Not all the England batsmen work with Gooch – Strauss and Pietersen don't – but you cannot grumble with Gooch's results in 2010/11. The batsmen had learnt to go big. I'll mention the saying once but not again because it has become a rather tiresome cliché: they are making what Gooch calls 'Daddy hundreds'.

And they are. In Tests in 2010 and 2011 England's batsmen made seven scores over 200, two each for Cook, Pietersen and Trott, and one for Bell. That is only one fewer than scores over 200 made by England players between 1986 and 2009, with Gooch himself featuring twice in that list, with his 333 against India in 1990 and 210 against New Zealand in 1994. The other six are Pietersen (226 v. West Indies, 2007), Collingwood (206 v. Australia, 2006), Rob Key (221 v. West Indies, 2004), Marcus Trescothick (219 v. South Africa, 2003), Graham Thorpe (200 n.o. v. New Zealand, 2002) and Nasser Hussain (207 v. Australia, 1997).

Double-hundreds were not required in that World Twenty20 final. Only 148 runs were needed to win there. Australia were not just beaten, they were thrashed, by seven wickets with eighteen balls remaining. After thirty-five years of failure – that is nine World Cups (a tenth went without success in 2011), six Champions Trophies and two Twenty20 World Cups – England had at last won a global one-day trophy. No wonder that the Harbour Lights nightclub in Barbados, situated conveniently close to the team's Hilton Hotel, was 'definitely lively' that night according to Collingwood. England's players celebrated long into the night. They deserved it.

What they didn't deserve were the events of the summer of 2010. The look of disgust and the slow shake of the head from

Collingwood as he spied the Pakistan team at Lord's on the morning of Sunday, 29 August said it all.

Until the night before it had been, considering the usual controversy that stalks a Pakistan cricket team, a relatively quiet season. The ball had generally darted around like a stickleback coming in and out of cover, but England had won the first two Tests comfortably before succumbing surprisingly in the third at the Oval. Now in the fourth they were in absolute control after a remarkable 332-run partnership for the eighth wicket between Trott and Broad.

I was travelling home on the train from Lord's with Scyld Berry that night when a call came. Apparently the *News of the World* had the scoop to end all cricketing scoops. But we did not know exactly what it was until 10 p.m. and the first sight of the story on the paper's website. It was shocking. There appeared to be clear evidence of two Pakistan bowlers, Mohammad Amir and Mohammad Asif, deliberately bowling no-balls earlier in the Test.

Sadly it was not a surprise. As a player I'd always considered the game clean. Corruption in cricket might as well have been on a different planet. But my experiences as a journalist, especially with Berry, of all the cricketing scribes the most relentless pursuer of fixing, as a colleague, have been very different.

Indeed earlier that season I'd almost had my own spot-fixing scoop. I'd become aware of something happening at Essex. It centred upon a NatWest Pro40 match at the end of the previous season. During the off-season concern had been raised by an Essex player about the actions of two of his team-mates. The ECB and the ICC's Anti Corruption and Security Unit were informed immediately, but they then decided to hand the matter over to the Essex Police.

It was a big story, and I had it. But it needed standing up. So on the Friday morning a call was made to the Essex Police. And they gave the following statement: 'Following allegations received about two Essex county cricket players involved in match irregularities, we have initiated an investigation and are working closely with Essex County Cricket Club and the English Cricket Board.'

The trouble was that the ECB then issued that very same statement late on the Friday afternoon. The Sunday scoop had been scuppered. The police had gone straight to the ECB to tell them that the media were on to the story.

On the Saturday morning Danish Kaneria was named as one of the players. At least I was able to name the other as Mervyn Westfield on the Sunday, but for me as a journalist it was one that got away. Kaneria was cleared but later named as the alleged corruptor when Westfield pleaded guilty and was sentenced to four months in jail.

None of this was a surprise because greed had long been the staple diet of too many cricketing people. Quite naturally that was going to spread into some dark and dirty corners into which the *News of the World* was now shining a welcome light. In February 2011 an ICC tribunal found Amir, Asif and their captain Salman Butt guilty of spot-fixing, and banned them for five, seven and ten years respectively. Butt and Asif had five and two years suspended. Then in November 2011 at Southwark Crown Court in London all three players, along with their agent Mazhar Majeed, were jailed for terms of between two years eight months and six months. They became the first sportsmen to be imprisoned for on-field corruption in the UK for almost fifty years.

To think the ECB had been helping Pakistan out by hosting their matches against Australia earlier in the summer. It was some raspberry they had been blown. But, as I kept stressing throughout the various storms that followed this horrible tempest, the show had to go on. Cricket could not cave in. There were more screams of 'Call it off!' during the subsequent one-day series than you find emanating from local councils when considering football on their pitches during a hard winter. But it was not called off, and England won a rancorous series 3–2, with a feverishly passionate display in the decider at the Rose Bowl.

England had won on and off the field. They were ready to go to Australia.

12

Sprinklings of Magic

Well, England weren't quite ready for Australia. First they had to go to Germany. Whisked away from Gatwick airport in the early hours of the morning, just a day and a bit after beating Pakistan at Southampton, and with only their barest essentials for company, they flew to Munich and from there were driven into the middle of the Bavarian forest.

The five-day trip was organized by Reg Dickason, the ECB's security adviser, and run by members of the Australian police force. None of the players knew where they were going beforehand. And, boy, did it cause some controversy, especially when it emerged afterwards that James Anderson had cracked a rib while boxing with Chris Tremlett; Tremlett himself suffered bruised ribs. It could have been worse too, or better, depending on your standpoint. Joe Calzaghe, the former world champion boxer, had been due to go to Germany with the players, but pulled out at the last minute with food poisoning.

It was reported that Anderson might miss the start of the Ashes, maybe even miss two Tests according to the wildest and most pessimistic speculation. But the truth was that he had suffered a small crack and indeed had completed all the physical work in Germany, only realizing upon his return home that he was in some pain.

Personally I was surprised that England went on this trip, especially after such an arduous summer. But the feeling among the England management was that, if they were going to do it, they had to do so immediately after the season ended so that the players could go away and rest completely for a month before reconvening for the Ashes.

But then I've always been sceptical in general about the value of such 'bonding' trips. And that's not just because I narrowly avoided nasty injury or worse on the way home from one of them in Brecon with the Glamorgan team in 2000. We'd done all the usual nonsense: orienteering, assault course, carrying logs up a steep hill, skinning chickens for supper, a night-time trek while some 'real' army men endured a mock ambush nearby, sleeping on the floor in a barn with no heating or lighting, morning aerobics in the snow, and another assault course. Then we had to go home, and drive ourselves. The player who was driving me, Keith Newell, fell asleep at the wheel on the A470 just outside Pontypridd. Thanks to the screams of Mike Powell, who was in the front passenger seat, Newell somehow managed to regain control of the car after it had hit the central reservation. Somebody really should have considered how we were going to get home after such an exhausting weekend.

A lot of baloney is spouted about the value of such things, and a lot of money is wasted. Initially it was interesting to me that two of England's best performing players in the Ashes had not seemed to gain too much from the trip. Jonathan Trott certainly didn't gain anything: he didn't go at all. His wife was expecting their first child and it would not have been possible to return swiftly had she gone into labour. So Trott stayed at home, even though his wife didn't give birth during the trip. And

Alastair Cook missed the first three days because he was attending to best-man duties at his brother's wedding. He didn't box. 'All I did was go abseiling,' he said, 'and I'm not scared of heights at all!' Graeme Swann absolutely panned the exercise in his autobiography: 'For me, it was easily the worst four days of my life. I hated every minute of it.'

But over time I have spoken to some others who were there and they have convinced me more and more of the benefits of the trip. Talking around a night-time fire can be a bit of a dreamy cliché, but those who were there said that was the best and most valuable part of the trip. The players learnt a lot about each other. And the support staff learnt a lot about the players, and, crucially, vice versa.

The team psychologist Dr Mark Bawden, an Olympic Games veteran and lead psychologist for the English Institute of Sport, was on the trip, and, if nothing else, the experience helped him gain the trust of the players. I know Andy Flower was amazed at and delighted with how easily Bawden worked with the players in Germany. After this it was noticeable how Bawden's name began cropping up in player interviews. Take Cook's explanation of his return to form in 2010. 'I went back to my old technique and worked with our sports psychologist, Mark Bawden, at the same time,' he said in the summer of 2011. 'Everything clicked. There's always a bit of a stigma seeing the guy we call the "Head Doc", but the mental side of cricket is so powerful. I've improved a lot over the last six months in that area. A lot of what we discussed was quite personal but the basic idea is to improve confidence and understanding.'

But post-Germany was the first time Flower started to cop some genuine flak. Even his father noted the shift. 'I don't buy all the papers and have the internet but I could see that turn,' said Bill. Flower had been on the defensive before the trip even began. 'First of all, I wouldn't describe it as a boot camp,' he said after the final one-day international against Pakistan.

'That's got quite a lot of negative connotations. It is designed to educate all of us, to give us a good sense of perspective on things, to allow the guys to become more self-aware, and allow the guys to understand each other better. We can live in a cosseted world, in the sporting world, and this is there to broaden minds. It's not related to the Ashes at all, it's more about our development as a group of blokes.'

In private he was a little more animated. 'It wasn't a boot camp!' he insisted to me one day. It may have been prefaced by an expression that rhymes with 'clucking bell'. Flower considered it a success, and Anderson played in the first warm-up match against Western Australia, bowling thirty-three overs in all. So really the fuss was misplaced.

I had never been to Australia before. I wish I had. A year or two playing Grade cricket might have been good for me. And I will admit that I did not see England regain the Ashes this time either. I was home for Christmas, just, after some pleading with my very sympathetic employers at the *Telegraph* had resulted in my planned return after the third Test in Perth. The only trouble was that this was around the time of the awful Arctic weather in Britain, and when I arrived at Perth airport on the evening of Monday, 20 December for my flight to Hong Kong, I was informed that it had been cancelled. 'There might be some flights available on Christmas Eve,' said the ever-so-helpful lady. Shit. I was rather looking forward to seeing my family.

But thankfully the wonderful staff at Commodore, the *Telegraph*'s designated travel company, and indeed the generosity of the *Telegraph* itself which agreed to pay extra for my return flights, ensured that I could return home via Sydney, Abu Dhabi, Brussels and Birmingham. It took a while, of course, and when a couple of current Glamorgan players, Mark Wallace and Gareth Rees, kindly arrived at Birmingham to collect me (my wife was snowed in) they declared that I'd aged at least ten years. Grey stubble can do that. You'd think the cheeky bastards would have been happy with their bar of Toblerone each, mind!

When I left, the series score was 1–1. England had just been hammered in Perth. And at dinner on my last night there was some concern among the travelling press corps. I wasn't budging from my pre-series prediction, though, as I emphasized in my last blog before leaving: 'England should not be too down-hearted, I reckon. This was one pitch on which they were always going to struggle. They are simply not used to such conditions. And crucially the lynchpin of their bowling attack, Graeme Swann, was wholly negated. I still stick by my pre-series prediction that England will win the series 2–1. Perth was always marked down as an Australia win in my book. Of course some of us got a little overexcited after Adelaide but reality has now returned. The battle is on.'

Others were less confident. But I had always been confident. Cocky even. Before I left for Australia I'd penned a piece for my Final Whistle column for the *Daily Telegraph*. The nature of that column is that it can often be tongue-in-cheek, and that was certainly the tone of this piece, with some truth, of course, lurking beneath. 'So I will travel to Australia very soon in a rare state of excitement,' I wrote.

But I will also travel in a state of some bewilderment. I'll admit it: I just don't get all the fuss. Hype and history are producing a cocktail that I'm not willing to stomach.

I'm led to believe that I'm travelling to another planet where visiting bowlers regularly disappear, sucked into some Kookaburra vortex, where batsmen become quivering wrecks on pitches simply too fast and bouncy for them, surrounded by fielders with PhDs in sledging and crowds so frightening that they all had parts in the film *Psycho*. Pah. I'm with Flower (A) on this. 'I don't think there's anything to be afraid of in Australia,' he said before departure.

The truth is that somebody needs to say it: Australia are simply not very good any more. They are losing for fun at the moment. They are the new England. Even Grade cricket is said to be going soft. Just like we used to in the eighties and nineties, they now seem to pick players out of a hat. Last Sunday they played a T20 international with players from only two states. They lost. In the past two years 45 players have represented Australia in Tests, one-day internationals and T20s. And they've only got six domestic teams! No wonder they've just sacked Merv Hughes as a selector.

Of course, the Ashes rivalry is ever-enduring, and I am indebted to Huw Turbervill, of this parish, for producing his recent book *The Toughest Tour* (Aurum, £16.99), recording the 17 post-war tours. It is full of some marvellous anecdotes and tales, certainly not 'The Toughest Read' as one of his friends mischievously ventured.

But will this be England's toughest tour? No chance. It will, though, be good preparation. India, the world's No. 1 team, are coming next summer.

Ha! I'd even fitted in a nice little plug for my *Telegraph* colleague Turbervill.

The piece caused a little bit of fuss, though. 'Below the line', as the comments sections on blogs posted on papers' websites are described, there was not exactly agreement with my sentiments. 'Juvenile' was one of the more repeatable comments. 'Steve, you know this article is going to be copied and quoted all round the Australian media? And when you get there, everyone who speaks to you is going to give you a hard time about it,' said another. Flower wasn't happy either. 'Oh yes, sure, Australia are shit!' was the gist of his sarcastic reaction. At least he reads my stuff, I suppose, and I could see why he was not keen at this stage for anyone to denigrate the Australians.

But when I did get to Australia, there was very little comment.

My feeling was that the locals knew what was coming. Of course, there was some bluster, but it was unconvincing. When the day before the first Test one of the Australian coaching staff emerged from the Brisbane nets to exclaim 'We're gonna fuck 'em!' to a journalistic acquaintance of his, the scribe just smiled obediently. He simply didn't believe him. Nobody in Australia did, really.

I have mentioned England's preparation already. It was good. They beat Western Australia. South Australia might have been beaten had it not rained on the last afternoon, and then they thrashed Australia A with their second-choice bowling attack. It was on TV too. In Australia and England, for all to see.

All the matches were eleven-a-side and accorded first-class status. When the tour began England had not won a match in whites in Australia since the last Test in 2003, a consolation victory to make the series score 4–1. They hadn't won any warm-up games on that tour either, so you had to go back to Cairns in 1998 when they scraped home by one wicket against Queensland for their last warm-up victory in whites in Australia. You could see why skipper Andrew Strauss was so keen to take these games seriously and develop a winning habit. When they beat Western Australia in their opening game it was the first time they had won their opening first-class match of the tour since 1965/66 when M. J. K. Smith's side also beat Western Australia.

But I still think the value of the preparation was rather over-hyped. England did not start the first Test well. Indeed they conceded a first-innings lead of 221. And to me the whole series turned on the first ball of England's second innings. Had Strauss been deemed to be lbw, as he so nearly was to Ben Hilfenhaus, then he would have bagged a demoralizing pair. England might never have extricated themselves from such a mess. As it was, the decision of the quite brilliant Aleem Dar, who gave Strauss not out, was vindicated upon review. Strauss had left the ball on length not line, as it cut back into him. Cook, his partner, said to me later, 'I immediately thought "That's close!"' He just about agreed with Strauss's assertion that the ball was too high. And fortunately it was. The England captain survived. Australia got him eventually but not before he made a century, and that was their only success in the second innings, as Cook made 235 not out and Trott 135 not out.

England's preparation was thorough. Just as they had before the 2009 Ashes, the England management had had a series of dinners with various groups of players looking ahead to the Ashes. Nothing was overlooked, on or off the field, from how best to use the 'Pro-Batter' machine to replicate facing the Australian bowlers before leaving to coping with the opposition's sledging, from their attitude to Twitter to dealing with the media. There was a cute move on the latter issue when, during the build-up, the press were invited to attend a training session with the team in Hobart, organized by the team sponsors Brit Insurance. One journalist remarked beforehand that it was going to be a bit like Christmas Day in no-man's land during the Great War. We journalists are easily pleased. Usually some free food will do, so this was really laying it on. The lads got a free T-shirt too!

I'm actually glad I wasn't on tour at that stage. I wouldn't have wanted to be involved. Indeed I've every admiration for my *Telegraph* colleague Derek Pringle for showing up. It's no place for an ex-pro, that sort of thing. But those members of the press corps who do not play, or have not played, seemed to enjoy it. The trouble is that I suspect, nay know, that the players were laughing at rather than with the journos, as they made fools of themselves. It was said that it helped media relations throughout the tour, and all the pieces the next day were certainly over-flowing with 'love' for the England team. But that might have had something to do with the results. It's easier to be cordial on both sides when the team is winning.

One interesting snippet, though, to emerge from the day was evidence of the remarkable accuracy of Anderson's bowling. Bowling coach David Saker had explained to the assembled throng that only three types of ball were of any use in Australia: the bouncer aimed at the head, the yorker, and the ball hitting the top of off-stump. To demonstrate he called up Anderson. To order, Anderson delivered the bouncer, hitting the badge on the helmet of a model batsman, the ball to hit the top of off-stump, and then the yorker, passing under an iron bar raised six inches off the ground on the crease. Impressive stuff.

There was also a close-up look at Graham Gooch's new toy, a device designed by a cricket-mad farmer from Writtle near Chelmsford in Essex called Frank Thorogood that appears remarkably similar to the plastic slinger used by dog-walkers to throw balls for their mutts, but is in fact something called the 'Sidearm' and is used to give throwdowns to a batsman. Quick throwdowns, in fact, with less impact on the thrower's shoulder and a trajectory that is more like a bowler's.

The proceedings were also filmed by Swann on a video camera. This was actually the third of his Ashes diaries, but it was the one that attracted most attention. Not because of the wheezing journos – and butter-fingered in the case of the *Sun*'s John Etheridge, who, for a once half-decent cricketer, had an absolute shocker in the catching part of the day – but because of the Sprinkler dance that is shown towards the end of the video. England, courtesy of Paul Collingwood so it later emerged, had created a new team dance. I actually thought the funniest part of that video was at the beginning when Swann was doing press-ups – '998 . . . 999 . . . a thousand . . . agh, [as he punches the floor in pain] the deep burn!' – but then I've seen Swann in the gym.

The Sprinkler became the craze, instant confirmation of a squad that was relaxed and happy. When they retained the Ashes at Melbourne, the whole squad performed it in front of the Barmy Army in the Great Southern Stand. It's the sort of thing you can do when you're winning.

I have heard only one murmur of dissatisfaction regarding England's build-up: that there was no game in Brisbane for the bowling attack that was sent there instead of remaining in Hobart where Australia A were being hammered. It could have been done because the Performance Programme players were in Australia until Christmas. They played a Queensland XI in a four-day match in Brisbane starting the day before the Test. Indeed Chris Tremlett (and Eoin Morgan) played. It would have been nice had Anderson, Stuart Broad, Steven Finn and Swann been able to play in such a game rather than just netting in Brisbane. But it was still a shrewd move to send them on ahead. Just as shrewd was the open declaration of strength in depth. Tremlett, Tim Bresnan, Ajmal Shahzad and Monty Panesar formed an impressive quartet. As Flower presciently observed at the time, 'Without a doubt, I would say, one or two of those guys are going to be playing Test cricket in the next couple of months – you don't have situations where the same bowling attack, or certainly not very often, play five Tests in a row.'

Indeed two of them, Tremlett and Bresnan, did play Test cricket in the next couple of months. Bresnan took the wicket that retained the Ashes in Melbourne, and Tremlett took the wicket that clinched the series in Sydney. Both were quite magnificent. Both were clever picks.

Tremlett had not been in everyone's Ashes squad. He had long been another enigma in English cricket. It is easily forgotten that he was in England's squad for the 2005 Ashes. Duncan Fletcher reckoned him the best net bowler he'd ever seen. But when it came to the crunch, the Oval that year when Simon Jones was injured, he could not be trusted. Nor could Anderson for that matter.

England went with Collingwood instead, and he was forever mocked by Shane Warne for the MBE he received as a result of his seventeen runs in two innings and four wicketless overs. He might not have deserved it then, but he certainly deserved it by the time he called time on his Test career at the end of this series. He did not have the best of series with the bat, but, with his enthusiasm never dimming and his fielding always outstanding, he departed on a high, a cricketer termed no more than 'bits and pieces' when first backed by the wise Fletcher who became an integral part of a hugely successful side. 'Few things have given me as much pleasure in my coaching career than watching Collingwood repay the faith we showed in him as a Test player by producing the goods over the years,' said Fletcher after Collingwood had announced his retirement. As for the man himself, he said, 'If, at the start of my career, someone had offered me three Ashes series wins and ten Test hundreds, I would have bitten their hands off.' It was a neat way of summing up both his modesty and his substantial achievements.

Tremlett had taken longer to fulfil his talent, including a move from Hampshire to Surrey. To me it was more about confidence in his body than anything else. Constant injury can do that to you. But when Saker watched the beanpole bowl for the first time in the nets prior to the Pakistan Test at the Oval in August 2010, he knew what he was seeing. He'd watched just three balls when he turned to Flower and said, 'This guy is coming on the Ashes tour.'

Flower replied, 'You think so?'

'Well, what I've just seen is world-class,' said Saker.

He was right. When Broad's tour was ended in Adelaide with an abdominal tear, Tremlett was the obvious choice for the next Test at bouncy Perth. The management may well have been considering him anyway. They had seriously considered using Shahzad's skiddy reverse swing in Adelaide, but Finn's six wickets at Brisbane secured his place.

England's knowledge of Australia and its conditions was vast. First there was Saker, who had played in Melbourne for six seasons for Victoria and then been assistant coach for five years. As mentioned earlier, Flower had also played a season for South Australia in 2003/04, although injury ruined it and he did not return for two more scheduled years. And Strauss had, again as previously mentioned, lived in Melbourne briefly as a child, attending Caulfield Grammar School in 1985/86, and had played for Mosman in Sydney for two seasons from 1999 to 2001. Before that he had endured a rather less fruitful season on the field with Sydney University in 1998/99 when he had been mostly stuck in the third Grade side. But off the field he had met his wife-to-be, Australian actress Ruth – a chance meeting in the Bourbon and Beefsteak, one of the late-night bars in Sydney's King's Cross, during that first season.

Strauss was one of seven players (Cook, Pietersen, Collingwood, Bell, Panesar and Anderson being the others) who had suffered during the 2006/07 Ashes, but many of the squad had also experienced Australian Grade cricket. Pietersen had played for Sydney University in 2002/03 (unlike Strauss they'd decided to play him in the first team); Collingwood had not only appeared for Richmond in Victoria but won the prestigious Ryder Medal for the competition's player of the year; Bell had played for University in Perth in 2003/04, after being recommended by John Inverarity, his Warwickshire coach; Cook played for Willetton in Perth in 2003/04; and Panesar played for Glenelg Seahorses in South Australia in 2005/06. England were not exactly entering uncharted territories.

Bresnan had always been earmarked for Melbourne by Saker. The ball was always going to reverse-swing there, but Bresnan could make the new ball bounce and bowl accurately when England required.

That was why Finn was dropped for this Melbourne Test, despite having taken fourteen wickets in three Tests. He had simply become too expensive. And England's bowling plan was very simple: attack with the new ball and defend with the old until it started reverse-swinging. Sometimes this happened very quickly; indeed in the second innings at Melbourne as early as the eleventh over.

But that was because England's husbandry of the ball was an art in itself. After the new ball had finished swinging conventionally (say usually in the first fifteen overs), some overs were bowled of cross-seam so that once one side of the ball was sufficiently roughed, vigorous shining began on the other (usually from fifteen to thirty-five overs). Cook, who famously does not sweat, and Anderson were in charge, holding the ball between thumb and forefinger, ensuring that not a droplet of moisture touched the ball. Hopefully for about twenty overs the ball would reverse-swing. And then for another twenty-five overs until the next new ball at eighty, England might have to revert to parsimony.

This rendered all the pre-tour fuss about the Kookaburra ball redundant (England use the Duke ball at home but had practised with Kookaburras frequently before leaving), especially about Anderson's average in Australia being 82 before the tour. He lowered it to just under 36 with twenty-four wickets, the most in Australia since Frank Tyson's twenty-eight in the 1954/55 series. Such was his timing and imperturbability that he also managed to pop home midway through the series to be at the birth of his second daughter, Ruby.

Twitter is a wonderfully modern medium, so when my colleague Scyld Berry tweeted thus: 'James Anderson has taken most wickets in a five-Test series here since Frank Tyson. Tyson was The Typhoon. Anderson is a Piercing Draught', you knew people were getting excited. About Anderson. And social networking sites.

The debate over four bowlers or five was also silenced. A lot of people, especially Berry, kept maintaining beforehand that England could not win in Australia with four bowlers. 'The last time England won an Ashes series in Australia with only four bowlers – and no all-rounder or fifth bowler of any kind – was in 1911-12,' Berry wrote, 'when grounds were open to nature. Relying on four bowlers in Australian heat, when the pitches and the make of ball favour batsmen, will put an immense strain on England's three seamers.'

Yes, it was one of Australia's cooler and wetter summers, indeed the coolest and wettest in some parts, but that should not be used as an excuse by the apologists. England were simply the better side. And you still need to score more runs than the opposition. As Strauss wrote in his Ashes diary, 'We've examined a lot of information on England teams in the past, and the statistics say that when England play five bowlers, they lose more games and they don't win any more. So the theory that it's a positive move and it's more likely to win you games doesn't stack up.'

Of course, England had some luck too. They managed to wrap up the second Test on a day recorded as Adelaide's wettest ever in December. They took the last Australian wicket at 11.27 a.m., and only a few hours later the nearby River Torrens was bursting its banks, such was the ferocity of the storms that lashed the ground.

Australia also lost their dependable opener Simon Katich after that Test to an Achilles tendon injury. And England could have lost Swann before the series had his thumb been broken rather than just bruised in the spicy nets at Perth.

And, less to do with luck but just as important, Ricky Ponting had a stinker of a series, averaging just 16, and that only because he made 51 not out when England were going through the motions at the drawn death in Brisbane. I thought before the start of the tour that he was slipping down the other side of the batting mountain, and that the series could be decided on how far that slide was from the apex of greatness. It was further than anyone could have imagined. His decision to play in

Melbourne with a fractured finger was typical of the fighter he has always been, but though he was heeding the advice of my friend Mr Thomas of Laugharne about raging against the dying of the light, his rage merely cost him 40% of his match fee for his remonstrations with umpire Dar over an unsuccessful caught-behind appeal against Kevin Pietersen. That's what can happen when you lose the Ashes three times. It didn't help that his long-determined deputy Michael Clarke averaged only 21 in the series as well.

There were also some unfathomable selections from the Australians. When they announced a squad of seventeen for the first Test, there was mirth unconfined, even if the huge number was as much to do with the desire of Cricket Australia's marketeers to hold a bells-on Ashes launch in Sydney, with a round of the Sheffield Shield still to go before the first Test, as much as the selectors' uncertainty.

But none of that explained the choice of left-arm spinner Xavier Doherty for the first and second Tests, or of Steven Smith at number six in Perth and Melbourne (he moved to number seven in Sydney), or of the clearly rather-too-well-fed Doug Bollinger in Adelaide.

Doherty's inclusion can have been for no other reason than to try and exploit Pietersen's sinistrophobia. We knew that Australia had had problems with spinners since the retirement of Warne, but this was ridiculous. Doherty was as ordinary as baked beans on toast. Indeed he was the ninth spinner they'd tried since Warne. Another shock selection and another left-armer, Michael Beer, became the tenth in Sydney. He'd been called up for the third Test at Perth, the selectors desperately claiming that it was because it was his home ground that he had been picked. It was as if he'd been bowling at the WACA since he was a nipper. He hadn't. He's actually from Melbourne and had only moved to Western Australia that season.

One of my great regrets of the series was that it rained after tea on the third day of that second Test at Adelaide. Pietersen was 213 not out, having made his first century for England since March 2009. He'd had one early scare when he got a leading edge off the spinner over cover, but by now he was treating Doherty with the sort of regard a schoolyard bully reserves for a newly arrived bespectacled nerd with a basin-bowl haircut. He was destroying him. I am convinced Pietersen would have made 300 by the close. As it was, he was dismissed for 227 the next day, but England won, with what Flower described as the 'perfect game', and with Swann taking five wickets. I think I might have mentioned that the latter might happen in my pre-match blog (or at least Swann's excited and very proud father Ray said I did when I saw him later, so that's good enough for me).

It was a busy trip. Or three Tests anyway. Blogs, daily pieces, Sunday pieces, even a debut in the Oped page of the newspaper (that is, the page opposite the editorial page). The Ashes must have been big news. So as I was heading out for dinner after the second Test had been won in Adelaide, I received a call asking if I could do a piece on how Australia as a nation was coping with defeat, especially as they had just lost out to Qatar in their bid to host the 2022 Football World Cup.

'To be a Pom in Australia right now is to dip oneself in Schadenfreude every morning,' I wrote. 'It is to walk into the Adelaide Oval and hear the gateman joke about the size of the crowds – "There must be a game on here today" – and respond with: "Yeah, but there's not much of a contest."

'The strange thing, though, is not just that the 24 years of hurt since England last won an Ashes series Down Under may be about to end. It is the way that the roles have been reversed. In response to my gag, the gateman just shrugged his shoulders. Negativity, it seems, is at last entering the Australian sporting psyche.'

Of course, very soon the Perth Test was being won and I could easily have been selecting whether I wanted the egg on my face scrambled, poached or fried. Mitchell Johnson, who'd been dropped for Adelaide, returned to the Australia side and produced a truly devastating spell of fast left-arm swing bowling, taking four wickets for just seven runs and turning the match on its head.

But it was a mere blip. By tea on Boxing Day the resignation had returned. There had been talk of a record crowd, but in the end the 84,345 on the first day at Melbourne could not surpass the 90,800 that attended the first day of the West Indies MCG Test in 1961. It didn't even beat the 2006 total of 89,155 when it was freezing cold and England were already 3–0 down.

But by just after tea there were many fewer than 84,345 in the MCG. It was estimated that some thirty thousand had already left in disgust. England had won the toss and, after some deliberation, bowled. It was a decent decision. In just 42.5 overs Australia were all out for 98, and by the close of the first day England were 157-0. Sisyphus had better days with his boulder than Australia had there. You just don't recover from that sort of position. By just before noon on the fourth day it was all over, and England had retained the Ashes for the first time for twenty-four years.

The celebrations were quite rightly long and hard. But if anyone was worried that, with the urn retained, England might relax a little in Sydney, they only had to refer back to preparations before the Melbourne Test. England had trained on Christmas Day, but not with the usual frivolity, with laughing photos taken with Santa hats on. England had practised as usual. When it comes to cricket, Flower just doesn't do frivolity.

It was right and proper that England won in Sydney by an innings and 83 runs. To win three Tests by an innings was not only unprecedented but also a fair reflection of England's superiority. The humiliation was duly completed, as Australia batted first when England would have bowled, and were summarily dismissed for 280. In reply England made 644. Yes,

644. It was their third highest total against Australia, and their highest in Australia. Cook made 189, taking him to 766 runs for the series (only Wally Hammond with 905 in 1928/29 has made more for England in any series) and making it a rather simple decision that he should be the recipient of the Compton-Miller Medal. Bell made his first Ashes hundred and Prior made a century off just 109 balls.

Australia made one more run in the second innings, 281, than their first, but just before midday on the final day it was all over when Tremlett dismissed Beer – 'replacing Beer with champagne', as one or two writers observed. England had won the Ashes, and were now ranked third in the world.

13

The Triumvirate

When Enland won in Melbourne, the first person Strauss had mentioned in interview was Flower. 'He has been immense,' the England captain said. 'He is an incredible bloke, a guy that we all respect hugely for what he has achieved but also for how he holds himself in the dressing room. Often you can't describe what he brings to the side because it is just a multitude of things, little conversations he has with people and little thoughts he puts on to paper that he actually brings into fruition in practice. The way he works with the team and back-room staff is as good as anything I have seen.'

Flower's contribution was all the more remarkable given that he had missed the second and third days of the first Test of Brisbane. A stomach bug maybe? No, skin cancer.

Gulp.

As a journalist you are obviously not supposed to reveal your sources, but I think this is an exception worth making without causing offence or rancour. I was staying in Brisbane at the Royal on the Park Hotel, and on the second morning I was waiting in reception for some colleagues to go to the ground. The huge figure who appeared through the doors was unmistakeable, if a little out of context. It was Eddo Brandes, Zimbabwe's famous chicken farmer who had destroyed England's batting on more than one occasion. He is now a tomato farmer on the Sunshine Coast.

We got chatting.

'Have you seen Andy?' I asked.

'Yes, he's in hospital having a melanoma removed.'

What?!

'I probably shouldn't have told you that,' said Brandes.

Well, it was a scoop, but it was also a shock. Even the most hardened hack would surely consider the health of their friend first. And Flower is a friend. But it was rather awkward because he was also team director of the cricket squad I was being paid to comment on, find stories on, praise and sometimes lambast.

'Is he OK?' was my only thought.

I got to the ground and made some calls. Later that afternoon I spoke to Flower himself. He was back at the team hotel watching the game on TV, with the volume turned down because of the local commentators' bias (it was that rare moment when Australia were in command). He was clearly in a lot of pain, because the operation had been performed under local anaesthetic. He said he could feel them scraping at his cheek. It was the only time I have ever detected any frailty in him. He was scared. But who could blame him?

Just consider the words of Dr Shobhan Manoharan, who operated on Flower in Brisbane, commenting on security adviser Reg Dickason's advice that Flower should get the growth under his right eye checked even though it had been there for eighteen months and he had previously received an all-clear from a dermatologist in the UK. 'For that reason, I suspect that Andy probably wouldn't have gone for another check-up for quite a while,' Dr Manoharan said. 'It's no exaggeration to say that Reg Dickason probably saved his life. I know that the England team have extremely busy schedules, so it was fortunate for everyone that we were able to get him in this week.'

Nobody had noticed on that second day that Flower was absent. Nobody in the written media, that is. During the afternoon whispers were starting to emanate from the broadcast media, who, of course, have the privilege of being out on the field before play starts, and so interact with the players a lot more. The story was not going to hold long. So I put it to Flower that I write it. He was worried because of our close relationship. He didn't want it looking like he'd given his mate a scoop. So he asked James Avery, England's excellent media liaison officer, to release the story through the Press Association. It may just have been on the *Telegraph* website a few moments before it was anywhere else.

Flower spoke to the media when the team had moved to Adelaide for the second Test. His press conference, deep in the bowels of the Intercontinental Hotel alongside the River Torrens, was a truly humbling experience for anyone present. 'I always feel lucky, every morning,' said Flower when asked whether he felt lucky that the melanoma had been diagnosed so swiftly. 'Seriously, I do. We are really lucky to be involved in cricket and get paid for it and I've always felt like that as a player. We've got so much to appreciate.'

Flower looked awful, with a large V-shaped sticking plaster over a wound with some fifty-five micro-stitches in it. 'I was surprised by being worried as much as I was,' he admitted. And, of course, he did have Hugh Morris for support and advice. 'Hugh had a much more serious issue and he was a great guy to have around,' Flower said. 'But it was more worrying for my family because they're miles away. They would have liked to have been here with me.' Mind you, if his mother Jean had been there she might have had some stern words for him. 'I don't want to make my parents feel guilty but when I was a child we were always out in the sun, all day every day, and we never used sunscreen,' he said.

Jean disagrees. When I phoned to ask if I could speak to her and Bill for the purposes of this book, she said enthusiastically, 'Yes, I'd like to put the record straight!' She would like to say that she did put suncream on her children, even if it was 'only Zimbabwean' stuff and maybe not as potent in blocking the sun's UV rays as cream purchased in more developed countries. Andrew, you have been told.

What with Bill also suffering his New Year's Day heart attack, it was a seriously stressful winter for Flower. I worried for him. It was why in January 2011 I wrote a piece suggesting he needed a break. All the talk was of how the team was tired, and indeed they were, but what about the coach? 'It was a year ago on Monday that England completed their winter tour of South Africa,' I wrote.

Since then, not including today's first one-day international in Melbourne, they have played 43 international cricket matches: that is 13 Tests, 17 one-day internationals and 13 T20 internationals.

It says much about England's improvements and consistent quality that they have lost just 10 of those matches. But it also says much about the crowded international itinerary that not one player has appeared in all 43 matches.

The closest are Paul Collingwood and Graeme Swann, with 40 appearances each, but both had to be rested last year, Collingwood skipping two home Tests against Bangladesh (he also missed a one-day international against Pakistan at the Oval due to a virus) and Swann being left out of the three home ODIs against Bangladesh.

Stuart Broad is next with 35, having sat out the same home Tests as Collingwood, while missing an ODI in Bangladesh with back trouble and then, of course, leaving the Ashes tour after the second Test with a nasty torn stomach muscle injury.

Modern cricket schedules simply do not allow players to stay on the treadmill all year. Collingwood is now to hop off for Tests, Andrew Strauss has done so for T20s for some time, but for the remainder their wellbeing and longevity are at the discretion of the team management. Like it or not, rest and rotation must now be an accepted part of international cricket.

Which brings me to England team director Andy Flower. When does the man doling out the rest periods get a rest himself?

Flower left home on Oct 28 and will fly back on Feb 7. Then there will be four nights in his own bed before leaving for Bangladesh and the World Cup. All being well, and England reaching the final, he will return home on April 3. Consider also that Flower will be away for around 100 nights next summer and that amounts to more than 250 nights away in a year.

Compare that with other sports. This year, a Rugby World Cup year, will be a busy one for Martin Johnson and his England coaching staff, but even if his team reach the final in Auckland on Oct 23 [which they didn't, of course, being knocked out in the quarter-finals], they are unlikely to be away for more than 180 nights during the year. And Johnson is reportedly on a higher salary than Flower. Fabio Capello? An obscene annual wage of £6 million for, so I'm reliably informed, just 64 nights abroad last year, including the World Cup in South Africa.

Flower did miss a one-day match in Ireland at the end of the India Test series in 2011, but he might have also liked to miss the Ireland match in Belfast in 2009, three days after the Ashes had been won. As Swann said of that, 'It was ridiculous that we went to Ireland the day after the final Test.

'All credit to the fellas who actually went out there and performed in Ireland because I know I didn't; I was in no fit state to play a game of cricket two days after the Ashes and that's how it should be, I think.

'The sad thing is that you don't get that England rugby

moment when they all got to fly home with the World Cup, passing it around. That would have been quite nice. But when it comes to cricket's schedules, there's not a lot you can do.'

I wasn't sure about too much celebration in 2009, but in 2010/11 they certainly deserved a fanfare. But they didn't get it. Instead they had to play two T20 internationals and seven ODIs out in Australia. They were knackered. But it was nothing new. In 2006/07 England had actually played ten ODIs against Australia and New Zealand before heading off to the World Cup in the West Indies. And it could have been eleven had they not beaten Australia 2–0 in the best-of-three Commonwealth Bank Series finals. Remember also that they had been at the Champions Trophy in India before the Ashes.

Understandably Flower was not happy. 'There will be a communication between me and the people who decide on these itineraries,' he said. And there clearly has been communication. The itinerary has been altered. It does mean that there will be back-to-back Ashes series home and away in 2013/14, but the cycle will be broken. Henceforth England will not arrive at World Cups broken.

The next World Cup is in Australia and New Zealand in February and March 2015. That winter England will play two T20s and five ODIs in Sri Lanka before Christmas, then go to Australia in the middle of January to play five ODIs as preparation for the tournament.

They will have a damned sight more of a chance than England did in 2011 in Asia. They were tired, and without their best one-day batsman Morgan, who had broken a finger in the very last ODI in Australia. But they were also confused. They were confused as to their best side. One match into the one-day series in Australia they had been forced by the ICC to name their World Cup squad, and had decided to pick Prior as opener, thereby dropping Steven Davies, who had done decently against Pakistan at the end of the previous summer.

The trouble was that Prior didn't do very well, so then the decision was made to open with Pietersen. And then he was injured, and had to go home after South Africa had been beaten in Chennai. Morgan returned, but it was too late. The Netherlands had already pushed England close with a score of 292, and Ireland had famously beaten them in Bangalore. Now Bangladesh beat them too. The quarter-finals were reached, but Sri Lanka strolled through by ten wickets. It was time for that drawing board to be revisited. England were still, according to the rankings, fifth in the world in ODIs. It was time for a new captain.

It had been flagged up by the *Mail on Sunday* during the tournament that Strauss was intending to step down, a story dismissed by Strauss in a TV interview as 'strange journalism'. Well, it wasn't strange, even if it pains me to add another feather to the cap covering the bald pate of the lovable Peter 'Reg' Hayter, who reckons he's scooped the resignation of every England captain since W. G. Grace decided at Trent Bridge in 1899 that fifty might be a little elderly to be skippering one's country.

It was right that Strauss went. It was time for Cook to have his chance. It was simply not possible to play both of them in the same one-day team, especially with the next man in the order being Trott, who was still being criticized as England flew home even though he was then the tournament's leading run-scorer. Clichéd or not, World Cups are staging posts. England had lost captains after the previous three World Cups (Alec Stewart in 1999, Nasser Hussain in 2003 and Michael Vaughan in 2007), and they duly lost another when Strauss eventually announced his resignation about a month later. It was his decision, but I'm pretty sure it was a decision with which Flower agreed.

Cook was made one-day captain, and in a ground-breaking tripartite arrangement (Strauss was still, of course, Test captain), Broad was given the Twenty20 captaincy. Cook's promotion was in general lampooned. I just couldn't understand the negativity of the response. Yes, he'd made a shambolic beginning in international captaincy in a Twenty20 international against South Africa at Centurion in 2009, but, as mentioned earlier, in Bangladesh in 2010 he had improved. And I always thought his batting could expand even further than Strauss's, who had made such strides after taking the one-day captaincy in 2009. Strauss was thirty-two then; Cook was only twenty-six. The evidence was immediate: England beat Sri Lanka 3–2 in the first series of the 2011 summer, and Cook made 298 runs with one century at an average of 74.50 and a strike rate of 96.75. In his previous twenty-six ODIs his strike rate had been 71.38. In the following five-match series against India England won 3–0, with a tie and an abandonment. Cook made 169 runs at 42.25, with a strike rate of 94.41. Of course, his side were then thrashed 5–0 out in India and he only made 133 runs at an average of 26.60. But at least his strike rate was 84.71. And even better was to come when Cook made two successive centuries and an 80 (at a strike rate of 88.36) in the first three matches of the series against Pakistan in the United Arab Emirates in February 2012.

Most notable among Cook's critics was my old university mate Mike Atherton, who'd described him as a batting 'plodder' and a fielding 'donkey'. Cook was furious, and so were the England management. They were harsh observations before Cook had even taken the job. But in fairness Atherton's comments were made on Sky's *Cricket Writers on TV* programme, which often lends itself to light-heartedness. He would not have used such words in print. And he was actually criticizing himself because he was worried that Cook might be another one-day captain not really worth his place, just like himself, Hussain, Vaughan and Strauss before.

Cook could not then justify a place in the Twenty20 side, but Collingwood was still captain in that format, captain of the world champions no less, and was unceremoniously sacked. Collingwood was devastated. It was 'like a juggernaut had come along at full steam and completely wiped me out', he said. 'I understand the thinking that the team moves forward and people only have a certain shelf-life. But it doesn't make it any easier to take and it doesn't mean I agree with it. I'm still very disappointed and hurt by what has happened.'

Again it was the right decision. During the World Cup Collingwood's body had been telling him things he did not want to know. Niggle had followed niggle. I could understand his disappointment, because it didn't just mean that he wasn't Twenty20 captain any more. It meant his whole international career was over. But again, that was the right decision.

If you think I am constantly praising Flower's decisions for the sake of it, then please think again. It is just that he, and indeed Strauss, just seem to make good calls. They make big calls too. This was a big call from Flower. As was dropping Pietersen at the end of the 2010 summer from the one-day internationals against Pakistan. He also missed two T20s, but that was because the second of them in Cardiff coincided with the start of a championship match for Surrey against Glamorgan at the Oval that Flower wanted Pietersen to play in in order to begin his long-form preparation for the Ashes. It was the T20 stuff that upset Pietersen most, prompting a Twitter outburst, which was quickly deleted but still landed him with a fine from the ECB. 'Done for rest of summer!! Man of the World Cup T20 and dropped from the T20 side too. Its a fuck up!!' he'd written.

Pietersen was also dropped for the India one-dayers at the end of 2011. It was said he was rested, but that was rubbish. He was dropped because he had simply not scored enough runs. Just check the figures: in 2009 in seven innings he had scored 132 runs (average 18.86), in 2010 in nine innings he made just 153 (17.00), and in 2011 in fourteen innings before being left out he scored 401 (28.64). And he still had not got a century in ODIs since his 111 not out in Cuttack in 2008, and, as one of the coaching staff present that night has pointed out to me since, even that innings was too slow (taking 128 balls), as England's 270-4 was easily picked off in just 43.4 overs by the Indians. But at least in February 2012 Pietersen got that elusive century when he made 111 not out against Pakistan in Dubai, then adding another hundred in the very next game.

There had been a lot of talk in the previous year of his one-day retirement, but he couldn't do that. It would have meant he could not have a central contract (Collingwood's Test retirement was different: both parties agreed on that). The ECB had him by the balls. So when Morgan was still injured for the away ODI series in India in the autumn of 2011, they picked Pietersen again. He only did reasonably. His 170 runs at 42.50 in four innings (he missed the last game with a broken thumb) still only took his average for the calendar year to 31.72.

Flower made another good decision in omitting Broad from the final one-dayer against Sri Lanka in 2011. He had not been bowling well, and it was said it was a tactical decision to omit him for Samit Patel on a dry Old Trafford pitch. But it was a rocket fired up Broad's backside. He went back to Nottinghamshire, and realized that he had been bowling too short. I actually always thought he was a hit-the-pitch type bowler, but he turned up for the first Test at Lord's against India with his place in jeopardy and suddenly swung the ball like Fred Trueman, taking seven wickets in the match.

Flower had been intrigued by Broad as a leader ever since an internal twenty-five-over-per-side warm-up match in the West Indies in 2009. He made Broad and Anderson skippers of the two sides in a match at the Everest club ground in Georgetown, Guyana, and the results were interesting. Before the start of the match Broad took Flower aside and asked whether he could expose some team-mates' weaknesses. There were some players he wanted to bounce, and he also wanted to test Pietersen's recently discovered aversion to left-arm spinners.

So when Pietersen came to the crease, Broad immediately

summoned Strauss to bowl his filthy left-arm spinners – and they are filthy because I faced them once in a Glamorgan v. Middlesex match that was fizzling out into a draw. One ball very nearly bounced twice. Thankfully Strauss didn't get me out, and Pietersen didn't succumb in Guyana either. But the skipper – the real skipper that is, rather than Broad – did only concede five runs from his over. Flower took note. Of Broad's captaincy, not Strauss's bowling, that is.

As I mentioned, this split captaincy could not have happened under Fletcher. His successful model of the coach being the consultant required one strong leader, with whom Fletcher formed a tight-as-a-drumskin relationship. Even during the brief Hussain/Vaughan overlap in 2003 there were problems.

But Flower operates in a very different system. The ECB now consider Fletcher's model 'old-fashioned', and Flower more accountable than Fletcher was. He is conspicuously in charge. And that has suited Strauss. It did not suit Vaughan when Peter Moores wanted to act similarly, and it certainly would not have suited Hussain.

If there was surprise at England's three captains, it was nothing compared to the shock I got while travelling up to Chelmsford on 27 April to interview Ravi Bopara, whom I'd been told was going to play in the first Test of the 2011 summer, against Sri Lanka, as England were worried about a safety-valve bowling option at number six after Collingwood's Test retirement. And I'm sure that was the plan. But Morgan's 193 for the Lions against Sri Lanka at Derby, just after returning from the Indian Premier League, was a scream that could not be ignored.

Anyway, somewhere between Newport and Paddington on that April day, I received a text message: 'Fletcher has taken India job'. I was genuinely shocked. My next thought was 'Well, he doesn't listen to me anyway.' Not that he should, of course. But he had sought my advice. I'd told him he'd be mad to take it. I'd even written a piece which, without referring to Fletcher because that would have broken a confidence, tried to warn him off.

In it I'd talked about India's superiority in world cricket, on and off the field. They were, and still are, World Cup champions. Then they were ranked number one in Tests, and had just had five players – Virender Sehwag, Sachin Tendulkar, V. V. S. Laxman, Mahendra Singh Dhoni and Zaheer Khan – selected for *Wisden*'s Test XI in its 2011 edition. The same publication had named its Leading Cricketer in the World as Tendulkar, and in both 2009 and 2010 it was Sehwag. I'd talked about Gary Kirsten and how well he had done as coach, especially as he had so little experience when appointed in late 2007. He was simply missing his family too much and had returned to South Africa, where he was very soon appointed national coach. 'India now enter the coaching marketplace,' I'd continued, 'along with Sri Lanka, Bangladesh and South Africa [obviously before Kirsten's appointment there].

Presumably there are some busy cricketing agents at the moment, as well as some excited out-of-work coaches. But I wouldn't be too excited about the India job if I were them. It is surely the proverbial hiding to nothing.

It is a fiendishly difficult job, as two other foreigners, John Wright and especially Greg Chappell, found before Kirsten. Chappell attempted radical change, in particular the removal of captain Sourav Ganguly, and very quickly discovered the meaning of player power. The players are everything in Indian cricket. They are idolized to an extent that we find difficult to comprehend in this country, and so no coach can ever be bigger than them. It is the trickiest of balances, with the public's fascination and obsession easily turned to vitriolic condemnation on a whim.

For this current crop wealth and immortality are now secured. For a new coach there is only one way for the team to go, and that is downwards. A trip to the West Indies in June soon should not cause too many problems, but the visit over here to England this summer could.

I will be surprised if England do not win the four-Test series. Hopefully, as we speak, groundsmen around the country will have their thoughts and energies focused upon producing pitches with pace and bounce. That should give England the edge. Home advantage should be just that.

Well, I got the last bit right anyway, about the series result (and at the time endured the most fearful and unrelenting volleys of abuse from India's notoriously one-eyed fans) and the type of pitches produced. But I didn't get through to Fletcher.

Kirsten was a far more persuasive influence. He had been charged with helping find his own replacement. He had met with Flower over breakfast during the World Cup. Did that help Flower when he sat down with Morris at the end of that tournament to discuss the financial details of his future employment? Maybe, but not because Flower would have used it as a bargaining tool. He is not like that. The plan was to talk with Morris anyway. Flower always wanted to remain loyal to England.

Kirsten had spoken with Fletcher at length. They have always done that. They had first met at the University of Cape Town where Fletcher began his coaching career. Kirsten was batting down the order, bowling occasional off-spinners and having a lot of fun at the bar. Fletcher took him aside one day and told him he was good enough to play for Western Province as a batsman. Kirsten laughed initially, but eventually began to believe in himself and his coach. Kirsten's father had just passed away, so Fletcher became his father figure.

When Kirsten became a coach, it was Fletcher to whom he turned. 'The coach is not the man to sit on the parapets in cricket – it's not like soccer,' Kirsten told me in 2008 during England's one-day tour of India. 'Duncan taught me that. He was a great mentor to me as a player, and now he is as a coach.'

The truth is that Kirsten was the only person who could have persuaded Fletcher back into full-time international coaching. 'I just don't think I could do the year-round touring these days,' Fletcher had told me as recently as early 2010. Of course, the money was a huge factor. It made him the highest paid coach ever in world cricket. Fletcher was sixty-two when he took the India job. It was always going to be his last post. He has two grandchildren whom he adores. He wanted to make sure they are provided for.

Kirsten was adamant in his talks with Fletcher that it would be a very different role from that which he had undertaken with England. He would not be heavily involved in selection; he would only have to do minimal media duties. As well as all that, Eric Simons, whom Fletcher once described as a 'legend' from their times together at Western Province, was remaining initially as bowling coach.

'You were the only one who advised me not to do it,' Fletcher told me. 'Just like Crofty with the England job!' I was worried about the stress it might cause him, as much as anything. Marina has had her health problems, and, having been out to his new home in Hermanus during England's tour to South Africa in 2009/10, it was obvious how relaxed and happy he was. He lives between the sea and the golf course, and his study, over-looking the 15th green with the Olifantsberg mountains in the distance, possesses the most stunning view.

But he wanted one last challenge. This was it. To bring India, the number one ranked Test team in the world, to England. 'Fletcher v Flower. A big summer just got bigger,' I wrote.

Or so we thought anyway. First India went to the West Indies with a depleted side. They won the one-day series 3–2 and the three-Test series 1–0 but were far from convincing. Five days after the conclusion of that third Test in Roseau, Dominica, they were playing Somerset in a three-day match at Taunton, with Strauss playing as a guest for the home side.

I could not believe there was such criticism of Strauss playing in that match. As mentioned earlier, for me it was a rare occasion when county cricket was paying heed to the importance of the England cricket team. Without that match he would have had just one county championship match in the month between the third Test against Sri Lanka at Southampton and the first against India at Lord's. He'd struggled in that rain-ruined Sri Lanka series, which England won 1–0 thanks to an astonishing collapse by the Sri Lankans on the last afternoon in Cardiff, where they were all out for 82 in just 24.4 overs, making just twenty-seven runs in four innings. He needed the practice and got it at Taunton, making 78 and 109 not out in the match.

But as he and Arul Suppiah were putting on 101 in the first innings it was already becoming clear that this was not an India side straining at the leash for the fight. They looked tired even then, with their bowling looking as flat as a can of Coca-Cola opened the day before. I spoke to Fletcher afterwards. 'They'll be up for Lord's,' he said, while also making the very sound point that those criticizing India's attitudes to fitness and preparation (they do not exactly adhere to the old 'Fail to prepare, prepare to fail' mantra) were missing the point that Indian teams have always been like that. They were like that under Kirsten, even when winning the World Cup. I recall shaking my head on numerous occasions during that tournament, and wondering about the justice and indeed validity of a team so poor in the field and between the wickets in winning the tournament. But that is cricket's paradox: unfit cricketers can sometimes prosper. I'm not sure W. G. Grace would have done too well on the Bleep Test.

I remember talking to Kirsten about this fitness issue among the Indians in 2008. He was, and still is, a complete fitness fanatic, and had taken his friend, Paddy Upton, the former South Africa fitness trainer, to India with him to work on that, but it was a difficult process of education. 'We're trying to bring in new thinking,' he said, 'but we're not going to force them [the India players] to do it. For instance after a game Paddy might say to those that haven't played: "I'm running a shuttle school. If you want to come, come." They're physically different. They must play the game their own way. They play with enormous flair, and they've got great hands on the ball. We've got to encourage that.' It was good, then, to see how athletic the young India side, missing the likes of Sehwag, Tendulkar and Yuvraj Singh, was in the 5–0 win over England at home. Trevor Penney's influence was stamped all over some of the performances.

The Lord's Test that opened England's series against India in the summer of 2011 was not just the beginning of the fight for the number one spot in Test cricket, it was also notable for a host of other reasons. It was the 2,000th Test of all time, the 100th between England and India, and, indeed, Fletcher's 100th Test as an international coach. Tendulkar also stood on ninety-nine centuries in all international cricket – a rather contrived statistic, I grant you, because Test and one-day numbers are rarely joined together, but a remarkable statistic nonetheless, and one which kept us journalists waiting excitedly all summer. The Tendulkar colour piece was done many, many times before it became obvious that, just like for his team as a whole, it wasn't going to happen. He returned home early during the one-day series, the eighth Indian to do so in a bewildering injury roll call: Gautam Gambhir (concussion while fielding during the Oval Test), Harbhajan Singh (stomach muscle), Zaheer (hamstring), Yuvraj (finger), Sehwag (shoulder that was still troubling him when he arrived late and promptly made that king pair), Ishant Sharma (ankle) and Rohit Sharma (finger).

If Tendulkar was the highest-profile departure, then the left-armer Zaheer was the most important and most untimely. It was obvious beforehand that India were going to rely heavily on him, so when he limped off at Lord's after bowling just 13.3 overs, and having bowled superbly in swinging conditions to dismiss both England openers it has to be said, the omens for the rest of the series were not exactly propitious. The suspicion then was that India would not be able to bowl England out too often in the series.

That was certainly the case. They did bowl England out twice at Trent Bridge but on the first day the pitch had more kick than a startled horse. England were fortunate that Broad and Swann dragged them from the mire with a partnership of 73 to take the total to 221. And in the second innings England had made 544, with Bell, promoted to number three through an injury to Trott, making a magnificent 159, before they were dismissed.

Otherwise India did not look like bowling England out, and some huge scores were amassed. At Lord's in the first Test Pietersen made a double-century, in the third at Edgbaston Cook ground out a mammoth 294, and at the Oval Bell made his first Test double-century. What with Trott making an invaluable 70 at Lord's when conditions were tough before succumbing to a shoulder injury at Trent Bridge, Morgan making a century at the Oval, Prior blasting a rapid century at Lord's, Strauss eventually finding form with 87 in a 186-run opening partnership at Edgbaston, and even Bresnan making 90 at Trent Bridge, it was a summer in which England's batsmen resided on Mount Olympus.

Only the remarkable Rahul Dravid among the Indians joined them, a solid brick 'Wall' among a team of sandcastles. The rest simply could not cope with England's aggression, accuracy and relentlessness. Some of them, especially Suresh Raina, Yuvraj and to a lesser extent Abhinav Mukund, played the short ball as if suddenly placed in front of a firing squad.

England's bowlers were feasting on ambrosia and nectar too. They also quite liked the 2009 and 2010 batches of Duke balls rather than the 2011 versions which didn't swing as much. This was another example of England's attention to detail. They used the 2010 balls until stocks ran out, then switched to those from 2009.

Broad took a hat-trick at Trent Bridge (in the middle of a spell of five wickets for no runs no less) just when India looked like fashioning a decent first-innings lead, ending the series with twenty-five wickets at 13.84. Anderson, now consistently world-class, took twenty-one wickets at 25.71, and Bresnan, who could easily have played instead of Broad in the first Test but missed out and only then played in the remaining Tests because of injury to Tremlett, took sixteen wickets at 16.31. At the end of 2011 Bresnan had played in ten Tests and England had won all of them. For Bresnan read England – almost disbelievingly brilliant.

When England won the final Test at the Oval, with India entirely out of pluck by then, by an innings and 8 runs, it was England's seventh victory by an innings in their last thirteen Tests. The closest India had come in their 4–0 drubbing had been losing by 196 runs in the first Test at Lord's. Ouch.

England became the number one team in the world on a weekend at Edgbaston, having achieved the aim required before-hand of winning the series by at least two Tests. It was on Saturday, 13 August 2011, in fact, that they won the third Test. The journey from Sunday, 22 August 1999 had certainly been long and eventful.

I'll not pretend I was there when they won by an innings and 242 runs, inflicting upon India the third largest defeat in their Test history. Saturday is usually my busiest day of work, but my sister had decided to get married that day. It would be stretching a point to call her an avid cricket fan, but she followed my career closely enough to know the game pretty well. Had she envisaged England being anointed as the number one team in the world on her wedding day? Had she heck. We're only eighteen months apart in age and we grew up in an era when cricket and England meant inevitable disappointment, however promising things might appear briefly. When planning a long time before she had been more worried about a clash with the Wales versus England rugby match that day.

Not that I could be idle in the build-up to her nuptials. A column was still expected for Sunday. And rightly so. England were top of the pile, and it needed explaining. Maybe I'd told too many people about the topic of this book, because there seemed to be a lot of articles based around its timeline, of that trek from 1999. But then I suppose it was where the progress to number one status began. So that Sunday I wrote:

There really is no mystery as to why this England side are so good. Possessing an outstanding group of international cricketers is a given, but it is not always enough. Leadership is key, and this team are superbly led by Andrew Strauss and Andy Flower. The players work hard, making them the fittest team in world cricket. They adhere religiously to simple plans. And they care passionately about the team ethic. 'The team is not a lease car' is their slogan, and it is mightily apt.

This team's journey began in 2009, just after they had been humiliatingly bowled out for 51 and beaten by an innings by the West Indies in Jamaica . . .

But the longer journey had begun in the late nineties when English (and Welsh!) cricket was generally an embarrassment, so lamentable that in 1999 they were briefly ranked as the worst Test team in the world.

Which is where we came in . . .

14

Dogberry's Comparisons

Ah, we're not quite done yet. There is still the awkward bit to come. The comparison, and the comparisons. As Robert Croft, my former Glamorgan colleague, said to me during the writing of this book, 'I can't wait to find out who you think is better!'

Fletcher or Flower? It's like choosing between a kindly professorial uncle and an old 'what-a-great-time-we-used-to-have' university mate. Duncan Fletcher is not my uncle, and Andy Flower did not go to Swansea or Cambridge with me, but you get the gist.

If you think Flower's England's comprehensive thrashing of Fletcher's India in the summer of 2011 (India did not win an international match in the entire tour) draws a firm conclusion then you clearly have not been reading carefully enough. As I mentioned earlier, Fletcher had had no time with his squad then, while they were ravaged by injury and fatigue. His 5–0 riposte in the one-day series in India is evidence enough of the worth of his work.

There is also another important point to be considered in

comparing the two: Fletcher has been to the end of his England tenure, Flower has not. Unless he shrewdly departs at the top, it will end in tears some time. It always does. And the 3–0 Test defeat by Pakistan early in 2012 was a chastening indicator of how swiftly things can change. 'Uneasy sits the crown' and all that.

Overall comparisons are odious anyway, or odorous, as Constable Dogberry said in the Bard's *Much Ado about Nothing*. I've always liked that malapropism and used it in 2011 when explaining the difficulties of comparing the side of 2011 with that of 2005, not least because three players – Strauss, Pietersen and Bell – played in both sides. Bell was undoubtedly a better player in 2011, but it might just be that Strauss and Pietersen were better batsmen in 2005.

The team of 2011 was undeniably a better 'team' in terms of its unity of purpose. As Matthew Maynard mentioned earlier, Fletcher has always spoken of the 'critical mass' of his team. He has always reckoned that you require eight solid characters in your side, who can then coax along the other three who might slack or disrupt. 'But as soon as that critical mass reaches seven-four or six-five you have problems,' Fletcher has said. That is unfortunately what happened in Australia in 2006/07, with Andrew Flintoff as captain.

Fletcher would have enjoyed coaching the England team of 2011. They had a critical mass of eleven; a group of genuinely good blokes. Believe me, that is rare. I have always been of the opinion that rugby dressing rooms are better places than their cricketing equivalent, because the characters found in them are generally less selfish. But the England team of 2011 seem to have bucked that theory.

Pietersen's name will obviously spring to mind in contradiction, but he trains exceptionally hard and that fits easily into the Flower and Strauss regime. One insider told me that James Anderson might once have been a problem in that critical mass respect, but apparently it is not just his bowling that has been transformed.

Sometimes as a team they might have appeared fractured on the field, because they could shout and bawl at each other when mistakes were made. I personally don't like that, and feel it was by far the most unattractive aspect of the side that went to number one. But those inside the camp insist it was just the team's methods of ensuring high standards. They say there is never any lingering animosity. And we have to believe them.

The other problem with comparing 2005 and 2011 is the standard of the opposition. In 2005 England were facing one of the greatest sides to draw breath, even if Glenn McGrath missed the two Tests England won after twisting his ankle on that stray ball at Edgbaston. Indeed before the start of that series Australia's points ranking (133) was at its highest at any time since the Test rankings were introduced. In 2011 it was an inevitable shame that India's quality was constantly questioned. They came into the series with a points ranking of 125, and finished it with 117. In direct contrast England began at 117 and finished at 125. Throughout this South Africa remained second with 118. It was close at the top, unlike, say, the end of 2004, when England were second to Australia: England had 109, Australia had 130.

In 2005, as I have touched upon, the reverse swing of Flintoff and Simon Jones was as good as anything the cricketing world had seen. The obvious differences are in the spin and wicket-keeping departments. Graeme Swann and Matt Prior would win personal duels with Ashley Giles and Geraint Jones without any argument. Anderson would have to play, as would Flintoff, who held hands with greatness for all of that series. Alastair Cook or Marcus Trescothick, though? Jonathan Trott or Michael Vaughan? Strauss or Vaughan as skipper? Steve Harmison or Stuart Broad? Tim Bresnan or Simon Jones? And so on.

In my column I went with the 2005 lot, for their individual brilliance as opposed to what I considered the more workman-like performances of 2011. 'It is 2005 for me, just, but, as Dogberry might have said, the 2011 side smell pretty good too,'

I wrote. And this even though I'd pick six from 2011 in my composite eleven: Cook, Trescothick, Vaughan (capt), Bell (2011 version), Pietersen (2005 version), Prior, Flintoff, Broad, Swann, Anderson, Jones.

Throughout the research for this book I asked many people about the similarities between Fletcher and Flower. One said 'Zimbabwean!' with a laugh, and then said that was it. They are very different, yes, but they are also surprisingly similar. Neither of them smiles much for a start. Fletcher's inscrutable gaze is well known, although he blames hereditary low jowls. He is generally happy, as it happens. And so is Flower, but the England team mock him for his miserable mien. 'Grumpy Flower' Pietersen called him jokingly after the team had reached number one and Pietersen was thanking Flower for keeping the team so grounded. And when at the post-match press conference in Sydney after the Ashes win in 2010/11 Strauss was asked why Flower was not on the field with the team, he said that it was because Flower was not very good at smiling. When told of that remark, Flower replied, with a smile, 'That's Strauss just being his cynical self.'

Scyld Berry's typically thoughtful assessment of the differences between the pair was that Fletcher is rural and Flower is urban. I have touched upon that. Fletcher grew up on a farm where words were not essential; Flower grew up in the cities of Johannesburg and Salisbury/Harare. It shows. He communicates more easily. He is more tolerant with the media, although one Sky Sports employee did tell me that getting an interview from Flower was like 'getting blood from a stone'.

'There is always a danger that by putting yourself in the paper you are aggrandizing yourself at the expense of the players,' Flower has said. 'They have to go out into the middle to play the matches; they go into the lion's den. As a coach, you should never lose sight of that.'

The majority of my interviewees reckoned Flower to be the

better man manager. I know that will irk Fletcher. He prides himself on his man management, and it was immediately proved by his treatment and the subsequently positive responses of the likes of Graham Thorpe and Phil Tufnell with England. Mike Atherton said as much in his autobiography when considering that early period when he was still an England player. Talking of Ray Illingworth's time as England manager, he wrote, 'He was as poor as Duncan Fletcher, later, was excellent.' And Fletcher's problem is that people easily remember the troubled latter stages of his tenure when he was mostly putting out fires started by the likes of Flintoff rather than the earlier more successful times.

But all those interviewees also said that Fletcher was the sharper coach. As Giles says, 'If I weighed the two up, I would say Fletch has more of the technical and less of the man management, and Andy is the opposite. But the mixes are still good, on both sides. They are just different forms of coach.'

Giles, a player under Fletcher and a selector under Flower, was interesting on their similarities. 'They have both got really good, simple disciplines,' he said. 'Respect and pride seem to be in-built into some of these Africans. There is not a lot of molly-coddling, but that doesn't mean they are not good man managers. It takes time to get to know them, and you have to break them down.'

Both keep their distance from the team. One current England player said to me, 'I wish we knew Flower a bit better,' but another told me that, as he was a young tyro, Fletcher had barely spoken a word to him.

But both have a desperate desire to win. There is a good story about Flower when he was coaching at Oxford University in 1997 (when, incidentally, he beat Fletcher as a coach for the first time when his Oxford team defeated Fletcher's Glamorgan – minus a few senior players, it does have to be said, including me! – in a run-chase after a rather generous declaration). His team had just been beaten early by Nottinghamshire and it was decided to play a game of football on the outfield between the teams. Oxford were hammered in that too, and their players headed for the showers and then, so they thought, their colleges. Flower had other ideas. He wanted to talk about the football. The players just didn't get it. It was only a game of football. 'It's about winning,' Flower told them. 'You must never, never accept losing.'

I found this story interesting because when Fletcher came to Glamorgan that year, one of the things he introduced was games of football and touch rugby as extra sessions of fitness. We had never done that before. Indeed I remember an occasion at Derby when Hugh Morris was captain and I'd brought a rugby ball along to kick around with, because I was planning a comeback season with Lydney. A game of touch was suggested. 'If you lot play touch, you'll be in trouble!' said Morris. But Fletcher encouraged it, before and after play. He encouraged the competitive side of it, splitting sides into youngsters and oldies, or East against West Wales. He'd always watch intently, scowling at slackers, enjoying the competition and never seeming to mind if tempers frayed.

Sadly you won't see England's cricketers playing football these days, as it was banned after Joe Denly was injured in a clumsy tackle by Owais Shah at the Oval in 2009. But Fletcher and Flower probably prefer rugby anyway, even if injuries prevented their playing the game for too long as youngsters.

Maynard, Fletcher's former assistant, says of the two Zimbabweans, 'I'd say there are huge similarities between them. Because Andy was more of a player in the spotlight his media stuff is far better, but, just like Fletch, he is very considered, very protective of his players and looks very well organized.'

It was the American philosopher and writer Henry David Thoreau who once said, 'The greatest compliment that was ever paid me was when someone asked me what I thought, and attended to my answer.' And that is one of Flower's great strengths. 'When you sit down with him you actively see him listening to you,' says Morris. 'And he is very considered in his response to you. He listens to people, he learns from them, he then plans meticulously and then leads that plan.'

Flower does listen, and he does seek advice in looking for what he calls 'nuggets' of information. He will talk to the likes of Ian Botham and Geoff Boycott in order to keep them onside. In both 2009 and 2010 he spoke to John Buchanan, the former Australia coach, about the Ashes series in those years and ways of planning for them. He regularly speaks to some journalists, giving them off-the-record briefings so that they understand what he is trying to do. And he has been cute in his relationship with the counties.

As Giles, as Warwickshire's director of cricket, says, 'He has managed it very well, probably better than Fletch. There is still a hell of a lot of cricket but Fletch might have got to the point where, quite rightly at the time, he said, "Sod the counties; we've got to look after these blokes for international cricket." Andy has been very clever in making the counties and the county coaches feel part of the process of producing the England team. That's how I feel anyway. When you get Bell and Trott back you feel he is doing you a favour in some ways. He is open to conversation about when you can have them back and it is more of a joined-up process. When I was playing, I might have popped back for a game but it was purely popping back for a game. They [Bell and Trott] are more Warwickshire players than I was.'

That might sound like heavy criticism of Fletcher, but it is not. Giles is an unashamed Fletcher fan. It was just, as I have said before, that Fletcher had the hardest part as regards the counties. Managing the beginning of central contracts was breaking over a hundred years of tradition, when the counties had always been in control of their players. It was always going to be messy.

Fletcher did communicate with the counties, always trying to go to every one after a winter tour, but even Maynard agrees that, with a better structure in place, it would have been good for him to have done more. He recalls speaking to Flower about this very issue when Flower was working at the National Academy in the winter of 2005/06 and Maynard had just returned from England's tour of Pakistan. 'We talked about one of the things Fletch needing to do was speak to the county coaches to make sure they knew about his philosophies and what sort of cricketers he wanted,' he says. 'But it never happened because of a lack of time.'

In 2010 Maynard was still cricket manager at Glamorgan before resigning after some shockingly underhand events at the club, whereby a new skipper, the South African Alviro Petersen, was signed in Dubai by three members of Glamorgan's hierarchy without Maynard's knowledge. Maynard was impressed that Flower made time to meet with various county representatives (it helps that he has Morris to sort out so many peripheral issues). Maynard went to dinner with Flower, Craig White (Yorkshire) and Richard Scott (Middlesex). 'I thought it was brilliant,' says Maynard. 'As a coach you could then go back to your county and say, "Right, this is what he wants."'

In one-day cricket Flower likes his explosive batsmen. And by coincidence that means he likes Tom Maynard, Matthew's son, now at Surrey after walking out from Glamorgan in disgust at the treatment of his father, and selected in 2011 for the winter Performance Programme squad. In 2010 Tom was asked to take part in a Twenty20 match situation the day before one of England's T20 internationals against Pakistan in Cardiff. Batting second, Maynard played exceptionally well, before attempting one heave too many and getting out with victory in sight. His team-mate Jos Buttler (Somerset) was bowled next ball to leave his side in trouble. Flower was not slow to communicate his feelings afterwards, using the example of the former footballer Eric Cantona. 'He [Cantona] knew he could play the magic ball,' said Flower to Maynard junior, 'but he chose to play the simple ones until he knew the time was right.'

Fletcher listens too, despite the common perception to the contrary, as Dean Conway confirms: 'I would say something to him subtly the day before, like I thought that warm-ups were too long, and he would not say "Yeah, you're right", he'd just say "OK". Then the next day that thing would have changed. I found him a good listener, but you had to be in that circle. Towards the end he got overly suspicious.'

Former team analyst Mark Garaway says that he did not become aware that Fletcher and Flower were so similar until Flower took over in the West Indies in 2009. 'I wouldn't have known before,' he says, 'but very, very quickly it was evident that we were dealing with a guy who was obviously a younger version of Fletch but had all the same beliefs. The difference between the two was that Andy was probably more prepared to challenge, irrespective of the person. So nobody got off lightly. He wasn't about respecting people's feelings. It was all about the team, and if somebody shed a tear at something he said he couldn't give a stuff. That was a very strong message to send out. I'm not saying that Fletch wasn't good at challenging, but during his time Flintoff, say, had got quite big.'

Yes, it is interesting that Flower has appeared more prepared to drop his big names. Pietersen, Broad, Collingwood, Bell and Anderson have all felt the cold steel of his selectorial axe. But in truth it is easier for him these days. England have far greater strength in depth. During Fletcher's time there was rarely that depth. That is why the team of 2005 unravelled so quickly. There was simply not the personnel to step in once injuries struck.

Garaway highlights the difference in coaching methods between Fletcher and Flower. 'It is a generational thing,' he says, 'but it is also because Andy's first coaching experience came under Pete [Moores] and that became very much a specialist and more scientific approach than Fletch's, which was a more integrated method. Pete had been a huge driver in getting the analysis department to grow and as a result we had a huge amount of people doing a lot of data mining behind myself. It was always going to go that way.'

And that is the way it has gone. Flower had been given the book *Moneyball* (Michael Lewis's tale of the statistics-driven success of the baseball team the Oakland As under their manager Billy Beane) to read by Moores and was an instant convert. Flower is cricket's Beane. It is a measure of the increased standing of statistics and statisticians that that can be seen as a compliment. In days gone by, he might have been called Mr Bean.

When interviewed for the job of team director in 2009, Flower stated that he wanted American sports science and particularly the analysis of statistics to be used more in cricket. It was a point reinforced when I interviewed him later that year. 'I think we are only scratching the surface with cricket statistics,' he said. 'They will play an increasing role in how you formulate strategy or pick people.' They have done that, courtesy of the department at the National Cricket Performance Centre at Loughborough that is solely concerned with statistics.

Not that Flower eschews technical work or talk. 'Some players are scared of talking technique,' he says, 'because they believe it will slow them down in the middle. But if there's a problem with technique – if, for example, you're playing a forward defensive and the ball keeps sliding off the bat – then something's wrong and it has to be addressed. If you've got a solid technique, your confidence will grow.'

But he will often use statistics to reinforce a point. 'It can be a very pure, a very non-judgemental form of feedback,' he says. 'I'm not saying you're a good guy or a bad guy, a great player or a bad player; these are the figures, let's talk about them.'

England's main analyst is, of course, Nathan Leamon. When England got to number one in the world, his name and his nickname 'Numbers' came to the fore. He had planned England's ascent up the rankings, and a lot else besides. He had also played all the Test matches that got them to the top on his computer even before they had been played on grass. 'We feed into the simulator information about pitches and the twenty-two players who might play, and it plays the game a number of times and tells us the likely outcomes,' Leamon told the *Sunday Times*. 'It helps us in strategy and selection. I've checked the programme against more than 300 Tests and it is accurate to within 4–5%.'

The simulations are based on those first used in the 1940s by the mathematicians John von Neumann, Stanislaw Ulam and Nicholas Metropolis, who were working on nuclear bomb projects for the Manhattan Project at Los Alamos. It was called the Monte Carlo method after Ulam's uncle, who was a hardened gambler in the casinos of Monte Carlo. 'Tell me what Monte says,' Flower will often say to Leamon when faced with a decision upon which he cannot immediately decide.

One such obvious instance is the toss. Leamon reckons that from the five hundred Tests he has looked at, you are just as likely to win the game if you've lost the toss as when you have won it. It is a logic buttressed by Strauss, who thinks that, with Test pitches deteriorating less, the days of always batting first have gone. 'If you think there's going to be something there and you bowl,' he says, 'but there isn't a huge amount there after all, you haven't actually lost a lot, because not many wickets these days deteriorate massively.' 'When in doubt, bat' might have actually become 'when in doubt, bowl'.

Leamon makes extensive use of Hawk-Eye data in preparing pitch maps for opposition batsmen, breaking down the target areas for bowlers into twenty blocks, each 100cm by 15cm. 'A lot of the old ways of looking at the techniques of opponents leads to guesswork – feet position, how they hold the bat,' says Leamon. 'Hawk-Eye enables you to come up with answers.'

It is an interesting point from Leamon. There has always been analysis in cricket. But in the old days it was conducted in the bar, and then stored in bowlers' minds if they hadn't drunk too much and could remember.

But having plans is one thing, implementing them is quite another. That is where England were so brilliant in the Ashes of 2010/11 and the India series in 2011: their bowlers were un-remittingly accurate. Contrast that with 2002/03 and the infamous first Test at Brisbane, where Nasser Hussain inserted Australia. The home side made 492 but Fletcher says all of their batsmen bar Ricky Ponting fell to pre-conceived plans. 'It took so long because we did not bowl enough balls in the right place,' says Fletcher. 'Plans to dismiss a batsman do not work unless you can bowl five or six balls an over in that area.'

It was a similar problem in 2006/07 when, embarrassingly, England's bowling plans were leaked during the Melbourne Test. It would be easy to mock them in comparison to today's, especially as some of the words were misspelt, but in essence they are little different. They had the essential weaknesses of each batsman, and they had the shrewd field-placings (for example, a 'straight catcher on edge of pitch' for Matthew Hayden) that were so lauded in 2005.

However, I reckon England need to be careful. They must not give too much away. Quite clearly Loughborough and the wonderful cricketing community working from there is a hive of invention and trail-blazing initiatives. They are giving the England team and English cricket an edge. But it will not remain so if other countries are able to copy and catch up. I've always felt a little guilty about the *Ashes Regained* book I did with Fletcher after 2005. Fletcher was very careful not to reveal too much about the Australia players he knew would be playing in the next Ashes, but before that 2006/07 series his opposite number Buchanan said, 'I've made the book mandatory reading for our coaches. I think it provides a very interesting insight into

Fletcher. He discusses his own philosophies and also gives his thoughts on the current players and the way they play the game in England.' Oh dear.

In 2011 I did a small piece for my Final Whistle column on the increasing influence of mathematics in sport, and especially in cricket. I obviously mentioned Leamon and Loughborough in despatches, but I had also come across the crib sheet used by a county team before one of their Twenty20 matches that season. I found it fascinating, especially the statistical detail it went into. I did not mention the county by name but I did drop in a couple of random statistics and terms used in it. 'Dot ball limit' was one of them, and, apparently, that gave the game away. That was their term. The county in question were not happy, so I was told. And in a way I was happy about that. They were protecting their own little version of the Crown Jewels. Caveat inventor. Look what happened to Australia after we copied their Academy all those years ago.

Of more importance, though, for England to beware of is the future of Flower. As you may have noticed, I am no closer to judging him against Fletcher. It is impossible. In their different ways under different circumstances, they have both done superb jobs.

Under Fletcher, England played 270 matches of all types, winning 119 at a winning average of 44%. Under Peter Moores they played 79 and won 30 (38%). Under Flower, up until the end of the 2012 Test series against Pakistan, they have played 135 matches, winning 69. That is a winning percentage of 51.11%.

Under Flower, England have won twenty of the thirty-nine Tests played (a stunning 51.28%). In eleven series England have won eight, drawn one and only lost two. With India in 2011 in the bag they had won six series on the trot, but so did Fletcher's team in 2004 and 2005, culminating with the Ashes at home that year. In twenty-seven Test series Fletcher's team won fourteen, with six drawn, so just over half compared to Flower's 72.7%. Fletcher won forty-two of his ninety-six Tests (43.8%). By comparison in the whole of the 1990s England only won twenty-six from 107 Tests (a miserable 24.3%). In the 1980s it was twenty Tests from 104 (an even worse 19.2%). In the 1970s it was thirty-three from ninety-five (34.7%). The numbers don't lie. The improvements are huge.

The England cricket team is back, and in 2011 was better than ever (at least in the modern era). And Fletcher and Flower have put them back where they belong. So I just hope Flower is better treated than Fletcher was at the end of his tenure. Zimbabweans might well want him to return home, but I cannot see that happening, even though he does still own that house in Harare.

Of course he has hankerings for his homeland. 'I miss certain things about Zimbabwe, yes,' he has said, 'but that's sort of dwindling the longer I am out of it. The most obvious one would probably be some of my closest friends and interacting with them again. But there are also things like the smell of the rain, or the smell of the bush, and being able to go fishing or into the bush, or just go to someone's farm. The freshness and innocence of that type of lifestyle, I do miss that. And I was really lucky as a kid, so lucky to grow up there.'

But I cannot see him continuing in the main England role for too long. Just read the words of this interview he gave in March 2011. 'My kids are twelve, ten and eight,' he said. 'So it's a very important stage in their development as young people and I'm not convinced I'm doing the right thing by the family by doing this job. I'm a bit greedy because I'm trying to get the best of both worlds by helping to raise a young family and also trying to make a difference with the England cricket team. I worry about the fact this time can't be regained. I worry about the fact the kids might at some stage resent me for being away during these years.'

Give Flower no more than two years, I reckon. England

might need to start looking for another Zimbabwean coach. They do seem rather useful. Two of them have taken England from the bottom to the top.

But England already have another Zimbabwean coach. When Flower left the Brisbane Test in 2010, it was the Zimbabwe-born Richard Halsall, not Graham Gooch or anyone else, who took over. It was the same when Flower missed the short trip to Ireland in 2011. As long ago as 2009 Flower told me that Halsall could easily be a county head coach.

Could Halsall, with greater prior experience of the requirements of international coaching than Moores, step up to the national job?

We may well discover one day. But Halsall, or anyone else who takes over for that matter, will know the magnitude of his task.

They will be big boots to fill. Very big boots indeed.

Appendix: England Test series results, November 1999 to August 2011

Season	Coach	Opponent	Venue	Result	Score
1999/2000	Fletcher	South Africa	Away	Lost	2–1
2000	Fletcher	Zimbabwe	Home	Won	1–0
2000	Fletcher	West Indies	Home	Won	3–1
2000/01	Fletcher	Pakistan	Away	Won	1–0
2000/01	Fletcher	Sri Lanka	Away	Won	2–1
2001	Fletcher	Pakistan	Home	Drew	1–1
2001	Fletcher	Australia	Home	Lost	4–1
2001/02	Fletcher	India	Away	Lost	1–0
2001/02	Fletcher	New Zealand	Away	Drew	1–1
2002	Fletcher	Sri Lanka	Home	Won	2–0
2002	Fletcher	India	Home	Drew	1–1
2002/03	Fletcher	Australia	Away	Lost	4–1
2003	Fletcher	Zimbabwe	Home	Won	2–0
2003	Fletcher	South Africa	Home	Drew	2–2
2003/04	Fletcher	Bangladesh	Away	Won	2–0
2003/04	Fletcher	Sri Lanka	Away	Lost	1–0
2003/04	Fletcher	West Indies	Away	Won	3–0
2004	Fletcher	New Zealand	Home	Won	3–0
2004	Fletcher	West Indies	Home	Won	4–0
2004/05	Fletcher	South Africa	Away	Won	2–1
2005	Fletcher	Bangladesh	Home	Won	2–0
2005	Fletcher	Australia	Home	Won	2–1
2005/06	Fletcher	Pakistan	Away	Lost	2–0
2005/06	Fletcher	India	Away	Drew	1–1

2006	Fletcher	Sri Lanka	Home	Drew	1–1
2006	Fletcher	Pakistan	Home	Won	3–0
2006/07	Fletcher	Australia	Away	Lost	5–0
2007	Moores	West Indies	Home	Won	3–0
2007	Moores	India	Home	Lost	1–0
2007/08	Moores	Sri Lanka	Away	Lost	1–0
2007/08	Moores	New Zealand	Away	Won	2–1
2008	Moores	New Zealand	Home	Won	2–0
2008	Moores	South Africa	Home	Lost	2–1
2008/09	Moores	India	Away	Lost	1–0
2008/09	Flower	West Indies	Away	Lost	1–0
2009	Flower	West Indies	Home	Won	2–0
2009	Flower	Australia	Home	Won	2–1
2009/10	Flower	South Africa	Away	Drew	1–1
2009/10	Flower	Bangladesh	Away	Won	2–0
2010	Flower	Bangladesh	Home	Won	2–0
2010	Flower	Pakistan	Home	Won	3–1
2010/11	Flower	Australia	Away	Won	3–1
2011	Flower	Sri Lanka	Home	Won	1–0
2011	Flower	India	Home	Won	4–0

Bibliography

Atherton, Mike, *Opening Up* (Hodder, 2002)

Fletcher, Duncan, *Ashes Regained* (Simon & Schuster, 2005)

Fletcher, Duncan, *Behind the Shades* (Simon & Schuster, 2007)

Flintoff, Andrew, *Ashes to Ashes* (Hodder, 2009)

Hoggard, Matthew, *Welcome to My World* (HarperCollins, 2009)

Hussain, Nasser, *Playing with Fire* (Penguin, 2004)

MacLaurin, Ian, *Tiger by the Tail* (Pan Macmillan, 1999)

Olonga, Henry, *Blood, Sweat and Treason* (Vision Sports Publishing, 2010)

Strauss, Andrew, *Winning the Ashes Down Under* (Hodder, 2011)

Swann, Graeme, *The Breaks are Off* (Hodder, 2011)

Thorpe, Graham, *Rising from the Ashes* (HarperCollins, 2005)

Vaughan, Michael, *Time to Declare* (Hodder, 2009)

Index

INDEX

Hauritz, Nathan 256
Hayden, Matthew 64
Haynes, Desmond 174, 176
Hayter, Peter 'Reg' 317
Hick, Graeme 11, 40, 197, 255
Hill, Tony 270
Hira, Hitesh 207
hitting the stumps 283–4
Hodgson, Myles 144
Hogg, Vince 105
Hoggard, Matthew 67, 73, 117, 124–5, 191
Hollioake, Adam 254
Hollioake, Ben 89
Hopps, David 151
Hore, Andrew 277
Hough, Nigel 100–1, 106
Houghton, Dave 75, 151, 230
Hoult, Nick 184
Hughes, Phillip 29, 285
Hussain, Nasser 21–4, 57, 74, 87–9, 117, 131, 137
  attitude to fitness 85–6
  as captain of England 21–2, 24, 82, 88–9
  and Fletcher 24–5, 87, 137–8
  and Gatting 156
  and New Zealand Test (1999) 1–2, 3, 4
  personality 23
  Playing with Fire 17–18
  resignation of one-day captaincy 87–8
  retirement 89–90
  run record 88, 289
  and Schofield Report 152–3
  and Sri Lanka Test (2000/01) 82–3
  and Zimbabwe World Cup match issue 92, 95, 96, 97

ICC (International Cricket Council) 107, 110, 114, 274
  ranking system 259–61
  and Stanford 175–6
Illingworth, Ray 334
Ilott, Mark 24
India 322, 324–6
  appointment of Fletcher as coach (2011) 10, 12, 127, 321–2, 330
  one-day internationals against 12, 179
India Test series
  (2001/02) 89
  (2008/09) 179–84
  (2011) 10, 11, 12, 210–11, 226, 235, 270–1, 320, 323, 326–9, 330, 332, 341
Indian Premier League (IPL) 4, 34, 41, 177, 225, 226, 275
International Cricket Council *see* ICC
Irani, Ronnie 4, 24, 99, 191
Ireland
  one-day international against (2009) 315

James, Bethan (daughter) 62
James, Jane (wife) 276–7

James, Steve
  autobiography 23
  broken hand 83
  composite eleven 333
  cricket journalism and column articles written 4, 53–4, 134, 162, 171–2, 214, 242, 262–3, 297–8, 308, 314–15, 322–3, 329, 342
  cricketing career and playing at Glamorgan 4–5, 22, 65, 76, 78, 136–7, 158, 188, 205–6, 216, 223, 239, 254, 268, 276–7, 278–9, 294
  father's advice 132
  ghosting of Fletcher's autobiography 6, 55–8, 125–6, 129, 140, 341–2
  knee operations 158
  relationship with Fletcher 5–6, 132–3
  relationship with Flower 199
  Test debut (1998) 23
  in Zimbabwe 6–7, 201
Jamieson, Campbell 176
Jardine, Douglas 235
Jarvis, Malcolm 7, 231
Jennings, Ray 57
Johnson, Mitchell 309
Jones, Geraint 48, 81, 98–9, 119, 133, 145–6, 332
Jones, Simon 46, 54, 59–60, 64, 65–6, 86, 89, 129, 332
Jordan, Chris 278
Joseph, Robbie 227
Jowell, Tessa 110

Kallis, Jacques 5, 123, 254
Kaneria, Danish 291
Kasprowicz, Mike 39, 55, 62–3, 287
Katich, Simon 284, 287, 306
Kendix, David 260–1
Kent 29
Kenway, Derek 48
Kenya 92
Key, Rob 46, 81, 289
Khan, Amjad 227
Khan, Imran 65
Kieswetter, Craig 51, 251, 252, 273–4
Kirsten, Gary 10, 224, 322, 323–4, 325–6
Knight, Nick 137
Knox, Adrian 49
Koertzen, Rudi 68
Kolpak, Maros 41
Kumble, Anil 212, 213

Lamb, Allan 251, 255
Lamb, Tim 2, 3, 16, 20, 21, 30, 33, 92, 94, 96–8
Lancashire 37–8, 167–8
Langer, Justin 55, 242–7
Langley, Ben 278
Lara, Brian 72
Laughton, Nigel 66

353

INDEX